White Is Not the Colour of Surrender

of Surrender

The Story of Syria's White Helmets

Jennifer Krausewitz

ACKNOWLEDGEMENTS

First and foremost, I would like to thank the men and women of the White Helmets for sharing their stories with me on and off the field of duty in war-torn Syria. Without your first-hand accounts through one-on-one interviews, phone calls and messages, this story could never have been written. I would like to thank the former President of the Syria Civil Defence, Raed al-Saleh, for taking the time to talk with me at the White Helmets Headquarters in Istanbul and allowing me entrance into the world of the Syria Civil Defence. I would like to thank the White Helmets in the SCD media department for providing a rich body of photographs for use in this book. It was difficult to choose a handful for publication out of the hundreds you provided. Each image is beyond extraordinary and tells a tale in and of itself. Likewise, I would like to offer heartfelt thanks to Amjad al-Dyab, the older brother of slain White Helmet Photographer, Anas al-Dyab, for letting me choose some of Anas' extraordinary images for posthumous publication in this book. Where I have been uncertain of the actual photographer of the photos among Anas' large collection, I am simply crediting both Anas al-Dyab/The Syria Civil Defence. Despite the SCD's tremendous influence on the field stories in this book, it should be known any political external opinions I have expressed about any players in the conflict are my own, and do not necessarily reflect the opinions of the organization.

For his beautiful foreword to my book, I would like to give my great appreciation and thanks to veteran conflict photographer and journalist, Paul Conroy. His heroism in journalism, particularly as he and Marie Colvin chose the "non-visa" route into Syria to get the true story of Assad's war on his people out, is the inspiration for many in a time when there is clear war happening between truth and propaganda. You and Marie will always be my heroes.

I would like to thank my son-in-law, Cameron, for his initial perusal of my manuscript, and his amazing advice on how to make it better.

I would like to thank my editor and life-long friend, Shannon Mann, for not only editing the final manuscript of this book, but for providing incomparable encouragement while I struggled through the four years of writing what is likely to be the most emotionally fraught story content I will ever deal with. She is the fixer of run on sentences, bar none.

I would like to thank my daughters for supporting me through my endless tales of the Syrian conflict (from which they had little to no escape) and for sometimes just being a sounding board for my ideas and frustration on how to put the story into words.

My deepest thanks to my husband Mark who helped me get through the hard work of activism for Syria and the writing of this book. He has been my buddy and cheerleader for a lifetime.

And of course, I would like to thank the team led by Tyler Croman at Parker Publishers for their great assistance getting this manuscript into something resembling an actual book.

The research for this book has been a monumental task. Much knowledge was gained from the following resources which I highly recommend should you wish more insight into the Syrian Conflict:

- *Under the Wire; Marie Colvin's Final Assignment* – Paul Conroy, Hachette Books, 2013
- *No Turning Back; Life, Loss and Hope in Wartime Syria* – Rania Abouzeid, W W Norton, 2019
- *Assad or we Burn the Country: How One Family's Lust for Power Destroyed Syria* - Sam Dagher, Little, Brown and Company, 2019
- *Syria's Secret Library: Reading and Redemption in a Town Under Siege* – Mike Thomson, PublicAffairs, 2019

- *Mayday: How the White Helmets and James Le Mesurier got pulled into a deadly battle for truth,* Intrigue, *BBC Radio 4 Podcast* – Chloe Hadjimatheou, BBC, 2020

DEDICATION

This book is dedicated to my husband Mark, my daughters Alicia and Juliette, and my bonus sons, Cameron and Andrew.

And of course, to every Syrian hero who ever put a white helmet atop his or her head.

Contents

Foreword

[Veteran conflict photographer and journalist, Paul Conroy, has captured stories in war zones all around the world. He worked faithfully alongside acclaimed Sunday Times journalist, Marie Colvin, on her final assignment in Syria that blew wide open the truth about President Assad's dedicated war on his civilians. He has written *Under the Wire* about his time in Syria with Marie; produced several documentaries; and his time as Marie Colvin's loyal conflict photographer was depicted in the movie *A Private War*. He is currently covering the war in Kyiv, Ukraine.]

Time heals, but it also takes. My memories of Syria – especially my final assignment to Homs, where my dear friends Marie Colvin and Remi Ochlik were murdered by the Assad regime – remain etched into me.

Jennifer's exquisitely written account of the White Helmets, and of a nation brutalized by a dynasty of tyrants, took me beyond the memories of that cold winter day. Her narrative is both haunting and urgent: beautifully evocative, precise in detail, and relentless as it lays bare the true scale of horror in a country torn apart.

A part of me will always remain in Syria. This remarkable book not only captures its devastation but also its strange, enduring enchantment. Above all, it illuminates the unbreakable spirit of those who have survived revolution and war, shining through the darkness like a beacon.

I cannot recommend this book highly enough. Thank you, Jennifer.

Paul Conroy
Kyiv
14 September 2025

INTRODUCTION

During the writing of this book, and still, I have picked up the habit of looking skyward at my Canadian heavens every time I hear an aircraft enter the atmosphere. Blocking the sun with my hand, I am for some few moments captivated by whatever it is flying through my safe suburban skies – a helicopter, a commercial airliner, a Cessna, or perhaps an old Lancaster B-10 Bomber from the nearby warplane museum. The habit first originated with helicopters years ago, as I was trying to get some feel of what it must have been like living as a Syrian during the early days of the conflict- before the sophisticated Sukhois and MiGs- when sheer terror was delivered by the angry whirring propellers of the choppers. When the incoming sight of the black beasts for those people looking up presented only the imminent prospect of hell about to be unleashed, usually, the horrific barrel bomb drops. Christ, what must that have felt like? In some small way, I suppose it was part of trying to empathize with the reality of what the Syrians were dealing with during their government's war on them. Or at least the best I could do. The White Helmets knew all the warplanes in Assad and Putin's arsenals by sound as well as sight. They'd had over a decade to learn, and it was a part of survival to keep their eyes trained on the heavens. My own continued ritual of looking skyward is perhaps a way of paying homage to the courage of the

Syrian people, to their rescuers, to their story. Anyway, I can't seem to stop.

I wrote the first draft of this book during a 10-week stay in an old part of Istanbul back in the autumn of 2021. It was the closest thing I was going to dare get to Syria, and besides, by that point, Istanbul was full of Syrians. Their exquisite culture was everywhere. Baklava, falafel and hummus, famous Aleppo soaps at market stalls and televisions screens loudly broadcasting *Real Madrid* football games, not to mention, fragrant hookah and backgammon played by old men on sidewalks well into sun-drenched afternoons and beyond. Good pilsener beer – however, was nowhere to be found, such was my sad luck. I sat working away on my laptop at a kitchen table in an apartment high on a hill in ancient Eyupsultan, an alien place where no taxi seemed to ever dare want to venture. It was a wonderful place to write. Huge old windows provided an incredible vantage point to survey my neighbourhood. Stacks of residential apartments surrounded me on the hill, their daily washing hanging out to dry on balcony lines, gorgeous Turkish graveyards at my feet down those hills shining ghostly come evening with misty yellow light, a majestic mosque across the scenic cove of water which glowed golden every night and rang out Call to Prayer blissfully starting at 5am and calling out four more times throughout the day. On my far right, down one wickedly buckled, rutted, and steep hill that was torture to climb, was a lively soccer pitch where the kids played rain or shine – a vivid juxtaposition to the ubiquitous graveyards. And just beside me there at the little white kitchen table, comfortably blissful in her new home, was a kitten named Rosie. In a city overwhelmed with cats, clever and tiny Rosie, in her best bid for adoption, waited on my doorstep for me to get home from Istanbul travels each day, and each day I resisted the obvious temptation. One night poured rain, and still I found her there waiting for me, drenched and shivering. Needless to say, I took her inside and gave her a bath, and set out some warm milk. Rosie won the Turkish lottery. So, with Rosie curled up at my side, the glittering mosque always just a glance away, and occasionally Brahms playing on the old record player drifting in from the distant room, I scribbled and typed away. And it was a setting for a writer every bit as romantic as can be imagined.

With their organization's headquarters stationed in central Istanbul, I also had White Helmets nearby for countless interviews and access to photographs, and even to my unabashed delight, Effes Turkish beers in Karakoy. None of the Helmets drank alcohol, however, and opted for orange soda and hookah instead. Kindly, they had sought out the beer just for me. I looked through books with them of Syrian life and landscape before and after the war. I even tried on an actual field white helmet and grinned so gleefully, I must have appeared quite ridiculous. One or two laughed at my reaction over something that was so commonplace to them. I was also entitled to gingerly, reverently handle a GoPro Hero camera that only recently had been taken off the front of a helmet, but had once captured thousands of videos of Assad's destruction and war crimes. I even tried the beloved Syrian drink, mate, with its metal straw and herb-thick sugared tea, once, and...uh...never again. I recorded the former field Helmets' stories and tried to make sense of the hell they had lived in the country south of us. Having worked for the White Helmets' media platforms, writing and editing their stories several times a day for many years, I had become completely immersed in the world of the Syria Civil Defence. My respect for the organization was great and always will be. I had seen what they had been through and were going through, unprotected by the same Geneva Convention measures as other humanitarians. Theirs was an important story, and I only hoped the book would do it justice. More importantly, I hope one day these forsaken humanitarian volunteers *get* their own brand of justice. Their losses of friends and family and home are incomprehensible in a time and age where the United Nations is supposed to protect humanitarians.

By late November, the draft was finished. What I didn't know then was that first draft was just the tip of the iceberg that would keep me busy and invested in the White Helmets story for a very long time to come. My editor and friend Shannon once jested, *"Your manuscript is taking longer to write than the Syrian conflict lasted."* That's certainly how it felt at times.

This is by far the most difficult manuscript I have ever written, and the first non-fiction one. The research was never-ending. I struggled with one chapter in particular, *Killer Propaganda.* The more I delved into this part of the story, the harder it became. Writing about the Assad apologists who made it their vocation to defame the White Helmets and put a target on their persons while never being penalized, was a brutal undertaking. Almost 400 White Helmets died in the line of duty, died for nothing less than the crime of being a humanitarian rescuing the people the regime and Russia were trying to kill. And to know these Assadists played a role in their deaths, was an emotionally-demanding endeavour to even attempt to put it down in words that would do it justice. Sometimes I didn't want to touch the chapter; at times it made me physically sick. And as the cursor blinked away on the screen waiting for my words, I sometimes would literally put my forehead down on the computer in despair. Mark, having grown accustomed to this, would simply look my way and say, *"You can do it. Just keep going."* I would call my editor, who would listen to me say I cannot write this chapter, I can't. She would have none of that, and more than once would resolutely say to me, *"The only way to get past this is to get through it"*. They were right. It took an incredible nine months to do the chapter, but I finished it. And I never want to write another citation as long as I live.

It's been a difficult book for so many reasons. Writing chapters like *War Children* and *James* was also emotionally draining. Happy endings in a modern-day story of a dictator's hell inflicted on his people for 14 years are far and few in between, but there are some. Humanity is the main character in this book, whether his role is to share bread during a siege with a neighbour, or as a doctor trying to operate through a bombing raid knowing those few remaining sutures could cost him his life but he stays and stitches them anyway, or the neighbour who picks up a shovel and runs to the fallout of a bomb blast to save anyone he can in the rubble and eventually wears a white helmet atop his head. Yes, Humanity is the story's quintessential protagonist. I hope, in my writing of this book, that I have shown this main character in his truest, most dedicated form, even when weakened repeatedly by the prospect of defeat. I hope Humanity takes the central role in as many more stories as possible in the world today. Wouldn't that be something.

By the way, when I went back home to Canada, a White Helmet adopted the kitten Rosie. I thought you might ask.

Jennifer Krausewitz

July 24, 2025

PROLOGUE

Yallah!

"We shall meet in the place where there is no darkness."

- George Orwell, *1984*

[Rendering]

At the first peaceful protests in Daraa in early spring 2011, when crowds gathered with only songs as their weapons, the government militia that was sent to stifle this "insurgency" wore black helmets. Long organized rows of black beetle-headed regime military blocked the streets behind the people with veteran truncheon clubs in their hands, well accustomed to use, their frayed rough handles as devoid of merciful colour as their long tapered black bodies. Behind them, the regime police, or *Mukhabarat*, stood in black uniforms, toting black Kalashnikovs. Indeed, the colour black prevailed as the dominant feature of the regime and its unchecked power encircling the people. And why not black? It was the perfect tone to mark the horrors of that spring day. A day when people chanting for peace were opened fire on for singing songs. Their pleas for something resembling democracy were met with immediate violence. Shots were fired from automatic weapons indiscriminately into defenseless crowds. Snipers took to rooftops to pick off protestors from easy vantage points. The people ran for cover, jostling through the hysterical crowds to get away, and hiding behind any wall or place of refuge they could find. In a matter of moments, the streets were filled with bodies. Any attempt by a friend or bystander to aid a victim or at least remove him from the road, gained that friend his own bullet holes. And so, the dead amassed by the scores in that Daraa street. On March 18, 2011, the Syrian people had appealed to their dictator leader not for his resignation, but for the most meager concessions. His response was intended to teach them to surrender to the will of the regime as they and their parents had for the last forty years. But what met those regime henchmen was something that surprised not only the men in black but all of Syria; they had come face to face with a people who had no intention of surrendering. This day of unmitigated bloodshed would fuel a revolution of person and spirit that President Bashar al-Assad could never have imagined. Daraa had just become the Cradle of the Revolution, and the baby would quickly outgrow its bed.

The Syrian people had been afraid for so long. Of gathering for a party of friends and family without a permit, of speaking with apparent insolence when merely expressing a frustrated thought about the government, of simply wanting to get ahead with their lives. And it was this chronic fear, more than anything else, that propelled them forward in those days leading up to the Syrian Revolution. Fear, uncertainty, and hopelessness had put the backs of Syrians up against a wall until eventually, resistance was the only route beyond it. Their rallies and songs were never meant to be more than a peaceful opposition. A mere nudge to their dictator that they wanted just a little hope to cling to. Not once did they ask President al-Assad to step down. Only to step a few feet out of their way. They would even be satisfied with inches.

Historically, most revolutions begin in coffee shops, a place of safe neutrality with plenty of buffering background noise. In these discrete meeting places, disgruntled citizens come together with quiet but urgent conversations across tables. Agendas are whispered out between sips of coffee between nervous friends. As it had been in the coffee houses of the Ottoman era and those of Paris in the late 18th century, so it was in the coffee shops of Daraa. Phrases liked *"It's time"*,

"It can't go on like this anymore", *"There will need be organization"* were whispered daringly across tables in the spring of 2011. The young men making their plans in whispers had been bolstered by the successful revolutions across the Middle East that spring, starting in Egypt. In Daraa, however, those coffee shop schemes, once manifesting from social unrest, were eventually further propelled by sheer outrage. The ultimate catalyst for a decisive call to action among the people had been regular Daraa school boys in a vacant school room idly behaving like bored teenagers do. The classroom cleared for the day, the boys took a can of spray paint and headed for a stone wall. Four words were sprayed in big bold letters in red paint. There is disagreement on what those four words actually were. The majority believe the boys indelibly sprayed, *"You are next Doctor"* – a formidable threat to their leader, Bashar al-Assad, a former optometrist. Others believe the words spoke of allegiance with the Arab Spring, in particular the most successful nation within it, and the most recent to make their own revolt. *"We stand with Tunisia"*. Mere weeks earlier Tunisia, a country, oppressed and stifled by their authoritarian leader, overthrew their government, start to finish in a matter of weeks. They had done it! The people had won. In excitement, perhaps the boys had spelled big and wide across the wall, their allegiance to a people just like their own, with the hope that Syria could be next to take down their own cruel and tyrannical government. The recounting of this act has had so many re-tellings, it has almost become fable-like. The number of teenage boys varies from

story to story, as does the actual words written on that school wall that fateful day. What is reliable in every version is the fact that teenager boys wrote anti-government words, were found out and exposed to the government forces, who immediately sought out each of the boys and took them away from their homes for interrogation. But it was more than interrogation, the boys under the custody of the regime police forces, were brutalized and beaten within inches of their lives, before being thrown out of cars back to their home doorsteps, most unconscious. Presumably, the outcome would have been much worse and likely the teenagers would have been outright murdered, had the masses not taken to the streets demanding the return of these neighbourhood boys. The government had taken a step too far. The people would demand change, and they would demand it together as one, revolution-style.

Out of the coffee shops and into the mosques each Friday (the only public place Syrians were allowed to gather lawfully in groups), plans for full-scale revolt commenced. The mosque was filled to the brim with eager men. Most of the revolutionaries were between the ages of 15 and 30, with the majority being in their early to mid twenties. With the idealism characteristic of their very ages, the only thing that trumped their willingness was their naivete. They had been warned time and time again by older Syrians, parents, grandparents, neighbours who had lived through the brutal reign of the father Hafez al-Assad, long before the son had come to power. They knew well the response uprising and discordance elicited from the al-Assad government. They had lived through the 1982 Massacre of Hama when an uprising against the government was met with monstrous force and retaliation, leaving a death toll in Hafez al-Assad's wake of 40,000 people, still the single deadliest act of violence perpetrated by a government on its own people in Middle East 20th century history. The message to the youth by their elders was unequivocal: *This is a war you cannot win.*

But the mindset of the mostly twenty- somethings who would start the revolution, believed every leader can be negotiated with. They emphasized their revolution would be peaceful, resourceful even. They would be respectful in their request for concessions to Assad. They would carry no weapons. They would head to the main streets of Daraa peacefully and purposefully.

They were wrong.

Breaking through the internet firewalls set up by the regime, amateur videos of the slaughter which unfolded on the Syrian people on March 18th, 2011, were uploaded and viewed millions of times over in mere hours. Frantic and angry Syrians had run at further risk of life or arrest to internet cafes to upload for the outside world the killing of innocent men, women and children by their leader. Each hasty upload came with the same confidence – that once the outside world, the West in particular, saw what had happened this day to mere innocents, children no less, Assad would know his last days in power. There was no question in their minds. But they waited and they watched, and as days became weeks and no help came, the concomitants of the Syrian Revolution became as shocked as they were disillusioned with the knowledge they were completely on their own. The West was not coming. In fact, no one was coming. No one. So what next?

Meanwhile, back in Damascus, Assad was in swift damage control. His lies about the Syrian conflict would start immediately. Initially, he had announced from the presidential palace, his tall, gangly body so tidy and trim in an expensive navy suit, that a few rabble rousers, merely some bored youth, had caused a little trouble, but that all was well again in Syria and his people were, indeed, as content as ever. The Syrian Lira was up. The young people even had social media! After all, had this default heir to the throne not presented himself to the world for nearly a decade as the modern and progressive President of Syria? He now provided for his people a far more liberal-minded approach to the welfare of his people than his father, former Syrian president Hafez Assad, had done, and perhaps far more than his dead brother, the beloved Bassel, killed "inconveniently" in a car wreck, usurping his natural born place as leader, ever might have. Had the times not changed for the better in Syria under his fair rule, gaining the respect of the world? He and his glamorous London-born Syrian wife, Asma, had been guests of the Queen of England, had given winning interviews to America's Barbara Walters with big, confident smiles on their faces, and they had been written up and touted by many media outlets as being the change Syria needed. They prided themselves on having their finger on the pulse of their citizens in this new, modern Syria. So, when the deadly protest of March 18th, 2011 hit the outside world, and people saw countless images of the body-strewn and blood-filled streets of Daraa, resourcefully, President Assad changed his tune, saying that when protestors are shooting at law enforcement, the police have no choice but to defend themselves. The problem for Assad, here being, was that in every video broadcast, the Syrian people were shown to be unarmed, defenseless, and for all intents and purposes, quite orderly. Some protestors even took off their shirts to reveal they were carrying no weapons. Others offered forth literal olive branches to the security. Consequently, having to take a step back on his theory of necessary retaliation, he changed the narrative again, stating unequivocally, that he, himself, did not order any firing on civilians and that the appropriate steps were being taken to correct the offending military for its conduct, promising it would not happen again. However, the televised speech he would subsequently give back in Damascus undermined that promise, long and full of vitriol, as he referred to the protestors as vermin needing be eradicated. The Syrian people were shocked by each and every one of his words, delivered shamelessly and ferociously. This dictator was clearly at war with his people. No one saw this more clearly than the Syrian people, themselves. And so, the protests continued, still unarmed, but with more Syrians joining the crowds than ever. The revolutionaries were all in.

Yet the punishing violence continued full throttle. Within days, Daraa was under siege with troops and tanks moving into the city and cutting it off from all food and supply routes in or out. In terror, civilians watched as the Syrian military entered on foot, having been commanded to "shoot to kill"[1] pedestrians in the street. Snipers took to rooftops throughout the city, terrorizing the people from entering the streets, their shots strategically meant to kill as they whizzed bullets through skulls and hearts. The military killed anyone who brought medical aid or even a bottle of water to the critically injured in the streets. They blocked ambulances. Security forces took control of most of the hospitals in Daraa, killing or detaining the wounded being brought in. Interrogations of bleeding and half-conscious patients took place, the police demanding to know everything about the uprisings, particularly who the leaders were, and where the organization was taking place. Consequently, the sick and wounded avoided the hospitals altogether, finding their way, instead, to makeshift field hospitals where there were, of course, wholly inadequate supplies and care. Come nightfall, the dying and dead bodies remained in the streets, sadistically guarded over by the military police. Loved ones watched in secret from house windows their beloved children, brothers, friends, stranded dead and defiled on the concrete with suppressed horror, but didn't dare try to retrieve or aid them, understanding military would be posted throughout the night. This immoral refusal by the military to allow the bodies in the streets to be cared for or retrieved was a mere foreshadowing of things to come when the eventual humanitarian organization called the White Helmets would be deliberately and repeatedly targeted during their search and rescue missions of their fellow human beings. The death toll mounted unchecked in Daraa and beyond. Assad was literally culling his people.

From the streets of Daraa City, the regime sieges would move systematically through neighbouring cities and villages, and then eventually province after province, with Assad cutting off the same necessities time and time again - food, electricity and medical supplies to the people. The military would deliberately shoot holes in water cisterns to ensure the people were without water. Checkpoints were set up to cut off the roads so there was no coming or going. Routinely, aid and life-saving medicine were blocked from entering the city. Nothing was coming in and nothing was going out. Hospitals were hijacked. Mosques were bombed and desecrated. Call to Prayer was finished. When civilians banded together in abject desperation to halt a siege through protest on April 29, 2011, the Syrian Army massacred 200 civilians.[2] Then, a 13-year-old chubby-cheeked boy named Hamza, harmless and innocent, was brutally abducted at a rally and tortured to death by the deadliest rank of the Syrian Army – Air Force

Intelligence. It was a defining moment in the people's revolution. What had been done to young Hamza while in the custody of the regime military was so brazenly grotesque and horrific, his story moved like wildfire throughout the Syrian provinces. It had become abundantly clear that peaceful protests were not working. Many believed it was time for full-out revolt. Huge numbers of revolutionaries broke out into rebel factions and began to pick up guns to defend the people and the future. Everything had changed. They lived now in a Syria they didn't recognize under a leader whose hateful indignation of his people had been propped up by a merciless military that stopped at nothing. Battle lines had been drawn. Even the two-starred Syrian flag they had once been proud of, but which stood now only for brutal dictatorship, was about to get a makeover. Indeed, the revolution of the Syrian people had only just begun.

What had started as a whisper in the cafes and turned into quiet sermons in the mosques would become a loud battle cry for freedom in the streets. When all the people said, *Yallah! Let's go! Let's do this!*

CHAPTER ONE

Three Stars, Not Two

*"Those who make peaceful revolution impossible
will make violent revolution inevitable."*

- John F. Kennedy

[Rendering]

When a pilot's aircraft has reached V1, takeoff has come irremediably to the point of no return. The acceleration of the plane has reached such a speed that the pilot no longer has the option to bring the plane to a stop. Even should there be good reason to abort the imminent journey ahead, a critical phase of momentum has been reached, and key factors already at play compel the plane to keep going.

It may be said that precocious and chubby 13-year-old Hamza al-Khatib was the V1 catalyst that hurtled the nascent Syrian Revolution forward with absolutely no choice of turning back. Perhaps there were many reasons early on to ground the escalating conflict embarked upon by the Syrian people, including the meagre concessions an already violent Assad had dimly proffered forth, but schoolboy Hamza changed all that. The unassuming kid from Daraa who liked to fish in the river with his dad and cared passionately for homing pigeons on the roof of his family home would swiftly bring about the Syrian Revolution's point of no return. In those early days of its inception, Hamza al-Khatib would, indeed, become the very symbol of revolt itself.

On a clear spring day in April 2011, Hamza followed a singing crowd of locals waving the two-starred national flags of Syria and holding aloft banners begging for freedom, liberation, bread. He walked with these neighbours 12 km to take part in a revolution rally just beyond Daraa in the city of Saida. This particular rally had gained momentum and vigor among the people during the week leading up to it, and every able revolutionary vowed to go. To someone as young as Hamza, it must have been incredibly exciting despite the long walk ahead. Described as something of a little humanitarian by a family member, Hamza had once asked his poor parents to give 100 Syrian Lira – 2 American dollars – to a poor beggar man on the road. At first, his parents refused, saying it was too much money, but eventually relented with their son's compassionate pleas, childishly explaining that they had beds to sleep in while this man had nothing. His altruistic leanings notwithstanding, Hamza's long walk to Saida that day was likely more inspired by the desire to just be part of the revolution like everyone else. Surely, the grade 8 student had no great aspirations to overthrow Assad by attending a protest rally that blue-skied, warm Syrian morning.

Having foreknowledge about the popular and potentially large rally descending on Saida that day, a department of the regime's military police was ready and waiting at the city gates. They were very different police which the approaching peaceful revolutionaries could never have anticipated might come for them. As with every other rally thus far, they carried only patriotic Syrian flags in their hands to make their point - not weapons. In fact, they had never carried weapons and the regime knew this. At this early juncture, they didn't want Assad's resignation; they merely wanted compromise. Mostly, they just wanted to be heard. That they posed little to no threat was clear. Yet, what had been sent by Assad was not merely a branch of the "anti-terrorism" military police, but the infamous Air Force Intelligence, itself. A branch well known for its sadistic methods and torture. There was nothing so fearsome to the people in all of Assad's arsenal. Clearly,

President Bashar al-Assad had drawn a line in the sand. He would tolerate no more uprisings against his government. Today was judgement day visited upon the people by the regime. True to form, the police started firing on the people before the flag-wavers had even reached the Saida gates, young Hamza's cousin easily recounted. They just mowed down everyone under the presumption they were there to protest, he remembered. Dropping their flags, the people scattered and retreated, while so many slain were already on the ground. Then the abductions began with people being chased and seized, their knees knocked out from under them with truncheons. Terrified Hamza, along with 50 other protestors, had been captured by Air Force Intelligence, thrown into their black vehicles, and simply vanished from the Daraa landscape. He was just all of a sudden gone, his cousin stated, punctuating with grievous recollection the last time he would see the little boy.

For one agonizingly long month, Hamza's mother and father waited, horror-stricken, to know the whereabouts of their son and if he were still alive. They would make no complaints to anyone about anything, certainly not about the regime – they just wanted their little boy back, no questions asked. Their response came on May 24th, 2011, when his badly mutilated corpse was dropped off like so much refuse at their front door. After a month in captivity at the hands of the Air Force Intelligence, the teenage boy was unrecognizable, having been tortured beyond all comprehension. It was clear to anyone who observed Hamza's body that his death had been recent, while the preceding torture had been weeks' long. His bloated and decomposing body was covered in the scars of horrific abuse. The purple bruising of electric shocks was stamped all over his flesh, bullet holes through his arms pierced clear trajectories into his sides and stomach, a broken neck, cigarette burns randomly deposited on his flesh, and in one final, gruesome act, his genitals had been cut off. The mother, so desperate to see her boy again, was permitted only to glimpse his grossly swollen face, wholly unrecognizable to anyone *but* his mother, while the sheet covered the rest of his body. Her screams seemed to have no end, until they turned to an unimaginable wailing. Hamza's father, however, was determined to bear witness now to all his son had endured, and no one would stop him. He turned his wife out of the room and, with trembling hands, removed the sheet, wanting to see exactly what they had done to his son. He had hardly taken in the sight of his boy's brutalized body before fainting to the floor. Photographs and video were taken for evidence. Word moved like a grassfire through not only Daraa but the Syrian nation about what had happened to the child, Hamza. The grotesque and monstrous things that had been done to a little boy by grown men acting at the behest of Assad were unfathomable. If there had been any doubt before about what grave abuses the people's "leader" would inflict on "his" people, they now had their answer. Hamza al-Katib had become everyone's child, and no parent could walk away from this grotesque injustice without wanting retribution. Shock and confusion on the part of the people had turned to abject anger. There would be no negotiation or reconciliation with a government that could do this; there could only be revolt.

The Syrian doctor who performed the autopsy videotaped it as he described the injuries in detail, cataloguing each injury, each violation, so the horrors of what this child suffered would not be lost on the world and could not be refuted. The video, finding its way onto YouTube, stunned and sickened thousands of people before it was pulled from the channel. News of this boy's murder reached the West. President Obama would make an official statement, as would Secretary of State, Hilary Clinton, clearly describing Assad's reprehensible actions as a message to the people of Syria that Assad would not back down, and consequently, international response had to recognize this fact, as did the people of Syria. Damage control on behalf of the regime was immediate. A physician from the regime and spokesperson for Assad, Dr. Akram Al-Shaar, claiming to have been present at the autopsy despite the operating physician's claims to the contrary, stated that there were no torture marks on Hamza's body, but that his condition was merely a result of natural decomposition as a consequence of being shot accidentally at an unlawful protest.[3] It may be supposed that the doctor did not know about the coroner's comprehensive video of Hamza's examination. His other blunder was that, whether he knew it or not, he had just made an admission that protestors had, indeed, been fired upon that day by the regime police.

The Syrian nation, beyond the confines of regime-controlled Damascus, exploded with outrage. Protests continued and proliferated steadily throughout the provinces of Syria, and well beyond those borders, continuing in Beirut and Egypt. Children marched through the streets with white candles and jasmine-strung wreaths commemorating the life of Hamza. Where once the Syrian flag had been held aloft, the face of Hamza, now iconic, marched above protesting heads through the crowds in outraged demonstration. Big brown eyes, short dark brown hair, chubby cheeks, and boyish innocence had usurped the unworthy flag with its two stars. A flag that no longer meant anything but brutality to the people of Syria.

And for a little while the world's anger was sparked and they again remembered Syria. Cries came globally for justice for this child, while near every Syrian city continued with the commemoration parades in the martyred boy's honour, but nowhere so much as in Hamza's hometown of Daraa. Indeed, the parents wanted justice. Hamza's father wanted to sue the Syrian regime for these horrific wrongs done to their son. Their demands were silenced instantly by a visit made to them by President Bashar al-Assad, himself. In a Russian Television interview, the president spoke about Hamza with a British journalist. Here is the stunning transcript.

President Assad: At the very beginning, during the demonstrations, during the first few days, we lost five policemen by shooting, by bullets.

How could we talk about peaceful demonstrations while you have policemen killed by...

Journalist: But how could you authorize the killing of a thirteen-year-old?

President Assad: ...I'm just starting from the very beginning. So, from the very beginning, I mean, the word "peaceful demonstrations" was not correct. There was shooting, and you can't tell who's shooting at police, and who's the one shooting at the civilians, because in most of the incidents at that time, the police didn't have even machine guns or pistols.

Journalist: Except this child was tortured?

President Assad: No, no, that's not true. He's not, we never had...

Journalist: cigarette burns on his body...

President Assad: No, no. He was killed, and there was allegation that he was tortured. He wasn't tortured, he was killed, and he was taken to the hospital, and I met his parents. They know the real story. This is only in the West, in the Western outlets, in the Western media outlets. This is not the story in Syria. So, that's why I'm surprised by those stories that are completely disconnected from our reality. He is somebody who died, how did he die, who shot him - nobody knows. It was chaos. When you have chaotic demonstrations, anyone could infiltrate that demonstration and start shooting in different directions and kill policemen in order to retaliate or vice versa.

Hamza's parents' pursuit of justice was, indeed, most assuredly over. What was also very much over, was the fragile belief so desperate for the Syrian people to hang onto, that President Assad and the Syrian regime were not entirely bad. They were far worse than that.

With Hamza, the fissure had happened. The nation had been split apart. For those destined to see the revolution through, the two-starred flag representing a nation that no longer existed and a government that had no meaning now to the people, a new flag would need be born.

The revolutionary flag chosen, the one with bands of green and black, three red stars in the middle, was not new to Syria or to revolt. In 1946, it had been the Syrian flag being waved when Syria liberated itself from France. Consensus among the revolutionaries revived it, and soon it flooded protests and rallies and posters, and social media. The three-starred revolutionary flag separated those crying for freedom and liberty from those violently refusing it.

Choosing the 1946 flag liberating Syria from France also showed the Syrian government that the revolutionaries now wanted that same autonomy that was sought after back then, that the time had passed for half measures and negotiations when reasonable demands were met with bullets and torture.

In the very beginning, these new three-star revolutionary flags were being made by the mothers and aunts and sisters of the protestors at sewing machines clandestinely in Syrian houses. As massive numbers were later required, factories would start making them. The flags were precious things, in and of themselves. One protestor would always be in charge of handing them out to the other protestors and then collecting them when the rally was over.

Daraa, the Cradle of the Revolution, would launch the new flag of revolt, and drop the first domino that would set off full-out rebellion and protest throughout the Syrian nation. Rallies now waving the three-starred revolutionary flag would continue for a long time to be wholly peaceful, but the message was now unequivocally clear: the Syrian revolutionaries wanted their dictator gone. Western and Middle East opponents of Assad also agreed this was the only option to restoring peace – to remove Assad from power and set up an interim government before a pro-democratic one could be chosen by the people. However, as Syria's old ally Russia began to become more and more active in the conflict, Putin strongly condemned any mention of removing Assad, reminding the West via the United Nations that Syria was a sovereign state and outside interference would be neither practical nor lawful and would not be abided. So once again, talks shut down, and protests continued.

Yet now, the Syrian regime, making use of its entire arsenal of weaponry and equipment, including its government armies, was responding with absolute force to stifle what it deemed a nation of insurgents. Serial bombing and sieges began, with army tanks blocking the routes in and out of city after city, starting unreservedly with its most populated city, Aleppo. The Syrian military was instructed to shoot down any and all protestors, women and children included. This brutal mandate would be the impetus for a huge defection of military personnel to join the opposition. Arbitrary arrests of civilians suspected of conspiracy were commonplace. Innocent, but "suspected" infidels were routinely led from the front doors of their homes right to Sednaya Prison, a torture house without equal.

Part of this brutal crackdown was the decommissioning of all essential services. All of the services formerly provided by the government were abolished. Ambulances were gone, hospitals worked now with skeletal staff and barren shelves emptied by sieges. The message was clear: the people were on their own to fill in for the missing infrastructure. As bombs rained down and shelling sprayed even the poorest villages, the Syrian people knew they had to pick up the slack. As hospitals were obliterated by regime bombs, makeshift field hospitals were quickly established, making use of any and all health practitioners remaining. And when residential neighbourhoods literally exploded and generational homes collapsed into rubble, leaving the inhabitants trapped inside, it was neighbours who dug the victims out, putting them hastily into the back of any and all vehicles available and transporting them to whatever medical facility or place of aid they could find. At that time, there was no equipment to move large slabs of roofs that had entombed inhabitants, and so they were left to die, needlessly. And there was even less education or knowledge on the proper way to handle victims. The death toll soared despite the best efforts of locals to save their Syrian neighbours. For two years amid the heaviest brutality rained down upon mere civilians, neighbours helped neighbours to the best of their ability. But there was no organization, no communication, no efficiency. The current search and rescue was evidently not working as well as it might. So, in 2013, in the Aleppo governate, the most regime-brutalized region of the country to date, a handful of individuals, men from every common walk of life, would band together and organize search and rescue so the maximum amount of lives could be saved after each bombing raid. They would find an abandoned government building to become their base, wear leftover government-issued uniforms to identify themselves as one body to civilians, and they would label themselves the new Syria Civil Defence. No weapons, no machinery, certainly no helmets at this early moment of inception, yet with organized structure, methodology, and the desire to save their people, beleaguered Aleppo had just given birth to what would eventually become the very first White Helmets.

CHAPTER TWO

Donning the White Helmet

"The white helmet provides no armour against missiles, but it is a bright symbol of humanity in a time of great darkness, and this is what fortifies every volunteer who puts it on."

- Hamid Kutini, White Helmet

[Hamid Kutini/Syria Civil Defence]

In the beginning they had nothing. No helmets. No boots. No walkie-talkies. The neighbourhood volunteers sometimes ran in bare feet or broken sandals to the bomb sites. They grabbed garden shovels and plastic buckets from home and made their way as fast as they could to the dust-encircled fallout. With so few tools, they often needed dig through near- insurmountable piles of rubble with their bare hands. The ubiquitous topography of rock and debris made it impossible to know where to start digging. And a wrong guess for the location of survivors would waste precious time and manpower, moreover, those lives depending on them. Still, for long hours they picked at Assad's handiwork relentlessly. Raw hands pulled and pushed the rubble aside, desperately clawing for a peak of survivors until their shredded flesh bled. Shovels broke, buckets snapped. Sometimes in climbing a step too far up the incline of mountainous rock a volunteer would lose his footing and fall hard. If, unwittingly, they stepped upon a weak part of a collapsed roof over a hidden basement, they might fall instantaneously with the collapsing concrete inwards, breaking limbs or dying in the drop - that volunteer's day of search and rescue assuredly done. The obstacles of search and rescue in those early days of regime bombing campaigns were overwhelming. The first responders who met Assad's massacre sites head-on in their cities and villages had next to nothing with which to recover the dying and dead. Nothing except hope and humanity. And of course, the understanding if not them to save their fellow civilians, then who?

Still, in those early rescues, when they unearthed the first crying children, alive and safe, the joy of these regular men - bakers, carpenters, painters, students - was like very little they had known before in their lives. When an entire family was, after so many painstaking hours, brought intact and breathing out of their rubble graves reborn into the light of day, the volunteers praised God and uttered Allahu Akbar in exaltation. Yet, when dead children from the neighbourhood were extricated like limp dolls with heavy bobbing heads, eyes sightlessly staring forward, they blamed themselves as much as Assad. There is little worse in this world than the sight of a dead child. And the volunteers would see many. Each time they held that innocent dead child, they pledged next time they would work harder, they would work faster, they would do better, so they never had to see another one. Despite all the chaos and uncertainty of those first rescues, one thing was absolutely certain for the majority of men, whether they knew it or not at the time, they had found their new vocation.

And so it was time and time again, those who beat the odds and survived the neighbourhood blasts and found themselves still standing in their aftermath, quickly mobilized to free those buried, to dig out the trapped, to transport the dead and dying lying helter-skelter on the streets, to collect limbs, to do whatever they could. In other days, long before the ritual bombing, it was the government that had provided the ambulances and the hospitals and the first responders for everyday emergencies, but even that basic infrastructure could never have dealt with this wholesale slaughter and wicked scale of destruction, that which the regime, itself, wrought down. For two years, the people had needed to adapt to form their own rescue system. And so started that routine of ordinary civilians running to the mountains of rubble after the bombs hit homes. Indeed, they became the first responders. Any and all vehicles became ambulances. All able-bodied individuals became the paramedics, the field doctors, the firemen. And it was far better than nothing. However, the limitations in what they were capable of doing were overwhelming, and worse still was the absence of any logistics and structure, and of course, the proper equipment. Lives were being saved, but not as many as could be. There were inherent, but often simple, problems that needed to be solved. While good intentions and manpower could save ten people after a bombing, the addition of organization and coordination might save a hundred more.

In 2013, two long years after the Syrian cries for democracy were met with bullets, President Bashar al-Assad had waged all-out war on his people with no cessation in sight. This was not a merciful leader. His bombing campaigns that systematically went through liberated province after province visited upon the people a brutality and murderous assault that was decimating and displacing tens of thousands of innocent Syrian civilians. When he set his sights on a particular province, the regime made no half measures - the cities within it experienced bombing all hours of the day, a destruction meant to annihilate, to raze the revolutionaries and their battle cries to the ground. Neighbourhoods crumbled to pieces under his endless barrage of ballistics. If Assad's treacherous goal was to leave nothing but ghost towns in his wake, he had succeeded on a scale not seen since the first two world wars. The inhabitants who couldn't get out in time or had nowhere to go were easily annihilated. Generational homes made of thick limestone were leveled in moments, families were buried inside, many dead, but some miraculously alive. And this sinister scenario would be played out over and over again. Assad was all in. The revolutionaries were to be taught a lesson never to be forgotten.

In the province of Aleppo, in the northwest of Syria, once thriving cities had the grotesque distinction of being chosen as Assad's first bullseye. The rest of the nation gasped as they observed the nightmare this ancient and historically rich province had fallen under.

***

It was in Aleppo City where a group of ordinary men, locals who had routinely taken on the job of entering the perilous bomb sites to do search and rescue of the buried, first discussed doing things differently. Between tea and cigarettes in an extraordinary time of clear skies devoid of warplanes, the rescuers began talking about the most obvious problems they were facing. Due to a lack of coordination, time was being lost getting to the victims. They had no proper tools or machinery for getting through much of the walls of concrete burying the victims. The tools they brought from home could do little when faced with a mountain of rubble – the leftovers of a two- or three-storey home. Worse still, too many recovered victims would die waiting for transport to hospitals because of the lack of vehicles and the delay when mobilizing those they had.

No one rescuer could be sure what another rescuer was doing. In summary, time was being wasted each and every rescue because there was no consistent planning in place.

So, these men began formulating a plan.

They would need a central headquarters from which to operate and where coordination of searches could be carried out with rhyme and reason instead of haphazardly. During field duty, they would need walkie-talkies to keep each other updated and accounted for, particularly when more than one city area was attacked at a time, forcing them to split up. They would need medical supplies and stretchers. And perhaps most importantly, they would need a team of devoted volunteers who would dedicate their days and nights to saving bomb victims. A schedule of shift work, which concentrated the volunteers at the centre, would be made. And of course, they would also need a leader to keep everything running.

With little care for the implicit irony of the situation, the place these Aleppo men decided on for a volunteer headquarters was an abandoned building previously run by the regime's original Syrian

Civil Defence. The former Syria Civil Defence that had become the regime's henchmen was defunct and non-existent as far as Syrians were concerned, likely having transitioned to regime military for the purpose of killing civilians instead of defending them. These men here and now, tasked with the true defence of Syrians, would take the old name and make it mean something entirely new. Unanimously, they decided they would become the Syria Civil Defence. In their urgency to get out, the old members had left their uniforms behind in that very building. Clothing that still bore all the insignia of the regime, marks of betrayal now for the Syrian people. Yet, for lack of any other uniform, the newly born SCD put on these uniforms, covering up the old two-starred regime flags, making them their own. In their newly founded but nascent humanitarian organization, the volunteers would need just such a cohesive uniform so civilians could distinguish them in times of need. There were, however, no helmets.

The volunteers knew securing walkie-talkies for communication was one of the more important issues in running an effective search and rescue operation. Not only would it provide more expedient mobilization of team members after a bomb strike, but it was an exceptional means of finding out from sources further out when the first sight of regime aircraft hit the skies and the trajectory it was on. This heads-up was invaluable when there was always a race against time when saving massacred civilians.

Recruits came by the scores. With planning, cohesion, and improved communication all orchestrated by an unanimously chosen team leader, the number of lives being rescued went up exponentially. Morale soared among the volunteers despite the bombardment and human casualty toll they were faced with daily. They were wholly incentivized by the fact that people were now given a fighting chance of surviving through Assad's bombs. And now civilians went to bed at night secure in the knowledge that with the presence of these rescue volunteers nearby, there was hope of actual survival should their home be bombed.

As Assad's genocidal campaign of ridding his nation of Syrians continued from Aleppo through province after province, additional Syria Civil Defence centres using the template of the first one in Aleppo also began springing up. Each centre followed the same protocol and command as the inaugural centre.

At its peak, the Syria Civil Defence would have 120 centres in eight provinces of Syria and over 3200 volunteers. People from all walks of life would take up the gauntlet and become rescuers of the innocent. People who had choices about what they were going to do with their lives. Many could have fled for the border, and others could have stood back and merely watched from a safe distance. But not these men. They were determined to form their own unique revolution by thwarting Assad's destruction of innocent life. They took chaos and made a system in which to work through it. They brought humanity to hell, hope to the forsaken.

The dedicated rescuers knew it was never going to be easy. But, hell, nothing was easy in Syria.

At its peak of operation, with scores of ballistics raining down and the newly devised double-tap (a secondary flyover by a jet to deliberately bomb and kill the rescuers at work) being faithfully carried out, the White Helmets volunteers had a one in five chance of being murdered by the regime and/or Russia while on duty. That is a 20% chance of not making it home to your wife and children. Most individuals in normal life, if given those odds, would not leave their house. But Syria demanded something else of these volunteers, something greater than self-preservation. It asked the question – if not you, then who? If your choice isn't to save the innocent and powerless, then what is your alternative?

Those who answered the humanitarian call, had refused to take up arms and join the rebel militias; they refused to flee the nation and seek asylum elsewhere. They refused, although they could have. Many did.

The sacrifice was huge.

When the Syrian men in white hard hats started being picked up in mainstream media for the phenomenal rescues they were carrying out daily in their war-battered nation, no one knew what to call them.

Countless videos showed these nameless warriors, frantically working through bomb sites, their white bobbing heads all coming together to unearth victims – newborns and children no less - from Assad's deliberate massacres on his civilians. Ultimately, it was the vision of their white hard hats seen time and time again that garnered them the nickname, the White Helmets. It became the organization's informal name and the insignia on their uniforms and vehicles soon bore it too. Suddenly, the symbol of a white hard had become their iconic signature.

Whether they knew it or not, in the next decade they would change things up in Assad's game plan of massacring his population, and bring back a word almost struck out of the Syrian vocabulary – Hope.

As the years of conflict carried on, one merging into the next, and with no cessation in sight, the organization of the Syria Civil Defence evolved to meet the needs of the civilians. They were no longer just performing search and rescue and fastidiously kept pace with Assad's brutal war. Their skills and manpower were needed in so many other places inside the liberated regions of their nation, which were struggling to have some semblance of normalcy. Despite the brutal conflict waged all around them, the people had no choice but to continue living their lives. Syrian children had to sometimes play. Trips had to be made to the leftover markets for food. Life had to find a way. The volunteers' new roles within the Syria Civil Defence would have been impossible without more training, more funding, and, for certain, the usual indomitable spirit of the men to do whatever needed be done to make life for their fellow civilians just that much easier. To allow life to go on at all. Help came their way in the form of two men.

Founders, one Syrian and one British, stepped forward to create a complete organization out of the existing and fragmented centres of volunteers within Syria. They quickly identified their needs and their lack of search and rescue experience, and with a focus on these things, the teams were, indeed, transformed into a cohesive and impactful humanitarian organization.

With the availability of an abundance of recruits and now significant funding from donor nations, sub-sects of the initial Search and Rescue of the Syria Civil Defence would be created. While saving bomb victims and documenting war crimes through photography and paper records consumed the bulk of the White Helmets, additional rescue teams were necessarily created.

Ambulance Drivers

With the addition of fully-functioning ambulances through national donors, the Syria Civil Defence allocated two to three team members to each vehicle, typically one driver, one co-pilot, and another member to sit in the back with the injured. All were trained in the basics of first aid. As straightforward as the job seemed and seemingly less dangerous than the jobs of other teams, the ambulance drivers soon learned this wasn't the case. After aerial bombings, the regime and Russia would send additional jets out to hunt down the ambulances, each bright white with their White Helmet insignia clearly marked on their vehicles, designating them as humanitarians. After the first two or three ambulances were picked off and destroyed en route, the teams decided to cover their vehicles in mud, so they were unrecognizable from the air. The topic of Assad and Russia targeting humanitarian ambulances transferring victims to hospitals was addressed at several United Nations Security Council Meetings, only to fade hopelessly from an agenda topic of concern into the political ether of apathy. The muddied ambulances would have to continue indefinitely.

Firefighters

Earlier, basic firefighters had sprung into action way back during the siege on Aleppo, when the regime and Russia were deliberately blasting farmers' fields with ballistics, setting them ablaze in order to ensure crops were demolished, perpetuating their starvation campaign on the people. The original firefighters, precursors to the more elite unit now formed, would be stationed nearby to quickly mobilize to the affected fields, extinguishing the fires and saving the crops. Over and over again, this had to be done. In the long run, some of the harvests were saved to feed the besieged civilians.

Long needed for their advanced ability to put out fires in the wake of both missile blasts and car bombings, or even just fires which occurred inside civilian homes, special training was given to the men designated as the Syria Civil Defence Firefighters. Now, with the availability of conventional, fully equipped fire trucks, the trained men finally had proper equipment with which to extinguish blazes and save exponentially more lives.

Visits to camps to extinguish accidental blazes were a daunting task the SCD Fire Fighters were charged with far too often. With the prevalence of makeshift cooking sources and heaters used inside countless tents at the camps, and inappropriate combustible fuels feeding them, fires were often devastating. Too often, the hasty inferno breaking out in the tents would have firefighters arrive at the skeletal framework of a burnt-out tent, to blast water at an accidental and needless blaze that had already taken the lives of the inhabitants within. Often, the fire found its way raging down a line of family tents, with the firefighters doing their best to gain control before refugee lives were lost. It was a weekly occurrence, sometimes more.

A much bigger challenge was the forest fires. In the treacherous heat and runs of dry days in Syrian summers, desiccated and dead trees inside the great forest of Syria, would start a fire that would carry on for days, and for acres upon acres of bush and forest, proving the greatest test for the volunteers. Forest fires were beasts unto themselves. Working near endless shifts in rocky and formidable hill landscapes, while the heat and smoke of the forest inferno was almost as bad as the flames themselves, the firefighters would often collapse during shifts, suffocating on the fumes and falling ill from exhaustion. Despite recalibration and sending men to hospital, or at the very least for a rest to get a drink of water, the men would continue battling the angry forests, days at a time, until the job was finally done. In 2021, some of the White Helmet firefighters were loaned out to the Antalya Province of Southern Turkey, where devastating forest fires had taken hold of the southern nation and desperately required fire fighter re-enforcements. The Helmets were allowed to cross the border to help with the mission.

More recently, in the spring weeks of April and May 2025, the province of Lattakia had an outbreak of flash forest fires that took the White Helmets several weeks to finally extinguish. One of their volunteers required critical care at hospital after his shift, while most other volunteers were simply overwhelmed with the inhalation of smoke and chemicals. The work, so horrifically onerous, saw the White Helmets collapsing during their rare rest breaks on whatever spot of ground was closest, water bottles held like treasure in their hands.

Divers

Strong swimmers in the Syria Civil Defence were given scuba diving and water rescue certification so they could take on the task of diving and rescue in local lakes and inlets. Come summer, during the brutally hot Syrian days, a favourite pastime of children and teenagers was to cool off in the nearby bodies of water. Most civilians, however, do not know how to swim. Often, parents would go to the volunteer centres expressing concern that they didn't know where their children were, with many suspecting the water. It was a sad reality that the White Helmet Divers were usually on a search and recovery mission when they hit the waters, dredging up unsuspecting children and adults who underestimated the ferocity of the water and waded out too far to beat the summer temperatures.

The Camps

As more and more women began signing up as volunteers for the White Helmets, their skills were essential and lifesaving, in capacities other than just search and rescue - which some also participated in. Working in the vast and numerous camps within liberated Syria, the White Helmets women were often former nurses or medical personnel who brought their experience to makeshift clinics within the camps, visiting them daily. Despite many of these women having children of their own, as well as the typical duties of a Syrian wife at home, they devoted their days to the service of camp residents. Providing first aid, neonatal and natal care, as well as psycho-emotional help to all in need, they had become a necessity among the people and were cherished as such. For most camps, the clinics run by the women volunteers were the only medical aid available to the people, particularly mothers and their children. The women White Helmets were responsible for visits to the people within their tent homes inside the camp, checking in on the state of the family, offering what support and supplies they could, to an overburdened habitat of people in near constant need. Camp women would come to the centres for ante- and neo-natal checkups, ultrasounds, and education, and the children born into the camps were usually delivered by the White Helmets. While vaccinations were given when available, the children still invariably came down with a variety of illnesses or diseases, such were the inhospitable camp conditions. Cholera outbreaks were treated in the clinic with oral rehydration solutions for mild to moderate cases, and with intravenous and antibiotics for the more extreme, but only if shipments had successfully made their way through to the camp and were available when needed. With Leishmaniasis infection spreading heavily in the camps as a result of poor sanitation and garbage buildup, treatment was urgent and ongoing. Weak and vulnerable children, in particular, were easy targets for Leishmaniasis, which is caused by the bites of sandflies, leading to painful ulcerated sores and dreadful itchiness. The women White Helmets would treat the persistent and menacing disease with anti-parasitic pills and ointments, but depending on the size of the shipment of medical supplies getting through the border, as well as the size of the outbreak of the disease, the treatment could quickly run out, only for the contagious infection to take hold in the camps again and again. The need for cleanliness and sanitation education by the White Helmets women is ongoing, but the facilitation of this is difficult in camps without clean and irrigated running water.

UXO

Other than search and rescue volunteers, likely the most dangerous White Helmet role exists in the Unexploded Ordinances (UXO) Team. These men were tasked with dealing with live bomb remnants and mines buried in the lands. As in every war, the leftovers in or on the earth after a battle or massacre are infinite, whether they be deliberately planted or not. The Syrian children are taught at a young age by classroom visits from the White Helmets that, should they spot a strange-looking piece of anything while they are walking or playing, they should stay far clear and report it to an adult. When unexploded ordnances are discovered, a team of highly trained and specialized White Helmets will go to investigate and are prepared to dismantle them. Outfitted in blue and black uniforms with protective vests and long plastic face masks attached to their helmets, as well as special protective collar pieces for their necks, the men still know they are susceptible targets for the hidden ammunitions. The program started in 2016, and the team members were tasked with cleaning up the ERW Explosive Remnants of War since the conflict began in 2011. The job is monumental. With 6 centres consisting of 12 teams of men, specifically dedicated to this operation, the work is both systematic and a piecemeal program of expansive survey and dismantling. Sweeps of lands are done with bomb-sensing equipment and necessary patience as the men wade cautiously through potential mine fields. Since the inception of the UXO, upwards of 24,000 ordnances have been discovered and dismantled. Their highly dangerous work focuses on allowing people to return to their homes in safety, allowing children to play without the threat of what may be lurking in the ground, and allowing farmers to freely work their fields mine-free. While the UXO White Helmets mitigate the dangers for their fellow civilians, they walk headfirst into them to do so. In December 2019, a team of three UXO White Helmets was killed instantly. Muhammad Nagooh, Saleh Arafat, and Ahmad Al-Hallah had gone to Qastoun Village in Hama to work on securing a target location of ordnances. Their work was nearly finished when the live bomb remnant exploded in the middle of all three men. Every day of duty, they had knowingly sacrificed their safety to ensure others would be safe. From the beginning of volunteering until the last moments of their lives, they had been part of an elite team diligently trained, but tasked with constantly tempting fate. A fate the regime and Russia had ensured would terrorize the Syrian people for many generations to come. These martyred UXO team members had contributed in their searching out and removal of leftover bombs from Syrian land, having recovered to the date of their death, 21,532 pieces of unexploded ordnances from various regions, fields, residential buildings lots, and playgrounds too.

Very recently, on May 23, 2025, UXO White Helmets lost their lives in a deliberately targeted attack in the Hama countryside. A call from the local police station alerted them to a suspicious object atop railroad tracks in the Village of Karah resembling a bomb of sorts, and the volunteers suited up and went out to investigate it. A team of four drove to the site in a clearly marked White Helmet vehicle. Three of the Helmets left their parked vehicle and from their vantage point, could see signs the bomb on the tracks was rigged and ready to go with the possibility of remote detonation. They reported as much to the remaining team member inside the SCD vehicle, who hadn't exited it. As they began to retreat to the vehicle, the bomb was detonated, and the three volunteers outside the vehicle were immediately killed. Based upon the eyewitness testimony of the sole surviving UXO team member, the Syria Civil Defence stated the following in what was a full and lengthy statement released by the organization upon the deaths of their volunteers:

"As they began to withdraw from the scene, the device was detonated at the precise moment of their retreat. Based on the timing and method of detonation, initial observations raise serious concern that the team may have been deliberately targeted by individuals monitoring the site.

We, the White Helmets, consider this incident a serious attack against humanitarian principles and international law, which protect humanitarian workers and criminalize targeting them. It targeted neutral humanitarian workers dedicated to protecting civilians from the dangers of war and appears to be a deliberate attempt to obstruct humanitarian operations and prevent teams from responding to reports of unexploded ordnance."[4]

Caring for and Educating the Children

Regular visits were made by both women and men White Helmets to existing schools and camps to educate the children on proper protocol for all varieties of war dangers, from bomb drops to spotting mines, to playing near open wells. Pamphlets with juvenile animation are handed out for the children to take home so they can remember the lessons delivered to them by the White Helmets. These visits provided the perfect opportunity for the children to voice their concerns and their fears. The White Helmets would sit down with the young students and address each one, doing their best to mitigate their fears. Inevitably, one child would always ask to try on one of the helmets, and the white hard hat that identified their heroes would make its way around the gathering of children, going from head to head, laughter abounding as each youngster got the opportunity to momentarily be a White Helmet.

The White Helmets understand too well the toll the Syrian war has taken on all of the children of Syria. The kids have witnessed and experienced tragedy and hardship that no child should have to endure. Those who have survived Assad's bombs and shelling, and gassings, do so having lost parents, siblings, and friends. When survival is the imperative in your world, remembering to do things like playing and dreaming is not necessarily granted. Anxiety and fear of losing yet more, fixate nearly every Syrian child. It is for this reason that when the skies were sometimes clear of warplanes, the White Helmets would go to orphanages and school grounds to set up carnivals for a day of festivities and merriment. The event would be festooned with balloons and streamers and everything colourful and bright. Slides and games were set up while White Helmets dressed up as silly clowns and teddy bears, and Smurfs, making their way amongst the children, saying hello to each and handing out candy and toys. Face painting centres were set up, and tables were equipped with craft supplies to make princess wands, complete with sparkles, or superhero masks for little warriors. And for a time, the children were transported from a nation thick with conflict to a wonderland where the laughter and antics of children were once again remembered.

The Transfer of Refugees

Each city in every province that was stormed and reclaimed by Assad saw a mass exodus of civilians. Assad even provided the buses for some to leave for the Camps. Some chose any available vehicles to pack up what they could take from their homes and leave before utter devastation, as promised by the regime, became a chokehold on their neighbourhoods. The White Helmets remained at the sides of civilians, offering physical and emotional support. Sometimes putting the last table or rolled rug onto the pick-up truck, ready for departure, was less important to the forlorn residents saying goodbye to their homes, than were the words uttered by the White Helmets, *"One day you will come home."*

When the region's former occupants did return to their battered and broken homes, the White Helmets were there again to receive them. Although the civilians had little to return to, on a daily basis the White Helmets did all they could to serve and equip these hundreds of thousands of civilians who made the difficult decision to return home from the displacement camps to the places where their generational homes had been blasted off the face of Syria. Today, millions of civilians are still waiting to return to their destroyed homes in order to escape the unbearable camp life.

Rebuilding

By late 2021, with few cities left to raze to the ground, the regime's systematic bombing campaign had significantly lessened. The province of Idlib, miraculously the last remaining rebel-held province, also benefited from its lighter bombardment. When the skies softened, and the days quieted, the focus of the White Helmets teams turned to rebuilding their broken lands. Restoration and rehabilitation of infrastructure, so long devastated and defunct because of war, could now be focused on. After essential services such as water and sewage networks, power grids, hospital and medical clinic facilities, and, of course, roads were restored and reconstructed, the revitalization of neighbourhoods would be the next phase of rebuilding. Schools were cleaned and repainted. Playgrounds were restored. Mosques were rebuilt. Marketplaces were restructured. Soccer fields were reborn.

The Evidence Gatherers

After saving civilians, the most important job the White Helmets have and will ever have is that of standing witness to the atrocities of a leader on his broken country. The evidence collected to date has filled an undisclosed building in Belgium, awaiting Assad and Putin's time in the Hague dock.

As the conflict waged on, the White Helmets organization grew stronger, bolder, more resilient. It had an unstoppable momentum that attracted recruits from all walks of life. Even former rebels and regime soldiers jumped ship to join this extraordinary band of humanitarians.

So just what kind of man or woman donned the white helmet? What separated these regular civilians from others and turned them into unassuming heroes to their nation and to the world? The characteristics were often the same: abounding bravery, loyalty and a sense of humour. Surely, it was impossible to be a White Helmet without these attributes.

Yet, the men and women, no matter their abundance of bravery and stalwart natures, were not immune to the reality of the work and how it would mark their entire lives forevermore. They entered the organization only to be changed irremediably by it. No amount of preparation could have truly readied the men who first enlisted. The technical training was the manageable part; the emotional readiness was an impossible wager. These regular Syrians – painters, construction workers, nurses, teachers, students - who volunteered to provide search and rescue for their fellow civilians could never have realized that they would be sacrificing far more than their own physical safety in this newfound vocation. Indeed, they had little notion they would be entering a world where the horrific and the macabre would forge to become a surreal commonplace, one from which many men have never fully returned. The field of duty in massacred Syria has kept many a man chasing the shadows and whispers of things they couldn't catch, things lost and gone. And it is back in that field where more than one white Helmet has helplessly remained, indefinitely stuck amid the rubble and the debris and the dirt, while their entrenched minds have taken over the job of digging, their hands momentarily stilled. The call to put on the helmet was and continues to be a vocation motivated necessarily by humanity tipping the scales of common sense and practical judgement, while in the balance, risk and peril are shrugged off as little more than collateral damage. It had to be that way for each man who put on the helmet.

A White Helmet named Shia describes the emotional toll of being a Syria Civil Defence volunteer, particularly the constant job of dealing with dead bodies, severed limbs, and so much blood.

"The White Helmets had to try to identify people through their limbs...uh...you get used to those terrible scenes of people being...killed or torn into pieces, sight of blood..."

"It kills a part of you or you intentionally kill a part of you in order to be able to do that [work]*."*

And for many, the prospect of they, themselves, dying was not the difficult part. Martyrdom was a righteous thing, a Godly thing. It was the deaths of others, the children, the neighbours, the man you worked alongside of whom you called brother. That good man who protected your life and for whom you were ready to give yours, who died needlessly, viciously, in the line of duty, perhaps before your very eyes.

A brother one moment working at your side doing search and rescue, and the next moment down on the ground, a brother not getting back up, a brother who shared cigarettes and laughter with you mere hours before he fell under a double-tap. A brother taken far too soon. Perhaps he had only been twenty-three, this brother. Perhaps he had been 39 and a father of five, this brother. To date, 392 White Helmets have lost their lives in the line of duty.

The volunteers have always refused to be called heroes, but everything they do for their fellow human beings define them as such. The organization's co-founder, James Le Mesurier, summed their character up easily:

"A hero is someone who runs towards danger when every human instinct says to run the other way."

Indeed, to the people of Syria and to those beyond the nation's borders who knew the humanitarians and their stories, these men in white hard hats risking life and limb to save as many lives as they could, they were truly heroes.

Heroes, yes, but also a persistent thorn in the sides of President Bashar al-Assad and his ally, Vladimir Putin. That a reckoning was coming for these humanitarians was inevitable in a nation where the leader wanted his people and their protectors dead.

CHAPTER THREE

Khaled's Aleppo

"Where is the world? Does anyone care?"

- Khaled Omar Harrah, White Helmet

[Associated Press]

I will never leave Aleppo.

Each time White Helmet, Khaled Omar Harrah, said these words, they were as much an oath of allegiance as they were an act of defiance. As the regime and Russian militaries inched ever closer to taking the entire province from its broken people, his pledge was clear: *"If there is one meter of liberated ground left in Aleppo, I will stand on it."*

Khaled's Aleppo was destroyed and under siege. He had watched for months the wicked devastation of his beloved province's regime-dedicated demise with the stoic resilience of a husband, father, and White Helmet humanitarian. He'd been toughened by the horrors he had witnessed perpetrated on his people and by the insult of neglect inflicted by the outside world that watched on cavalierly and indifferently as Aleppo fell. He shouldered squarely, and as a matter of fact, the blatant disregard for the sanctity of human life that all Syrians had endured. He had stopped listening to the UN Security Council emergency meetings. *It was all bullshit*, he would say between drags on his cigarette. *Expensive bullshit, then afterward handshakes with the devil.* The international cavalry wasn't coming, no matter their half-hearted promises. They had never intended on coming. Aleppo, beautiful Aleppo, was dispensable to those who didn't live within it. Khaled and those left in besieged eastern Aleppo were entirely on their own. Although they did have the faithful company of Sukhois and other Russian jets crisscrossing the Aleppo skies day in, day out.

Undoubtedly, it took the indomitable spirit of a man just like Khaled to even attempt to survive what was happening to Aleppo and counter the fallout with a vanguard of hope that would manifest in his team of humanitarians. He felt it was his imperative to keep others strong too, particularly in his White Helmets Centre, the first of its kind anywhere in Syria. He could still joke with his men after a reconnaissance jet flyover, chuckling that the pilot had turned back without dropping payload for the simple fact he was late for lunch back in Damascus. *It's spiced Kubba Halabiya at the palace today. What do you want from the guy?* He could provoke a laugh out of his most crestfallen White Helmet, even after a daylong shift of search and rescue that had ended with casualties. His constitution was unflinching, fierce yet mitigated with juvenile boyishness that boasted a contagious smile for all, and without an ounce of self-pity for his own situation. Robust Khaled, with the promise of immortality in the translation of his Syrian name. The *"Immortal Man"*, his fellow White Helmets teased him. He would laugh it off. Inshallah, immortal. But how many near misses had there been for him? For all of the White Helmets? *Immortal, my ass*, he would reply, his good-humoured nature the necessary sustenance for the White Helmets he managed. Khaled was something solid when the world around them was crumbling. His guidance was never more important to them, when Aleppo's compass had been all at once smashed to pieces, making it hard to tell up from down. *When are you leaving this place?* He was asked often. *Almost everyone is gone, Khaled.* In response, he might kick at the ground with the toe of his boot, hands on his hips, shake his head a little at the mere prospect of leaving. *"The dilemma is our children. There is no place to send them,"* he would respond. But it was more than that, it was a matter of principle to Khaled to stand one's ground, especially when it was your homeland. When there was respite from search and rescue, Khaled's habit had become watching the skies. The next attack was never that far off. The city suffered through upwards of twenty bombings daily. So, countless times a day, he jerked his head habitually upward, surveilling the heavens for Sukhois and MiGs off in the distance, hoping he could save rescue time if he beat the routine warnings that came through the walkie-talkies that aircraft was headed their way. Even a few seconds off the dispatch time could save one extra life, maybe more. The men could be in their Syria Civil Defence vans and maybe partway to the bomb site before the target area was even impacted. Such was his investment in watching the aircraft come in. In another time, another life, he would surely have made an excellent bird watcher. But instead, here in battered Aleppo, it was warplanes. He got good at it, too. He could distinguish the make and model of each one that was within a half mile of him. What he knew, too, was what payload was coming their way, depending on the warplane. To learn the jet, was to learn the payload. Khaled knew the full range of Sukhois and MiG fighter jets that had entered the airspace since Russia joined the war in Syria, he could distinguish everything in their subtle style variations, from the geometrics of their wing lifts to the gaps between engines, to the length of the fuselage with the Sukhois' flankers being longer and often leaner, and the MiGs significantly shorter. In particular, he easily spotted the routinely-used and old Russian Sukhoi 24, or Su-24, for its degree of wing sweep when it was coming in for a drop at a lower level than other jets, and the fast-firing cannons mounted on each side, full of hundreds of rounds of ammunition that would shell the neighbourhoods swiftly in mere minutes. Indeed, in the early days, that was a favourite bomber of the regime. Old but reliable, and cost-effective.

Then, as Russia became partners in the war, there were more sophisticated fighter jets employed, some tried out for the very first time, using Syria as a veritable trial by fire. A regular bomber was the Sukhoi-34, a newer, sleeker version of the earlier Sukhois - a more advanced Russian fighter jet that took its inaugural war flights in Syria in 2015, carrying both short-range and long-range air-to-surface missiles. The cluster bombs they dropped would light up the skies like fireworks as they obliterated multiple neighbourhoods at once, not just destroying homes but setting on fire all the people in them and leaving them to burn. These were also the bombs notorious for having duds that wouldn't detonate on drop, becoming, instead, live mines in the Syria lands, imperiling generations to come. These new favourites of the regime bombing campaign had stood out immediately to Khaled because of the sleeker design than its precursors, in particular the small lifting surfaces ahead of the wings known as canards. With these beasts, Khaled knew, the game ante on destruction of Aleppo City had just been exponentially upped. They were finely engineered killing machines, handcrafted in Russia. The helicopters with their deadly barrel bomb payloads were easier to take early notice of, louder, and without the swift stealth of the fighter jets. Khaled knew the sounds, too, each fighter jet seemed to have a different head-splitting wail or whoosh to them as they sliced through the helpless atmosphere. Perhaps Khaled knew too much, and it was an acute knowledge he wished he had never obtained, except that it did give his centre occasionally that precious head start on the hell about to be unleashed.

The streets of the neighbourhoods Khaled now walked, sometimes with his young daughters in tow, one on each hand, to buy a few groceries or search out available supplies, were each day as surreal to him as the last. He knew he would never get used to this destruction. It was a dagger in his heart that this was the Aleppo bequeathed to his daughters. Khaled remembered times that might never come back in his lifetime, if at all. He struggled with the question of how all this had happened. Who had given Assad and Putin the right to take this sacred place from generations past, present, and future. He remembered a place that was as if out of one of his daughter's storybooks. Once upon a time, Aleppo had been something very special. But that was before Assad picked it out as the first province in the land to be totally and utterly obliterated. Where was his old Aleppo? Where, indeed.

Long gone were the boulevards lined with cypress and cedars, all the timeless Arabian trees that fragranced the streets as easily as they provided legend for fables. Gone was the verdancy of the very colour green, the grassy parks breaking up the bustling city where children played and families picnicked. Long gone were the flower-trimmed sidewalks where women pushed their carriages and men played backgammon on tiny tables and chairs, chain-smoking and sipping their teas and thick glasses of sugared mate long into the late summer evenings. Even the abundant souks, great vibrant avenues of them, selling hand-painted pottery, soaps, spices, and of course, carpets – the heralded markets once flocked to by tourists and locals, alike, had receded into once upon a time. Only the bravest marketplaces remained open to the public - defying the bomber jets and reconnaissance planes - their selection of fruits and vegetables, flour and spices, sparse and expensive. The Syrian Lira had depreciated. Simple tomatoes, if they could be found at all, were sold at upwards of $4 each. They no longer came in truckloads from the farmers' fields in early summer like every year. Those fields were blasted away now. And gone with the tomatoes was something much more coveted by the people, the wheat to make the flour. The very ingredient, the staple of the Syrian diets, flatbread, depended on. Some was clandestinely harvested or brought in by smuggled shipments by the rebels. Even still, the bread shortage was felt brutally. Every day, lines stretched around city blocks leading to the baker's oven where it had been baked all night and rationed out during the day. Only half a portion for each family. The last in line, having waited for hours, were often told the supply was done for the day, and they would have to come back tomorrow. Yes, come back tomorrow. But their children were hungry tonight.

And perhaps harder to bear, for a people so greatly imbued with love of preservation of tradition and pride of posterity, was the inescapable destruction. They were living in a veritable post-apocalyptic wasteland of never-ending wreckage. The bomb-shocked homes where the children had once slept safely in their beds and wives and old mothers made food at the ovens, were a treacherous reality. Their beloved homes. Aleppo homes, built strong and lasting for countless generations, their thick white limestone walls cool in the summer heat and warm in the winter, were now little more than carcasses. They existed now as nothing more than the brittle artwork created hastily by fighter jets, harbingers of a dying city. Most roofs and outer walls gone, now, very few homes were habitable or safe. A rainstorm could easily bring down a precarious roof, collapsing in on those trying to live inside. Roads in and out of the city were mostly destroyed. The traditional city fountains on roundabouts were leveled, as were time-treasured statues and monuments. The archaic mosques and churches were decimated by shelling.

How great it had once been, Khaled considered.

Indeed, the fabled city, a jewel in the Arab landscape, that mecca of traditional Arab poetry, music, cuisine, and handicrafts, frequented by turbaned men of lore and fixed in romantic ideals, was all but gone. And it was not only the Middle East that was held enamoured by it.

The world had cherished Aleppo. In poignant elegy, it was even spoken about by Shakespeare's Othello...

Albeit used to the melting mood,

Drop tears as fast as the Arabian trees

Their medicinable gum. Set you down this,

And say besides that in Aleppo once.

Yes, *that* in Aleppo once. And gone forever now with its ancient Arabian trees. Indeed, the once upon a time Aleppo had now become nothing more than a fable or a fiction, and whatever existed in these leftover and solemn streets now was unrecognizable to itself. Perhaps, no one knew this better than Khaled.

At the age of 31, Khaled had spent his entire life in Aleppo Governorate. The largest governorate in Syria, Aleppo was situated on the Silk Road and at the crossroads of many trading hubs, making it commercially and economically successful. It was renowned for its textile industry. And of course, the traditional spices, perfumes, and jewelry. Its fertile lands had brought forth a successful agricultural industry boasting its superior fruit and olive trees, its abundant wheat, barley, and endless vegetables, so plentiful in the Middle Eastern climate. Yet, before the revolution, Khaled had steered to a different vocation, that of painter and decorator. There was always work for fair prices, and he was able to provide a modest but satisfying life for himself, his wife, and then his two girls came along, born into the Syrian War. The moment the bombing began in his neighbourhood, Khaled had set down his paintbrush and joined the search and rescue. For many who knew him in his past life, it was hard to reconcile his previous role with the brave volunteer they witnessed rushing into massacre sites for search and rescue. But this is the common catharsis of a people's revolution. It can bring out a fire and grit in people they never knew they had. It was just this fire and grit Khaled Omar Harrah had in abundance.

By the time the city had been gripped by the siege, Aleppo was down to a fraction of its former population. Most people had fled north to the camps. Very few residents remained now. His wife had also begged him to go, to take the girls and go to Turkey. He'd thought about it, of course, he had, just like everyone else. Yet, he once told a teammate driving with him during duty that he had to stay and that he could not send his little girls away either. As they peered out the windows at their forsaken landscape as if seeing it anew, he spoke solemnly, *"I'd rather they die before my eyes than have something happen to them far away. I would cry blood if that happened, honestly."*[5]

In other words, he was not leaving. Not ever. When Khaled Harrah's mind was made up, there was little that could change it. The original White Helmet centre in Aleppo, this one he had helped form and became manager of, had been created with the sole purpose of saving those who couldn't help themselves. What would it say about

66

him, about any of the White Helmets, if they left when the people needed them most? Khaled knew some Syria Civil Defence members had, indeed, fled from the other Aleppo centres bordering on Damascus as the advancing regime was just too close. He had no opinion about that. He knew well in his five years of Syrian conflict, that survival was a personal matter. No two people survived the same way.

Surrender or starve was the ultimatum given by the regime and Russia in the last months of 2016 for Aleppo City. The battle for control over the city had been ongoing since 2012, with the rebel Free Syrian Army [FSA] and the government's Syrian Army [SA] raging continuously and fiercely, splitting Aleppo in two with the FSA taking hold of the ancient Eastern side while the SA kept control of the Western side. In the very middle of this ancient city was a two-millennia-old citadel surrounded high on a hill by a fortress. The clash of sides had come so close in their east and west boundaries that they would actually, routinely meet face to face in the historical palace, cutting it in half with their respective camps, with gunfire coming through the walls and occasional man-to-man combat. The palace, once an Aleppo landmark of rich history, had become yet one more war zone battlefront, claimed by both sides in this fierce confrontation, slowly but surely being destroyed by the combatants, UNESCO'S designation that it was a rare heritage site requiring preservation notwithstanding. Amazingly, the FSA had kept the better-equipped, better-experienced, and much larger contingency of the regime military at bay for 4 years in Eastern Aleppo from 2012 to 2016, with only the off-again, on-again support of the West, the United States being their biggest but undependable sponsor. Their organization would in large part grow out of regime army defectors – those who had experienced what it was to be under Assad's military thumb, those who had seen his wanton bloodshed on innocent civilians, which they were commanded to carry out, and wanted no part of it. In the early days, Assad's checkpoints in and out of Aleppo were manned by his soldiers. In a coup of sorts, in 2012, many of these soldiers fled from their posts and either drifted into obscurity or, in large numbers of solidarity, became soldiers in the Free Syrian Army. Many of these new members combined to create a formidable faction called "Al-Tawhen Brigade", the biggest subsect in the FSA. The remainder of the FSA were Syrian regular civilians who were tired of seeing their fellow Syrians die at Assad's discretion. They were organized, they were well led, and they were determined that the rebels would win this war that Assad had waged on their country. For four years, their armed rebellion stunned the regime and emboldened Syria. It was a feat spawned from heart and soul.

Meanwhile, the inception of the first Syria Civil Defence Centre, not yet known as the "White Helmets" back then, took place in Aleppo City around this same time- 2012. While the FSA and other rebel factions fought hard to liberate Aleppo, the new first responders for the people made use of the building once occupied by Assad's original

Syria Civil Defence. With little to no funding in the very early days, the Syria Civil Defence had only a small arsenal of tools and equipment with which to carry out search and rescue.

As the first videos of their rescues, mostly captured on their cell phones, started to come online, sparking the interest of the world, it was Khaled, his right-hand man Najib, and the other centre volunteers seen repeatedly in the footage, running toward the massacre sights as everyone else ran away. Footage showing the team always deep into search and rescue, digging through mountains of rubble that had been family homes, pulling civilians out of the ruins, alive and dead, all while trying to keep clear of being targets of the military strikes themselves. They were always in the line of fire, and they wholeheartedly accepted this.

It was around this time that the barrel bombs started dropping from helicopters in routine fashion, a horror to the rescuers, as this egregious invention worked so effectively to kill and maim and destroy. In fact, the barrel bombs were so good at killing and destroying, while being so easily deployed, that Assad added them as a regular munition in his arsenal. To the Syrian people, the barrel bomb was the thing of nightmares. It shredded human bodies with its indiscriminate blast of shrapnel as easily as it took out whole buildings with its incendiary power. So, this was the new warfare Khaled and Najib, and their team found themselves ensnared in. This newest brutal fallout and devastation were what they had to navigate through at risk to their own lives. Shift after shift, for years, they had witnessed a destruction of human bodies that no one should see. They saw day after day a complete and utter disregard for human life.

***

Two years before the siege, in the summer of 2014, came what was perhaps the defining moment in not just the humanitarian career of White Helmet, Khaled, but in the fortification of the organization, itself. A man, known only to his White Helmet colleagues, would suddenly garner the stunning attention of what had become a hopelessly indifferent world.

On June 18, 2014, the regime rained down bombs on the southern region of Aleppo in the Al-Ansari district, striking and obliterating the small stone house of the Ibildi family in the early hours of the morning. White Helmet Khaled Hurrah and his team were at the massacre site in minutes. They were told by neighbours that there were four families trapped inside, the members named off on someone's fingers. This was the usual way of gaining information about the formidable task ahead and whom they needed search for. *The kitchen would have been here*, a family acquaintance offered, *the children would have been playing here, the living area just about here...*.It wasn't blueprints, but it gave the rescuers the general idea of where to start digging for life when time was always of the essence. The guys went to work lifting away the heavy slabs of concrete, praying there were survivors. They were searching for several families who had all lived together. Under the heat of the summer sun, working through the upheaval of concrete walls, ceiling, and all the detritus that had once been a Syrian home, the team began unearthing and recovering the victims' bodies. They had recovered the father of the home, the daughter, and the members of three other families, all dead. Remarkably, Umma Mahmoud, the mother, was rescued alive and transported immediately to the hospital. Another grim day. Only one survivor. The White Helmets were as forlorn as they were exhausted. With confirmation from the neighbours yet again, that those were the only people possibly inside, the team wrapped up. It was dark when they walked back to the centre in silence. Once there, each man retreated to a place to rest away from everything they had just been through. Exhausted and in grief, they smoked cigarettes, and called their wives, their children, their mothers.

Perhaps an hour later, back at the centre, Khaled received an urgent transmission on his walkie-talkie. There was likely one more victim under the rubble. The now conscious mother in her hospital bed had asked about her ten-week-old baby boy. Had they gotten him out alive?

The men had no time to let their shock register. Adrenaline surging through them again, the team raced back to the site. Prospects of this new baby being alive after the blast and with the time that had passed were slim to none. But Khaled knew he had to keep hope alive; he had to find the baby regardless of the outcome. First light had turned to night, and for another 9 hours, Khaled and his team leader, Najib, and the rest of the team, picked the bomb site apart as carefully as they could. If the baby was, indeed, alive, their methods would have to be painstakingly slow to ensure more concrete didn't cave in on him, and so the hours stretched on with four White Helmets in a valley of rubble, excavating a fragile baby boy. Exhaustion and dwindling hope set in as they always did. There was no way this baby could possibly have endured this attack and then lived for that long afterward. Khaled had to take a break, just for a moment or two. He didn't want to admit it, but their actions were futile. He lay down near the place where he had been digging, hopelessly discouraged and most likely thinking about his own two baby girls at home. What if they were under the rubble? He turned his head where he lay, and with his ear now directly against the rubble, he thought he heard the faintest muffled crying of a baby. He was quite sure it was delusion. His brain was as fatigued as his limbs. Surely, it was a trick of his mind. He told his teammate Najib to also lie down and listen. Najib bobbed his head excitedly, yes, that he had heard the crying too. New purpose shot through Khaled's body with this renewed hope. His big hands began picking away at the rubble again, but the light from their flashlights wasn't enough, and visibility was poor. He called to anyone and everyone for more light, and within minutes, neighbours were standing above the digging while shining their own flashlights, lanterns, even phones, down on the operation. Several more hours passed, and the cries ceased. Their renewed hope once again turned to despair as it seemed apparent this child had not survived, not all these hours with a building on top of him. Now they anticipated the recovery of a baby boy's body. They would not leave the deceased baby in there; at the very least, he would be returned to his mother for burial. As the excavation continued, and the men worked, clawing at a different part of the wreckage, scooping the loose rubble out with their hands, a peak of the baby's motionless head was suddenly revealed...lodged in between the floor and ceiling of the far side of the house. The wall of limestone was too heavy to be lifted. There was no heavy machinery back then to aid in the excavation. Khaled called for tire jacks from the cars. *Yallah! Yallah!* Several were slipped into place to help raise the slab of ceiling resting mere centimetres above the infant. It seemed to be working, and the baby's head was now clearly visible to Khaled. The immense weight of the ceiling, however, was too much for the jacks, and the right side of the ceiling slab snapped away. As if in response, the baby started crying. Too soon to rejoice, the men used their strength to support the remaining ceiling atop the baby even as they dug with their hands to free the debris around his now fully visible head. There was clear movement. He was alive. Another agonizingly slow hour would pass as the child was freed from the wreckage, and, with the same movements mimicking a doctor bringing forth an infant out of the womb, Khaled drew the baby through the narrow and jagged opening of rock and debris and finally back into the world. Immediately, the crying child was brought to Khaled's chest, and as the cell phone video of the rescue captures, White Helmet, Khaled's face revealed both shock and profound emotion as he was overcome with the understanding that the baby had been saved, that he was miraculously alive, that he had beaten Assad's grim odds. In the soon-to-be-famous video, another team member's hand is seen moving in to help take the baby from the exhausted Khaled, but with a quick brush of his hand in protest, Khaled refuses. The instinct of a father over his cub. He was not letting the baby, now safe and alive in his arms, go. Not for all the world would he let the baby boy be taken from him until he had it far away from the massacre that had fought so hard against the men to take the child into its vast oblivion.

It had taken 19 hours of digging, but now the child was visible to one and all, saved, and a chorus of Allahu Akbars rang out, praising God. Yet, in his state of near shock, Khaled could not find any words at all. He was numb with relief. He recalls that for two hours, he could not speak a word. Later, he would sit and weep not only over the fact that the child had survived, he had made it, but perhaps more so, about the evil brutality that had put him there and taken half the infant's family.

The baby's name was Mahmud Idilbi, born into a war and at 10 weeks old barely escaping it. He was nicknamed *"The Miracle Baby"* and Khaled Hurrah, *"The Rescuer of the Miracle Baby."* And as the grainy video of this incredible rescue hit YouTube and the world, attention returned to the horrors of Syria, and the White Helmets became famous for their humanitarian work, if only fleetingly. In a rare interview following the rescue of Baby Mahmoud, Khaled responded poignantly with indifference about this one child being the Miracle Baby. He believed that the rescue of one child did not discount all the others saved as well as all those lost needlessly in the horrors of this war.

"There are many stories about [the White Helmets] working from the morning to the evening trying to save children. The only difference is this rescue was caught on film."

His words rang true for every member of this Aleppo team. Baby Mahmoud was far from the only child targeted for slaughter by Assad, who had survived. Yet, countless others, their crime being born Syrian, had their lives taken in the blink of an eye by Assad's bombs. Mahmoud was just one of the lucky ones.

Some days later, Khaled and his teammates would be reunited with Baby Mahmoud and his convalescing mother in the hospital. It was a bittersweet moment for all. While Umm Mahmoud cradled her surviving son, she was also mourning the loss of her husband and young daughter.

Khaled Hurrah would say later in reflection, *"For me this is the real jihad [non-violent defense of his country]. If I die saving lives, I think God would definitely consider me a martyr."*

***

Two years later, the *"Miracle Baby"* long forgotten by the world, the siege in Aleppo worsened day after day. Khaled and his team kept up the good fight with their shovels and pickaxes, and signature white helmets. The story of the ongoing battle of Khaled Harrah and his teammates of his original White Helmet Centre was captured in a Netflix documentary, *Last Men in Aleppo.* Filmed by White Helmet, Hamid Khatib, and directed by Feras Fayyad, in one of the most dangerous filming locations on earth, the movie is raw but brilliant in its storytelling. The film reveals drone footage of the expansive, seemingly never-ending graveyard that fills up the film's frame, of Aleppo and its unimaginable ruins alongside the White Helmets' continued work inside this carcass of a former city. The mission of the filmmakers was to both reveal the last days of dying Aleppo as well as preserve it for posterity. And perhaps more than this, to show the truth of what had happened to Syria and its people. The result for the audience is the cold, grey, desperate feeling of almost being there. *"This film gives an artistic form to the absurdity of war"*, says director Fayyad.[6] The film hides nothing. Not the limp, lifeless infants being pulled by the volunteers out of their graves of debris, nor the raw emotions of the men working through the nightmare of it from which they cannot wake up. Khaled's big smiles and innate sense of humour keep his men going, and keep the audience from losing all hope, but the close-up countenances captured of Khaled when he is with his children, pensive and anguished for them, despite his outbursts of silliness for their sake, tells the true tale - he is a man who is afraid for his family and for his country. He is a man who has had enough. But to be fed up is not a choice Khaled Hurrah can consider – it simply is not in his constitution. And what else is plainly clear by Khaled himself, and the choices he makes, is his refusal to leave Aleppo. Come hell or high water, he makes it known he will stand his ground and see it through.

It seems more than just a little peculiar at first, that the documentary about Syrian humanitarians, *Last Men in Aleppo*, opens with high- resolution shots of goldfish filling the screen, close up and oddly captivating, their big bulging eyes and their waving fins and tails, swimming round and round in a fishbowl, just round and round. The more the viewer focuses in, the more determined the common goldfish appear to be, almost as if they are trying to figure out a way beyond the narrow boundaries of the universe prescribed for them.

The goldfish eventually reappear in the documentary as Khaled stops to buy some from a streetside vendor who has his tank set up. Not unlike a kid at a pet store choosing his fish, Khaled looks close into the glass, picking out his favourite for the vendor to scoop out. He tries to hide his excitement with his characteristic jokes. He tells Najib and the others who accompany him on this quest, that the fish will just be pets, but that if the siege gets much worse, he will have to eat them. The big grin emerges helplessly on his face. Or better yet - Khaled tells them - if they multiply, he will set up his own market stand and become rich. There is laughter. Khaled takes the four fish home in a small bag, and then the construction of a backyard fountain and basin begins. Everyone helps. It is something to do, after all that is outside of war. When the newly constructed fish home, a three-tiered fountain of sorts, is finished, Khaled pours in the water and releases the fish from the top tier to make their way all the way down to the largest part of the basin, which is now their home. It's a spectacle to the men, and they watched amused, wondering if the fish will like their new home and dubious about their chances of survival. At one point, Khaled reaches down and scoops up one goldfish, letting it wriggle breathlessly in his big hand for a few moments, observing its resistance to life beyond the water, and then releases it back into the small pool. The men take chairs around the fountain, smoking and relaxed as they take in this new chance entertainment. There is a pensiveness in Khaled's expression, however, as he watches the fish swim round and round, complacent yet somehow determined in their shunted journey that is a basin only 1 meter across. Would they prefer to be in deeper, more exotic waters? Yes, of course. Khaled takes another drag off his cigarette but continues to watch them. Of course, they would, but they have no choice in the matter. Whether he knows it or not, an affinity is struck then and there in those moments between Khaled and the fish. Khaled wonders how long the fish can last in this makeshift sea, or even if they will be alive when he checks on them tomorrow. What is clear to him, however, is that the fish cannot exist at all, outside of it. Instinctively, Khaled knows that this is his predicament in Aleppo. To stay is to bide his borrowed time, to leave would be impossible. Aleppo, so foreign to him now, is still the only place he can survive.

Once, Khaled had been given an offer to leave Aleppo. A once in-a-lifetime shot at getting out of Syria altogether. Following his astounding fame rescuing the 10-week-old baby, he was invited to Washington, D.C., and New York City to speak about the ongoing conflict in Syria from the perspective of a White Helmet. Through a translator, he spoke his truth. Afterward, the offer was made by the American government to move him and his family to the United States permanently. Khaled said no. He went back to his home in Aleppo to spend the rest of his days, whether they be long or short. He knew it was the right thing to do.

At home, any available downtime was generally with the loves of his life, his daughters, one four years old, and one eight, usually on the floor of their living room or on walks through debris-filled streets hunting down the stray cats his girls loved to chase. Time at the centre spent in between rescues, found him usually on the cell phone with them. The younger of the girls, his baby, would coo loving words into the phone and smack kisses into her dad's ear. He would smile big. This made it all worthwhile. The older daughter invariably asked, *"We miss you. When are you coming back?"* To this, Khaled would try to reassure them that he would be home soon and that he loved them very much, too.

Come August of 2016, Aleppo was all but lost. Regime and Russian troops were now entering the city on foot, even while the shelling continued. The siege had intensified. Very few people remained in the city. The White Helmets were some of them.

On February 22, 2023, I spoke with White Helmet Najib, Khaled's right- hand man at the centre, via text messages. I asked him to recount a fateful day in the lives of the White Helmets which occurred in August 2016, as well as he could. Speaking only in Arabic, he used an English translating system to communicate with me. He provided the following information for me.

On the morning of Thursday, August 11th, 2016, fierce attacks rained down on the area of the Ramouseh neighbourhood. Residential houses once more took the punishing ballistics. Khaled's centre responded and was quick to mobilize to the hardest hit bomb site, a mountainous pile of what had been people's homes. It was one of the most dangerous search and rescues the men had been exposed to, with snipers abounding and troops just off in the distance. Khaled and his team worked quickly, and then the double-tap came. Instantly, Khaled was peppered with shrapnel from shelling, one deadly piece of it lodged in his neck. Najib took an incapacitating hit of shrapnel to his lung. Najib saw his partner, Khaled, go down, but there was nothing he could do. He knew he was dead. The blood from his throat was too great. There was a pool of it around Khaled. The shrapnel had hit an artery, clearly. Najib, himself, could barely get air into his damaged lungs and was quite certain he, himself, was going to die.

Najib: *"I was injured, and I saw Khaled dead. I left him and left, and Khaled stayed the first day."*[7]

Jennifer: *"Khaled's body stayed there? For how long?"*

Najib: *"For the evening...."* [Trying to understand through the context of his translated message, I was made to understand Khaled's body was left at the bomb site throughout the night and into the next day, as the area was just too dangerously surveilled by regime and Russian forces to attempt his recovery.]

Najib: *"I went out in the* [next] *morning....and he pulled him out in the evening."*

One of the last things Najib wanted me to know during this conversation was that he would not have left without Khaled, had he believed he was alive.

Najib: "Yes, I did not leave him until I lost hope."

On August 11th, 2016, Khaled Omar Harrah took his last breath in Aleppo, the place he had vowed never to leave. He was, until the very end, a man of his word. The news broke to the world that the rescuer of the "Miracle Baby" had been killed during search and rescue. The Syria Civil Defence posted his picture, a big-smiling Khaled, mourning him and honouring him - with the hashtag #sothatothersmaylive. Condolences poured in from around the world.

James Le Mesurier, the co-founder of the White Helmets organization, in his statement on Khaled's death, also honoured the man he was and his indefatigable work ethic. *"There are literally dozens of images of him carrying women, children, old men, the dead, the wounded from buildings in Aleppo over the past two years. He was one of just under three thousand White Helmets who have the same experiences, and is a symbol of the humanity, dedication, bravery and commitment of these extraordinary volunteers."*[8]

Among a community of heroes that are the White Helmets, Khaled Omar Harrah, has become synonymous both in life and posthumously known as the great man. His name in Arabic means "immortal," and that the legend of the man is.

He leaves behind his wife, two daughters, and the son his wife was pregnant with at the time of his death.

Khaled Omar Harrah

Born: Aleppo, Syria, 1985

Died: Aleppo, Syria, August 11, 2016

CHAPTER FOUR

Enter Russia

"I do not think I have the right to determine the political future of Syria, be it with or without al-Assad. This is for the Syrians themselves to decide. Nobody has the right to claim the rights that belong to the people of another country."

- Vladimir Putin, President of Russia

35 36 00.69 N – Longitude
36 36 28.06 E - Latitude

These were the coordinates read out to the Russian pilot from ground control as his Sukhoi jet crossed the airspace over Idlib Province in Syria. Moments later, the fighter jet's payload was released and two precision-guided munitions, "Smart Bombs", neatly found their bullseye in the town of Kafranbel, Idlib, all but obliterating Nabad al Havat Surgical Hospital, an underground civilian medical centre. The mountainous cloud of dust and debris rising up over the cavernous place where the hospital had been just moments before had incredibly clean margins. A feat only possible with Russian aircraft, as Assad's air force didn't have this capability in its outdated arsenal. In fact, the regime had, up until then, been using conventional carpet bombing, indiscriminate and messy. Russia would change all that. When military budget allows, the modern and elite precision bomb finds its target so accurately that it can be launched with the directive of taking out a single vehicle in a street, leaving incredibly little to no collateral damage. A Jeep can be destroyed so effectively that, other than a few leftover metal fragments, it might never have existed. When the precision bomb is multiplied in number and dropped on a larger target, such as a building, it maximizes destruction while minimizing output. And this was the regime's objective this day. Having been on a bombing campaign for weeks beforehand, wantonly targeting civilian neighbourhoods in southern Idlib Province, this spring day, the regime only wanted the area's hospital, one of the very few now left in Syria. And Assad took it swiftly. The Russian Sukhoi was back at its base long before the dust had settled, no party to the wicked fallout the pilot would leave in his wake. This was on May 5th, 2019. For the next 12 hours, Russian jets would scour Idlib Governorate, debriding its landscape of three more hospitals, destroying four in all in less than one day. The tactic was clear and shameless. To take out the hospitals would ensure civilians and the rebels alike would have no lifeline to critical medical help. For a surgical hospital like Nabad al Havat, whose jurisdiction treated over 200,000 Syrians, this was no small loss to southern Idlib, while so easy a victory for the regime. No longer could doctors treat village children or wounded rebel soldiers. And in the eyes of the regime, both were terrorist opposition in defiance of the State.

Attacking a civilian hospital is one of the most illegal acts of war. They are dedicated safehouses, neutral in their dispositions. Ensuring hospitals are protected during wartime goes as far back as 1920, when nations first convened in Geneva in the wake of the unbridled atrocities of the First World War. The First Geneva Convention prescribed the rules that there should be no *"obstacle to the humanitarian activities"* and that the wounded and sick *"shall be respected and protected in all circumstances."* Article 19 of the Convention made hospitals off limits. Anything less was a war crime. Current International Humanitarian Law was predicated on the tenets of the Convention and is purported to be upheld to this day. But crimes against humanity were nothing new for the regime. In fact, they had become Assad's tried and true modus operandi. And with their new ally, Russia, the execution had never been easier.

The exquisite precision of the initial singular strike was immediately baffling to anyone from the outside, looking in. The hidden hospital should have been safe and gone unnoticed, underground. The tunnels for the entrance were almost invisible. They were fastidiously constructed to be that way. For all intents and purposes, Nabad al Havat Surgical Hospital didn't exist. For certain, Assad's reconnaissance jets had never been able to pick it up before. Moreover, the precision bombs used in the hospital's destruction were completely reliant not only on the exquisite accuracy of the measurement system used for determining location but also on exactitude in setting the coordinates of the target. These coordinates are wholly dependent on intelligence information. Guesswork is not part of the equation.

So, where did the exact coordinates for not one but ultimately four hospitals come from so readily, and how did the enemy acquire them so effortlessly? This was some of the most classified intelligence to be had during any war because not everyone played by Convention rules. The answer was in a word, incomprehensible. Quite simply, they came from the self-proclaimed pinnacle of humanitarian protection and justice itself, the United Nations. In an apparent effort to protect vital infrastructure, schools, hospitals, factories, and even first responder buildings like the White Helmets Centres, a newly established department called the *'Deconfliction System'* of the UN had deliberately collected this information and then provided it to third parties within the United Nations organization to *safeguard* these targets. Russia, a specious UN member, eagerly received the intel and wasted no time in putting it to advantageous use. In this way, no less than 26 medical facilities in rebel-held Idlib Governorate were systematically destroyed. It was a fact that shocked and gave pause to many politicians, statesmen, and humanitarian organizations. With incredible naiveté, the United Nations had simply handed over top-secret hospital coordinates to the enemy on a politically tarnished silver platter that had all the trappings of blind bureaucracy, no matter how well-intentioned. The rules of war had never been so skewed.

***

Even before the Syria Civil Defence dispatch came in that a hospital had been struck, the White Helmets in the Kafranbel and Khan Sheikhoun centres knew, without a doubt, it was the underground surgical centre. They had grown attuned to surmising a bomb's target merely by the initial fallout of the explosion itself in terms of its telltale sounds, the direction of the plumes of wayward smoke, and even by the very trajectory in which affected civilians immediately ran for cover. While centre White Helmets rapidly mobilized, off- duty volunteers hastily threw on their uniforms and helmets too, knowing near instinctually this was a massive attack bearing excessive casualties and that every able body would be needed for search and rescue. What they knew also was that a significant number of critical and convalescing children had been housed in that destroyed hospital and that they were, in these very moments, dead and dying, but perhaps there were some still holding on to life who could be saved. SCD vehicles raced along the bomb-pocked and pitted roads, their sirens blaring, their Islamic prayer beads bouncing chaotically from their rearview mirrors, silent prayers being uttered in mental litanies, until they arrived at the crater in the ground...the remains of Nabad al Havat Hospital.

As the White Helmet teams rushed into the enormous wreckage and fallout of the hospital, they were confronted with unspeakable carnage. Bodies were strewn over the floors amid overturned hospital beds, tables, and all variety of destroyed medical equipment. It was an attack so overtly brazen as to border on the diabolic. As the White Helmets took their first survey of the massacre, they realized there was little to no movement in the ashen clouds of grey dust and dirt that still swirled through the air, unmitigated. The devastation of this supposed safehouse was confounding. The White Helmets recognized dead patients they had maybe a day earlier rescued from previous bomb attacks. Shredded and bloodied hospital gowns, no longer standard hospital blue but massacre grey now, delineated the patients from the medical staff. One White Helmet froze as he parked his roaming gaze on the far corner of the hospital. The Helmet at his side was compelled to look that way, too. Then he froze as well. For off in that corner, there was the child Ahmed, not far from his overturned wheelchair, discernable even now, covered in blood and the grime of bomb dust. Ahmed. The one they had nicknamed the "smiling boy". Both his legs had been fractured when the regime bomb hit his house on Saturday. One so severely that it had needed amputation. Here now, looking at his lifeless body were the very White Helmets who had pulled him from the wreckage and then visited him in this hospital on their day off. They had sat on the side of his bed just over there in that corner, and the 8-year-old had smiled big to see them. Likely for Ahmed, it was nothing less than a visit from superheroes - no capes required. In a world fraught with instability and chaos, one certainty was that White Helmets rescued and saved while their government hunted and murdered, and to the people they were, indeed, saviours. To be in their presence was a blessing. "قطعت إحدى ساقي" he told them without losing the smile. ["One of my legs was cut off"]. They nodded. They knew. They reminded him he was a survivor and a hero, strong beyond words. They assured him he would learn to walk with one leg, and when they had told him several of the White Helmets also had missing legs, and that not only had they returned to helping the people, but that they even played soccer again, Ahmed smiled bigger. This latter bit of knowledge was the best medicine. *"I will play soccer again, too."* His subsequent confident grin had earned him a pat on the head from one of the Helmets. That was then. By the hand of cruel Providence, which had never particularly favoured Syrians, Ahmed had survived one indiscriminate bomb attack only to be taken to a place of convalescence where he would die of a second one. Now, they picked him up carefully, reverently, where he lay on his side in a pall of ashen dust, and carried him away, the smile once and for all erased by the regime. The overturned wheelchair was no longer needed by him. Assad had eliminated one more *terrorist* – an eight-year-old soccer fan, beloved by his mother. And just who exactly would tell the mother that the very place meant to heal her boy had, ultimately, killed him. In the list of White Helmet duties, the task of telling a parent their child was dead, ranked pretty much the worst. One Helmet caught the eyes of the other in acknowledgement of all these searing truths, but no words were spoken. There was nothing to say. For many of the volunteers, their on-duty adrenaline kept emotions at bay, kept them in survival mode so they could keep going, keep doing what needed be done. Unflinching focus was key. They depended on this to get through. Tears saved no one, they had needed decide long ago. When the job was done, perhaps then they could allow the abject horror of the images seared indelibly into their brains to manifest so as to make some sort of sense out of them. No, in the field they would stay strong, unflinching. It was later at home when they would relive the horrors on their own time, perhaps sobbing uncontrollably before children and a wife, alike. In a mere moment, they might be mentally snatched from the present and returned to the site of their search and rescue, where too many had died...on their watch. Or all by themselves, sitting in a corner in deafening silence, wanting the world to stay away from them for just a little while, they might collapse in horrific reverie. Just one brief moment in this eternity of horror to be allowed refuge from everything. Sometimes the sound of silence worked better on the pain than any opioid or tranquilizer possibly ever could. Their tallies of the dead they had recovered just kept growing. They felt somehow responsible for each body that they could not bring out alive. But that was a menacing fact they would deal with years into the future. Now they had only to keep going. Keep fighting the good fight. Surely that was the unspoken but truest motto for this beleaguered organization, which was tasked with saving all those targeted.

The few surviving doctors helped with the search and rescue. A seemingly calm but emotional voice from the corridor of a remaining tunnel announced resignedly, almost matter-of-factly, that they had lost their orthopaedic surgeon. The *only* orthopaedic surgeon. A colleague and friend of this rare, specialized surgeon, crouched down prostrate to the dirt floor and pounded his fists in the stony rubble, raging at the futility of it all. There was likely only a handful of orthopaedic surgeons left in all of Syria. Before the war, there had been many. The surviving patients could be counted on two hands. Incredibly, one still lay in his upright hospital bed, barely conscious but alive, the room around him turned upside down. He was found muttering *Allahu Akbar* (God is greater) in a near stupor. Indeed, Providence had been fickle this day.

Amazingly, many bottles of ointment and packages of medication remained in their original rows on an opposite, sheared-off wall, like no explosion had occurred, while everything else was scattered like detritus upon the mangled floor of debris. After the dead and wounded were attended to, the White Helmets gathered all things medicinal alongside the doctors. These things were worth their weight in gold. The SCD team photographer documented the scene with photos and video throughout. Surely the world would do something now, they considered. A hospital, it *was* a hospital. The other thought that pressed each of their minds...where would they take the injured now when the next bomb hit?

Indeed, the rebuilding of the hospital would begin immediately with the White Helmets at the forefront of the reconstruction, only for Russia to return with their precision bombs that very November. A déjà vu so cruel as to be almost surreal. Then, as had happened in the spring of that year, the Russians brazenly played the same trump card to those who would accuse them of breaking international criminal law...claiming empirically that they had merely bombed facilities being used as "hospital shields" where all varieties of terrorists were being housed. A United Nations security tribunal calling for punishment was thwarted by permanent council member Russia's veto power. The UN could proceed no further with the matter. And in the context of this incredible injustice, the entire tribunal struck many as an expensive farce. Only the first of many that denied the Syrian people any justice whatsoever.

***

In the Autumn of 2015, the balance of war in Syria was turned upside down. The aerial bombardments suddenly changed in the Syrian skies. The people had become accustomed to the clockwork strikes of the regime, taking immense relief when night fell and the attacks would routinely stop. For whatever reason, Assad didn't send his jets out at night. So, with darkness came a reprieve from the threat of bombs and massacres. Syrian mothers could put their children to bed without fear of losing them through the night. Then suddenly that was all done. One White Helmet from a small village near Khan Sheikhoun recalls hearing the very first foreign missile detonate in the deep darkness from where he sat upon his home's concrete rooftop on a cool fall night, exploding and giving an electric jolt of light to the blackness on the horizon. Knowing the sound of every regime war plane or chopper, right down to their make, model and year, the White Helmet understood immediately it wasn't Syrian aircraft. And it was only the beginning of what would become an unrelenting campaign of indiscriminate warfare on a helpless population. A new fleet of beasts, mostly Sukhoi fighter jets and Mi-28 Helicopters, took to the skies within days, dropping bombs around the clock and unleashing a new brand of terror on the Syrian people throughout all opposition-held areas. Now there was no safe time to be alive. What had been horror for the Syrian people had, with the clandestine shake of hands in a Kremlin office, become hell on earth.

On September 30, 2015, Russia entered the war on Assad's people. The internationally- labelled "civil war" was up until then slowly but surely being won by the rebels, and the Syrian regime was losing its footing. No one was more aware of this than President Bashar al-Assad as he paced the halls of his Damascene Palace, which was less than one week away from a full-fledged onslaught of rebel fighters coming down the slopes of Mount Qasioun and storming his front doors. If truth be told, Assad was more irritated by the thought of revolutionary three-starred flags crossing the Assad Family threshold than he was by any Kalashnikovs or Bazookas. To relinquish his father Hafez's sovereign power held for five decades to a ragtag team of impromptu and untrained fighters would be worse than death. The shame would be all on him, the second-choice default heir to the Syrian dictatorship.

Since mid-2011, intense fighting and mass desertion had weakened the regime's Syrian Arab Army. Great numbers of Assad's soldiers even turned coat and joined the opposition, seeing the real picture of the monstrous regime they were owned by and wanting no more part of it. The "Shoot to kill" mandate on helpless women and children was not an easily-stomached order. Even the support of Iran's Islamic Revolutionary Guard Corps (IRGC), the paid-for Iranian militias, and Russian mercenaries, was foundering. Huge regular shipments of

Russian weapons weekly were also useless if the bodies holding the guns and driving the tanks were falling away steadily. Meanwhile, the rebels, including the ever-expanding Free Syrian Army, were advancing and occupying, growing in number and morale. In March 2015, Assad suffered a huge blow when the regime lost a second provincial capital – Idlib - to the opposition. To this day of writing, it has not been recaptured. It is virtually the only remaining liberated large city in Syria.

So, enter Russia. The new Russian arsenal, consisting of a sleek collection of fighter jets, stealth helicopters, submarines, and naval ships, would change all that. A veritable king's ransom of munitions delivered near instantaneously to dedicated Syrian air bases and naval ports, the narrow shores of Tartous being at the forefront, and generously brought to the aid of Assad's massacres and atrocities on his people. Liberated regions of Syria and the world wondered not just a little what Putin was doing there, why Syria mattered suddenly to the Russian Federation. In a televised October 2015 interview, Putin stated Russia's goal in Syria as *"stabilizing the legitimate power in Syria and creating the conditions for political compromise."* Creating the conditions for political compromise...undoubtedly, a bold-faced euphemism for aiding and abetting the slaughtering of innocent civilians into submission. But, of course, Russia had never been one to give out free lunches. Their collaboration would, of course, require compensation.

Putin had been watching Syria closely since the first wave of civilian revolutions in the Arab Spring. He observed with unmitigated disapproval when, in 2011, the Libyan government was overthrown by its people, mere mortals, unchecked and suddenly more powerful than their rightful leader. He had been Prime Minister of Russia at the time and openly criticized then-Russian President Dmitry Medvedev for enabling the defeat of Muammar Gaddafi. Putin viewed the successes of these vulgar upheavals as a cautionary tale and started getting his "*utki*" in a row as he cast his eye to his old ally, Syria, and the chaotic rumblings in their own streets. It was time to act. First, weekly shipments of weapons were provided to the regime out of the Russian arsenal - one so massive that the handouts were hardly missed. And in this way, he rekindled the relationship with what was one of his oldest and rarest allies in the world. For the Russian Federation, "friends" were, indeed, few and far between. Politically sanctioned by the United States, ignored by the majority of the Middle East, particularly Saudi Arabia, and snubbed by the European Union, Vladimir Putin was well aware of his isolated political positioning. And there was, of course, history beleaguering him. His nation came off in the history books as a scourge on the world. Stalin's Gulags were but one political and humanitarian obscenity needing be swept under Mother Russia's rug. The Iron Curtain and all that loomed behind it was but another indiscretion discrediting any perceived fair play. Soviet Communism had collapsed, and Putin saw this last defeat as an epic tragedy.

Restoring Russia's standing as a major world player was first and foremost on President Putin's mind and couldn't, somehow, Syria provide a vehicle for doing this? If Russia preserved Syria, perhaps Syria could preserve Russia. Motivation to lend a hand to his Middle East ally came in many forms. Primarily, the discussions over the proposed Qatar-Turkey pipelines that were to be built in Syria, and bring natural gas to the Middle East and Europe from a new route. Negotiations for this had gone back as far as 2012 and were a significant threat to the Russian nation. If the Qatar-Turkey pipelines became a reality, Russia would lose billions as the number one supplier of natural gas to the Middle East and Europe. The Russian company Gazprom, the majority state-owned multinational energy corporation headquartered in Saint Petersburg, kept Russia on the map in a big way. Nicknamed a "state within a state" due to the fact that it had, among other extraneous resources, its very own military protecting it, sales are noted at the time of this writing to be over $120 billion US dollars. It is nicely situated as the largest publicly-listed gas company in the world and the largest company in Russia by revenue. To protect and continue to empower it, Putin needed into Syria. And the Russian government was not shy about discussing the thwarting of the Qatar-Turkey pipeline. In an October 2016 TV interview, General Leonid Ivashov, openly addressed the fact that Russia's engagement in the Syrian conflict would allow it to block proposed pipelines between the Middle East and Europe, and thus ensure the dominance of Gazprom.

Of course, they presented this as a fair proposition. For wasn't Qatar and Turkey's support of the Syrian opposition driven by those very plans to get *their* pipelines through? But now Syria outright rejected the Qatar-Turkey proposal, explicitly stating it would *"protect the interests of* [its]*Russian Ally, which is Europe's top supplier of natural gas."*

Hanging in the balance of all this political and backroom maneuvering were, of course, the Syrian people. The victimization they had known until now was about to witness a completely new, wicked dimension. One, perhaps, wholly unimaginable.

Immediately and generously, Russia emerged, with its military might and its awesome fleets of weaponry, like a wrecking ball to the Syrian nation. At the time of this writing in the autumn of 2021, documentation provided by the White Helmets indicates Russia has to date launched 5,586 attacks across Syrian governorates. Stalwart Idlib was exposed to the largest number of attacks (3,759), while Aleppo and its countryside were targeted 1,175 times. Hama was targeted 521 times, rural Damascus was targeted 255 times, and Daraa was targeted 205 times, in addition to 50 attacks on Homs and more central Damascus. Breaking it down, Russia hit Syria with 194 attacks in 2015, 1,064 attacks in 2016, 1041 attacks in 2017, and 804 attacks in 2018. 2019 was the most violent year, with Russian forces carrying out 1,567 attacks, 821 attacks in 2020, and 98 attacks in 2021. The numbers, however, sterile in their characterization, do little justice to the horror each attack unleashed. Putin had easily upped the ante of terror and brutality for the Syrian people.

His choice of weapons was varied. There were the conventional missiles dropping payloads that decimated everything that was a target. Then there were cluster bombs meant to take out a city block of homes and ignite to continue burning everything in sight into the next day.

The White Helmets were a clear and credible problem for Syria's machinations and, therefore, for Russia's. Perhaps the biggest. Not only were they saving many of those Russia targeted for massacre, they were filming the atrocities in real time, defying the propaganda Russia was feeding to the world with clear and concise eyewitness accounts of the real story.

The question for Putin, as it had been for the regime, was what to do about the White Helmets. When state terrorism against civilians and humanitarian workers, alike, is consistently unchecked by the world, despite their impotent protestations, the terrorist knows only impunity and an "anything goes" warfare mentality. If hospitals can be obliterated without so much as a slap on the wrist by NATO or the United Nations, then anything is within the realm of possibility. Russia and the regime would push the envelope on this certainty just as far as they could conceive ways in which to do so.

The presence of the White Helmets came to the attention of President Assad early on. As plot lines go, they were absolutely foiling his. Assad's dedicated campaign of destroying infrastructure early on, including medical facilities to rescue the wounded after regime attacks, was necessary to weaken the morale of the people and purge the civilian population who would not capitulate. When he saw this was being hijacked by teams of neutral humanitarian workers who took on the role as first responders, he initially thought they would grow weary and fall away. But as they turned from disorganized neighbours heading to bomb sites into an organized group of rescuers, that just kept growing, and began setting up centres in all liberated cities that were operating as a whole, Assad could no longer ignore this force to be reckoned with. So, in interviews and reports to the world, he would designate the White Helmets as terrorists, aligned with Daesh and al-Nusra terrorist factions. But what was even more important than this was getting rid of them by any means possible.

With the aid of Russia, the infamous double-tap was introduced, with its singular aim of taking out the White Helmets during the search and rescue of bomb sites. The operation of the double-tap strike was easy. After an initial air strike on a civilian area, the White Helmets would quickly arrive for search and rescue. An entire team of these first responders would be deeply invested in excavating rubble and painstakingly extracting buried members of a family, children, grandmothers, from under the rubble, when over their heads another warplane would drop a second bomb on the exact location approximately 20 to 30 minutes later, killing attending White Helmets and civilians alike. The White Helmets could only feel shock and unabated horror with this first double-tap, but quickly understood it wasn't a one-off; it was a regime/Russian strategy designed to decimate the Syria Civil Defence. More than ever before, they understood they were prey. It provided just more insight into the fact that the regime was not hunting terrorists but civilians. It was only logical that they wanted to take out those first responders trying to keep them alive.

The routine for the White Helmets, thereafter, was to work more expediently than ever in the first 30 minutes at a bomb site. Through the sounds of machinery moving mountainous rocks and their own digging through rubble and debris, each had their ears pricked for the far-off sound of that second warplane. When it came, they hoped they had the victims in arms already so they could make a run for it before the second bomb hit. However, this was not always the case. Often, they were faced with the worst scenario when they were almost at the point of freeing a crying baby, and the Russian jet was all but right above them. To leave this living child half buried in rubble but almost home and run for his own safety was, to many White Helmets, unconscionable. That is when the adrenaline kicked in hard, that is when the rescuer saw only pink flesh and wide eyes and rocks in his tunnel vision. That is when, so focused on saving life, he barely heard the engines of the jet, never mind his colleagues' beseeching cries for him to get out now. Many a Helmet, in his virtuous obstinacy, had captured their victim, running with him in their arms to safety. Other Helmets stayed too long and died in the blast, the double-tap. In those moments, surviving colleagues who had escaped the impending blast, would sob for their lost White Helmet brother after their shock subsided. Some stood paralyzed as they looked to the place where their colleague and brother had been, intoning whispered Allahu Akbar in voices that broke with uncertainty. Some fell to their knees and wailed at the injustice of it all. That day or the next, after going back for clean-up at the bomb site, they would have a burial for their retrieved fellow White Helmet. On a slab of white rock, his name and details would be written. And the very next bomb attack, they would do it all again. The Russian double-taps would take out scores of White Helmets during the war. They continue to this day.

There was no confusion among any of the White Helmets that a huge target was on their backs. Back at the centres during moments of respite from attacks, as they chain-smoked and sipped their tea, they would joke about their absurd importance to the powerful regime and Russia. That simple men from all walks of life, painters, teachers, construction workers, could pose such a threat.

"Like pretty girls, we are always on their minds," one joked to those sitting on the floor around him. Laughter. *"Ah, such pretty girls we are,"* said another, butting out his cigarette, his countenance long and his voice caught somewhere between jest and lament.

Assad and Putin's message to the White Helmets bore no ambiguity – they should stop rescuing civilians or pay the price. The volunteers received this edict loud and clear. It didn't matter. There was nothing the regime or Russia could do to make them cease their humanitarian work. Each volunteer who stayed the course, discovered in their own time, that there were, indeed, worse things that could be abided than death. Yet, even as the lethal double-taps continued, danger came for the White Helmets in many other ways, one of which they might never have expected.

On August 12, 2017, at the White Helmet Centre situated in the city of Sarmin, in the south-eastern region of Idlib Governorate, volunteer shift change was set to commence in the early morning hours. White Helmets began arriving at the SCD building to take over for those who had spent the night on duty. As the first two Helmets entered through the door, they were confronted by a scene of inconceivable horror within. Seven of their colleagues lay scattered dead about the centre floor, entirely drenched in their own blood. One White Helmet fell instantly to his knees as he took in the sight while the other rushed into the room, crawling through the thick congealing blood to the first of his brothers nearest him. The bullet hole in this Helmet's forehead would be found in each head of the assassinated volunteers. They had been shot while asleep, execution style, in what was clearly a targeted massacre. As the other members arrived for their shift, the same horror was relived. In all their years of work, they had seen nothing like this. Their White Helmet brothers were all dead, all of them. As grief and wails poured out, someone called for backup. It was the darkest day in the humanitarian's organization the White Helmets had known. Unknown assailants had carried out the attack but their affiliation was clear immediately in the minds of the men. In a city overrun with Daesh-affiliated sects, the international community was quick to blame the terrorists. But, white hard hats were taken, and two Syria Civil Defence vehicles were also stolen. Vehicles? Sure. But hard hats? Why? And Daesh? Perhaps. None of the White Helmets were convinced of this. Though not affiliated with any terrorists, the Helmets didn't feel targeted by them in any way, either. They had had to co-exist with them in Sarmin, each group forging its own path. And besides, there was no motive for terrorists. Several pieces of evidence pointed to different attackers. Regime/Russian mercenaries. Guns fitted with silencers had been used, and therefore, nearby residents had heard nothing of what had been a full-scale attack. Terrorist groups had never bothered using silencers for the simple reason, they didn't care who heard. Also, why would the helmets be taken by terrorists. Or were these the helmets that would later show up in staged Russian propaganda videos showing "White Helmets" played by actors wearing official helmets on their heads.

The slain White Helmets would be buried the next day, their plots side by side, just as they had spent their last living hours in the volunteer centre. Their broken colleagues could not hide their unprecedented misery. Tear-stained faces and dejected countenances stood elbow to elbow before each grave. White Helmets came from far and wide to bid goodbye to men, who, like them, had tried their best to save their fellow Syrians. However, these men had paid the ultimate price because of this. All while the world looked on and allowed another crime against humanity to go unchecked – the killing of humanitarian workers. The violations the United Nations knowingly allowed go unpunished was an obscenity on the institution.

Silver linings in Syria are hard to come by. Faith in God for even the most devout can become bruised and broken at times when the blows raining down seem unending. The brutal reality of living in Syria, never mind trying to defend its people, can take a hard toll. But the heartbreak and the anger burning in the hearts of those White Helmets standing in the cemetery before the plots of their fallen friends and brothers took on a life of its own. Each of them wanted to go back to work immediately. Right away. They would do it for the men who had been martyred, for every child that the regime and Russia had ensured would never see her first birthday, for every Syrian soul who had ever sang on high with a three-starred green and black revolution flag in his hand, they would carry on, stronger than ever.

CHAPTER FIVE

The Gas Even Hitler Wouldn't Use

"For the powerful, crimes are those that others commit,"

- Noam Chomsky, Writer

[Syria Civil Defence]

In a chemical factory tucked into the picturesque Rhineland of Germany, Third Reich chemist, Gerhard Schraeder, was tasked with finding an effective insecticide to combat the weevils devouring German crops and orchards. It was 1936, and the German nation needed to preserve its dwindling food supplies to last them through the winter, and perhaps longer still. The German government, on the precipice of another war, lauded highly the national self-sufficiency of German farmers' lands, but the insidious bugs were devouring everything that grew. They had to be stopped. In his clinical laboratory with every type of flask, beaker, and test tube at his disposal, as well as a veritable arsenal of chemicals lining the lab shelves, Schraeder went to work. Genius and perseverance paid off, and he was at last able to present to his impatient superiors something of value. But in his urgency, he had gone too far. It wasn't an insecticide Schraeder came bearing. It was a nerve agent, in essence a biological weapon, the likes of which had never been tapped into before. Phosphorous and Cyanide had been combined to insidious effect and tried out on wild rabbits at the behest of a few Nazi superiors. They demanded secrecy from Schraeder and his colleagues so they alone could see exactly what this new "invention" could really do before word got out that such a thing existed at all. Suddenly, weevils were the very last thing on their minds. As a substantial quantity of the serum was cautiously fed into the glass cage's ventilation mechanism, the rabbits were initially engulfed in a murky brown colour from the falling gas, and the faintest odour made its way past every gas mask in the room, a deceivingly fruity smell. The unsuspecting animals froze in place momentarily as if dazed before they transitioned into grotesque seizures, convulsing unabated until their hearts gave out – the final rabbit twitching and fighting the gas long past the deaths of the others. Healthy to dead in a matter of fifteen brutal minutes – one Nazi had timed it on his watch.

Despite the successful outcome of consistent demise among the subjects, the secret trial was a disappointment to Schraeder's superiors. They complained the animals had taken too long to die, and the brown colour of the gas, along with its sickly sweet odour, was too obvious. They encouraged Gerhard to do better.

It wasn't long before the secrets being kept in Schraeder's lab reached the German Army Weapons Office. Instantly, the department recognized the serum's deadly potential and named it *Tabun*, German for Taboo. The majority agreed that such a serum should not see the light of day. That it shouldn't be talked about, let alone considered – even during wartime. However, not everyone in the Reich felt this way. Taboo or not, some in the chemical warfare section of the Weapons Office, thought it had the capability to win a war – should one present itself. Perhaps it only needed a little refinement – in other words, they wanted something colourless and odourless, a lethal gas that left much less of a German fingerprint. Dr. Schraeder returned to the IG Farben laboratory and started tinkering with the Tabun, pulling it apart molecule by molecule and then stitching it back together until it had become a chemical Frankenstein. In 1938, Tabun had become something far worse. Schraeder could not have entirely grasped what he had done. Now, a mere drop of the gas could choke and devour its subjects with rapid but torturous death. The nerve agent on Schraeder's table had far crossed the line of being taboo; he had devised death in a vial, devoid of all colour and smell. It was named SARIN –

an acronym using initials from Schrader's surname and those of the three other scientists who had helped create it: *S*hraeder, *A*mbros, *R*itter and von der L*in*der. In mid-1939, it was ordered to be brought into production for wartime use – just in case it was needed. Enough of the nerve agent was stockpiled to kill millions of people. If used, it might have prompted the turning point of World War II in Germany's favour, except for one factor: Hitler said no. He outright vetoed its use.

Why? The conjecture for his unequivocal refusal has been ongoing for decades. For a man who used Zyklon B, a chemical created at the same laboratory, to exterminate millions of Jewish people without a shred of conscience or compunction, determining this to be an ethical decision on Hitler's part seems highly unlikely. Perhaps it was because of his own experience with a much weaker chemical agent, Mustard Gas, which he was exposed to and temporarily blinded by, during his time fighting in Belgium during World War I. The most pragmatic explanation seems to be that he didn't want his troops entering the cities they attacked in the aftermath of the gas, only to be affected by it themselves. Or worse, what if the enemy retaliated in kind? Regardless of the rationale, even in the last weeks of the Second World War, when Germany was clearly losing, the nerve agent Sarin remained untouched and unbothered on the Nazi shelves.

Decades later, Gerhard Shraeder's taboo recipe would find its way to Branch 450 of Institute 6000 in Barzeh City, just north of the Presidential Palace in the Province of Damascus, Syria. Of the more than 12 special "units" or buildings designed for the manufacturing and storage of chemical weapons throughout the country, Institute 6000 was the biggest and most important to the Syrian regime. Inside this massive complex, staffed exclusively by members of the president's Alawite sect with its proven and unremitting loyalty to the regime, scientists were clandestinely and defiantly turning out the precursors of every deadly, poisonous concoction banned by the OPCW – the Organization for the Prevention of Chemical Warfare. From this first staging point, which saw the lethal beginnings of the most brutal weaponry, including the chemical ignition for Sarin, the killer gases would be shipped out to the nearby Unit 416, where they would undergo finalization before making their way to warehouses pending usage. Nearby, in these same buildings, all types of warheads and vehicles for chemical dissemination were also on standby until the time was right. In the days leading up to late summer 2013, without hesitation or any meddling humane conscience, Sarin came easily off the Syrian regime shelves.

***

A mere 6 kilometers away from the lavish Presidential Palace lies Eastern Ghouta, a hearty agricultural belt where vegetables and wheat were once grown in abundance, and where vineyards and orchards stretched for as far as the eye could see. Verdant and flourishing, it was aptly named Ghouta, or *Ghuta* in Arabic, which means "garden". Beyond the agricultural lands, densely packed neighbouring communities, also once thriving, were now crippled and deteriorating under the brutal siege President Assad had imposed on the region for ten long months. Since winter, the rebel-protected city was languishing under starvation, illness, and immobilization. Farmers' fields could not be tilled or harvested due to the threat of being targeted by missiles. The farmers themselves would be picked off by snipers if they stepped into their fields. Even chicken houses were a favourite target of the regime. Many a hunkered-down family taking up desperate refuge within one had become collateral damage, losing their lives in a designated strike meant specifically for poultry, a staple of the Syrian diet. Every semblance of normalcy in the city had been hijacked by a dictator who, deep down at heart, wanted above all else to gain the upper hand on the opposition-held region, which had kept the regime on the chase far too long. He wanted this ragtag team of fighters that was getting the best of his trained "elite" army to be taught a lesson - that their time was up. No food or medicine could get into the city. The major hospitals had been picked off one by one in bombing raids, leaving inadequate makeshift clinics and field hospitals to try to pick up the slack and do the impossible for the Ghouta civilians. Countless doctors had been killed in previous raids, leaving very few behind. Medicines were dwindling despite cautious rationing by the doctors. Vital anaesthetics had been all but used up. Too often, operations on children had to be done without freezing of any sort. They were given teddy bears to clutch even as they needed to be held down on the surgical table so shrapnel could be removed from their small bodies or an immature limb amputated after a shelling attack. One veteran surgeon routinely put Beethoven on his record player as he set his scalpel to human flesh still tingling with nerve endings that could not be numbed. He did this, perhaps, not to soothe the screaming patients, but to keep his hands from shaking as he soldiered through the perverse circumstances which medical school could never have prepared him for. The odd pharmacy remained with a pittance of supplies, parceled out to those most in need, bandages mostly, perhaps a few precious bottles of rubbing alcohol. Fragile infants and seniors routinely died of sicknesses that could have been staved off by mere analgesics and antibiotics. Sometimes, if the FSA was lucky, they could get a shipment of medicine and food in through tunnels just before their coordinates were discovered by the regime army and blasted out of use. They would recalibrate and merely start digging again. Schools were closed. The children, for fear of snipers, could not play outside. Only the bravest ventured out into the streets, all but running from one doorway to another. Indeed, the once vibrant city, following in the footsteps of Daraa and Aleppo and Homs, was merely another chess piece waiting to be taken off its square and put on Assad's side of the board. The rebels on the front lines were struggling to keep their grip, as they, too, were starving and sick. Many were maimed into inaction or dead. Ammunition was becoming scarce. Even still, rumour had found its way to Assad's inner circle that the opposition planned to storm Damascus with one last battle cry, pushing as close to the Presidential Palace and their dictator as they could. Whether this threat was a reality or not, for a paranoid leader, the proposition of this needed be dealt with. For a people already crushed both physically and emotionally, what would come next in those humid last days of Ghouta summer was inexplicably and wholly unimaginable.

At around 2:35am on August 21, 2013, while the darkness and cool began to slowly usher in the Syrian morning, the citizens of Eastern Ghouta were asleep in their beds in the Ein Tarma neighbourhood. All at once, peace became frenetic turmoil. Most residents were awoken by the sound of an explosion and the subsequent reverberation of the detonation hitting the ground. However, it was not the sound of a conventional bomb, and many slept through it, never to awaken again. Mere minutes later in the adjoining district of Zamalka, the same detonation occurred. Two surface-to-surface adapted 330mm artillery rockets had been launched from Damascus, full to their brims with Sarin gas. Fearing another conventional strike, many residents fled like every other time to their basements for optimal safety. They had no inkling that Sarin, the weapon they had been attacked with, stays airborne for mere moments before it settles as low as it can get. Those in their basements died down there, or, if the gas was faster than them, they fell prone and unconscious on the very steps leading down to them. Others ran outside as it was still falling, only to have their nervous systems immediately overridden by the gas. Everywhere near the bomb site, people were falling instantly to the ground in convulsions, choking for air, having been attacked unawares by something they could not see or smell.

Then, a hellish mayhem broke out in the besieged city immediately and ferociously, as had never been experienced before. Less than ten minutes later, within a makeshift hospital in Eastern Ghouta, the two sleepy physicians on duty heard the first rumblings of a hysteria that would continue unbridled throughout the next 24 hours. It burst through the roughshod doors of the emergency clinic, bringing with it a tidal wave of horror never witnessed before in this city. Terror was everywhere. The doctors' hearts surely skipped a beat in their chests, inside the hospital as they bore witness to the chaos. Hell had been unleashed from the unknown, this much was apparent.

Syrian doctors will admit there is little worse than the sound of horrified and panic-stricken parents, teetering desperately between fragile hope and abject despair - the cause, invariably, their dying children. The agonizing screaming and wailing voices came nearer and nearer as the first infants and children, the most vulnerable, were raced into the surgical room in the arms of parents and neighbours. There was brief confusion for the doctors at first. None of the usual warning signs had alerted them to what was coming now. There had been a thud to the earth, yes, but no sounds of shelling or serial bombing had preceded this. And the more pressing question was - where were the injuries? What appeared before them now were not mangled bodies, missing limbs, or seeping blood where they were peppered with shrapnel, and there was no hanging, lacerated skin either. No. Nothing of the sort. This was completely uncharted territory of the most treacherous kind. Rosy-cheeked children still in their pajamas were hastily put onto operating tables and then eventually placed on any available surface in the clinic. Not a blemish or mark on them from injury. But their convulsing, twisting bodies, their glazed-over eyes, wide, but unseeing, and the froth collecting at their mouths, each trying impossibly just to breathe, told the tale as well as their words might have. The physicians in short order recognized what this was... poisoning en masse. There had been a full-scale chemical attack on Ghouta. Every available physician and medical person was called for urgent assistance. It was barely 3am, and already the room was overflowing with gasping, dying children and adults, now too. The medical providers knew this was an emergency of near apocalyptic proportions, and they had little to no resources with which to deal with what was happening all around them. Staff tore the chemical-saturated clothing off the children and washed them down, before turning on the few oxygen tanks they had left. The oxygen masks would have to be shared among the victims, each being given a minute or two, before the mask was moved on to the next mouth gasping for life. The oxygen meters on the tanks slowly dropped to empty. The physicians peered at the levels anxiously every few minutes. Some children were already dead, having become motionless at last with the convulsing done. Mere babies, days old, fell away into death, having never had a chance at life at all. Their disbelieving parents needing be pulled away from their children, before being washed down themselves. The shrill sounds of mothers' screams filled the already noisy and chaotic room. They were forcibly led away to have their clothing removed. The same poison that not only killed when ingested was hazardous when it lingered as a residue on the skin as well. More help eventually arrived. One doctor from another centre had brought Atropine, the few vials he had left. Those lucky enough to receive it, were given new but fragile life as the Atropine injection was the antidote to what the doctors had now surmised was some sort of nerve agent. One doctor even guessed it might be Sarin. Among other symptoms of this killer gas, the tip off was the constricted pinpoint pupils of the afflicted as they stared straight ahead sightlessly. Every victim in the room had the same unseeing eyes. And then the Atropine ran out. Clinics in the vicinity were contacted for more. And more oxygen, too. Some arrived, but for so many of the victims, it was too late. Invariably, anyone who had been within a half-kilometre radius of the bomb sites would ultimately die. The exposure was just too great. Time and distance were direct factors in who had a chance of surviving the gas. Had the clinic's shelves been properly stocked, significantly more victims would have survived. Instead, scores perished at the helpless hands of the doctors. Needing the tables, the lifeless bodies of deceased children and adults were moved to a vacant room, and laid on the floor, side by side, turning it into a makeshift morgue. Parents knelt sobbing over their dead children, disbelieving. Perfect little faces turned up to their parents, convinced them their children were only asleep, nothing more. Those moving the bodies didn't have time to react to this obscene and monstrous reality they were dealing with - they just kept going. Little time passed before the next wave of victims came through the hospital doors. Eventually, the doctors had to say no more and stem the tide. They were already stumbling over the countless bodies that were being deposited everywhere. There was no choice but to send the dying Ghouta civilians to other field hospitals, though the doctors knew they likely would not survive the transport. The ground outside the hospital was littered with the dead and dying, the healthy and able doing their best to save lives by hosing down the victims, helpless to do anything more. An apocalypse had come to Eastern Ghouta that warm August morning, delivered directly from Damascus. Later, when plotted on a map, the trajectory origins of the dropped Sarin cannisters were traced to converge on a site that the Human Rights Watch stated was a large military base on Mount Qassioun that is home to the Republican Guard 104th Brigade.

There was no doubt in the minds of the physicians that this nightmarish assault was the act of the regime. Evidence was collected. Contaminated clothing was eventually bagged and labeled. Photographs and video gave a comprehensive albeit horrifying summation of the massacre at hand. Surely, someone needed to pay for the lives of all these dead and dying children. Many sincerely believed the evidence collected would ensure just that. Infants as young as one week old, perfect little faces, their lives just beginning, had been exterminated like alley rodents or petulant insects by a man cowardly hiding behind the ostentatious walls of his palace.

In the days to come, the UN's requests to investigate were ignored or waylaid by the Regime after the massacre until they had had enough time to clean up their tracks. However, what was found not far from the bomb site was a soviet era ballistic that had carried the gas and detonated it. Assad blamed the rebels, though it was well known they possessed neither the Sarin nor the weaponry to carry out just such an attack. That they would choose to orchestrate it in their own region, and the civilians they were protecting made the allegations even more ridiculous. A significant number of rebel fighters died in the massacre.

When the maelstrom of Syrian horror had a modicum of respite, parents and neighbours buried their children and friends in hasty mass graves to contain the killer gas that left its trace everywhere. Meanwhile, the international community played out its inevitable routine of inertia. Red lines crossed by Assad were promised to be met with American retaliation that never came. United Nations Security Council meetings were held in farcical fashion, as any investigation or punishment decided upon for the perpetrators was easily squashed by the perpetrators, themselves – Russia was a permanent member of the

United Nations with veto power that it would use over and over again to exonerate its ally, Syria, or itself. It was a kangaroo court of nations, acting out the saddest and most obscene performances, the impotent consequences and conclusions, sadder still. Justice was swiftly buried alongside all the Ghouta dead.

Months later, when political pressure made it so he could deny it no longer, Assad admitted to possessing some Sarin, yet vehemently kept up his denial that the regime bore any responsibility for the chemical attack. He was ordered to surrender his stockpile of Sarin. In a concerted Western effort, it was removed from Syria and painstakingly destroyed in NATO countries such as Germany, France, and Britain. All of this, coming too little and too late.

In all, estimates of more than 1700 innocent Syrians died in the August 21, 2013, Ghouta attacks, one third of which was children. Despite forgotten Red Lines, hollow UN threats, and the pretense of action on the part of governmental powers, the "never again" mantra that had been repeatedly chimed by the West since the horrors of the Jewish Holocaust, quickly evolved to *never mind*. Justice had come to none of the people in Eastern Ghouta, while an unspoken impunity was given by the international community to Assad. It was only a matter of time before he would do it again. He had been given a veritable license to kill, and he knew it.

***

Four years later, White Helmet Hamid was off duty and sound asleep in his bed when he was startled awake by the sound of a bomb detonating. His small house shook. The explosion had occurred in relatively close proximity to his home in the city of Khan Sheikhoun, in north-west Syria. It was 6:50am on a Tuesday morning, April 4, 2017. He shook his wife awake and told her to take the baby and their parents to the basement quickly. The usual terror and adrenaline propelling him forward, he was out of the house, and headed in the direction of the bomb site, less than five minutes later, just enough time to throw his uniform on and grab his helmet.

Hamid knew all too well the bomb drill. At the young age of 26, he had been doing search and rescue for the Syria Civil Defence for the last three years. He had saved scores of Syrians and lost many more. He knew what to expect and what to do. The fallout and subsequent protocol seldom changed. First, there would be the gut-wrenching squeal of aircraft piercing the sky before the payload was dropped, whooshing through the air. Then the bomb would fall, exploding its target, a house or school or hospital, turning the bullseye instantly into a mountain of rubble. Next, the fallout of a massive cloud of dust momentarily covered everything and everyone. Then the people screaming with horror in the streets. Chaos. Pandemonium. And of course, the White Helmets, sleeping in their uniforms, or perhaps taking tea and chatting, should it be daytime, would frantically exit their centres, jumping into their ambulances and racing through the streets to get to the war zone, hoping they would find someone alive. *Allahu Akbar* instinctively murmured by the volunteers again and again, even as the Muslim prayer beads bounced about in the raucous drive, hanging from the rear view mirror of the SCD vehicles. This day, as Hamid ran as fast as he could down the road and then through blocks of neighbourhood streets, he knew something was different. Something felt off. Where was the dust cloud? Where were the screaming people filling the streets, making their horrified exodus? Instantly, he knew he was running into something he had never witnessed before. In reflection of what happened that day to his town, Hamid recalled, *"The warplane dropped five missiles on the city at the same moment, four of which were explosive missiles and one carried sarin gas."* When he talks about the cannister that detonated and dispersed the killer gas, he states, *"It fell next to a baking oven* [public bakery] *and grain silos. The plane dropped the sarin bomb first, and there was a low sound, then the plane turned and dropped the rest of the* [conventional] *missiles on the city."*

As Hamid ran into the market square, right into the fray, he was stunned and horrified at what was revealed to him. Children, men and women stumbling about without balance or motor control of their limbs, until they fell to the ground with those already lying there. A collection of heaving, erratic life sporadically spread out on the ground before him. No one looked hurt. Yet all were slowly dying. Bodies were jerking, stiff arms raised in the air looked wooden, open eyes were not seeing, and gasping mouths drooled a frothy substance. Hamid knew it was gas poisoning, but he couldn't smell any chlorine, and there were no yellow clouds drifting downward – Syria had been attacked with chlorine gas at least seven times since the start of the year. Hamid was correct – it was not chlorine. This April day, whatever lingered in the Khan Sheikhoun air was something stealthily insidious. There was no odour. There was no colour. Something invisible was attacking these people. As he watched so many people convulsing and gasping to breathe, the white foam oozing from their lips, he called those unaffected to help him. They needed water to rinse the victims. Then needed to get the children and infants immediately to hospital. Later in brutal moments of reflection, Hamid would describe the events of that morning as nothing less than "Judgement Day".

Mere minutes after arriving, Hamid received a transmission on his walkie-talkie from his team leader that this attack was "unusual" and extreme precautions were needed in approaching the victims. They, too, guessed lethal gas. White Helmet ambulances approached even as he stood there. As if in a dream, Hamid watched as one, seemingly slowing to park, lost all control of the ambulance and crashed into a wall. Unwittingly, the driver had kept his windows down and succumbed to the gas that had made its way into the vehicle and into his lungs. As he saw other White Helmets go to help the ambulance, Hamid blinked away the sight as he refocused on the convulsing and dying children all over the ground. People brought buckets of water, and hoses were found. He helped rinse the people but there never seemed to be enough water. In mere moments, he caught sight of his best friend and fellow White Helmet, Anas al-Dyab. Anas had also been off duty that day, but with haste had made his way to the attack site. Even then, stressed and terrified from the madness all about him, so different than the other attacks, Hamid's heart instinctively soared to see the comforting imaging of his friend. He wanted to cry, but in running to him, he only embraced him quickly, thanked God he was alive, and then together they turned back toward the bedlam. Together they helped hose down the victims on the ground, providing all the first aid they could, while in turns running for stretchers to transport the victims to medical centres. Calls went out to every other centre in nearby jurisdictions for any and all available White Helmets to come to Khan Sheikhoun. In less than half an hour, the city centre was filled with the Civil Defense volunteers. None of them wore hazmat suits, nor masks, nor gloves. Protection of that sort was simply not available. With little regard for their own protection against this invisible killer, they gathered the children up first, sometimes two or three in their arms, and raced them into the closest medical centre. By now, the Atropine had been mostly used up. Those nearest the explosion, receiving the first of the gas, died. Those secondary to ingestion moreover died as well, with a few saved. Angry doctors closed the eyes of the dead innocents before they were taken away from the clinic to await burial. Less than an hour later, in another incredible act of evil, the makeshift clinic receiving the Sarin victims was hit by a conventional bomb, killing patients and doctors alike. It was unparalleled brutality and cruelty, the kind so easily devised by the Syrian regime. As always, Hamid and Anas were keeping an eye out for each other as they carried out their duties. At one point, Hamid looked for Anas, who had been working fast and hard to save as many victims as he could and saw his friend failing. Anas was doubled over at the waist, his hands on his thighs, his body heaving as he tried to regulate his breathing. For certain, he didn't look right despite his protests to the contrary. Hamid ran to him and, heaving as he took breaths, Anas once more declared he was okay, waving Hamid away. But his symptoms were evident. Hamid swooped an arm around Anas and walked his staggering friend quickly inside the nearest clinic. He pushed him down on a chair and signaled for a doctor. Immediately, the doctor washed Anas's face before applying an oxygen mask over his nose and mouth. Hamid waited until his friend's breathing normalized and Anas gave him the "thumbs up" before reluctantly leaving him to run back to help more victims. A mere five minutes later, outside, Hamid was lifting more children onto stretchers, when out of the corner of his eye he saw Anas back in duty. He ran to work along side him, only to see the symptoms gradually return to Anas. Maybe fifteen minutes later, Anas ran himself into the clinic, took the oxygen mask for a minute, and then immediately ran back outside to keep working. On one of the clinic visits, they eventually injected him with Atropine. On his next visit for more oxygen, the clinic doctors found a "hazmat" suit for this stubborn warrior, not first-grade gear but enough white plastic to cover his head and body, a surgical mask over his mouth. *"Anas was like a machine"*, Hamid proudly recalled about his friend, *"Gentle, brave, and enthusiastic always* [but] *like a machine."*

Eventually, the White Helmets centre team leader insisted that Anas be checked over and made to go home, firmly advising that his shift was most certainly over. After many protests to keep working, Anas followed the orders. He would have to return some hours later for more oxygen and another injection, and he noted, like all the others, that his vision was becoming blurry. Anas had done all he could on April 4th, 2017. When he wasn't providing first aid, he was photographing hundreds upon hundreds of images of the dead and dying, of the bomb site itself. He had gathered enough evidence to try and convict Assad for the use of prohibited chemical weapons and crimes against humanity several times over, at the Hague.

For six grueling hours, White Helmet Hamid Kutini also stayed in the field that day with only a surgical mask on his face to protect him from the residual gases on every surface and on every body he touched. Despite how his stomach dropped and his heart broke at the massacre fallout he was immerse in, with every victim he helped, particularly the children, he gained more momentum, stoically kept going, doing what he was trained to do. He was doing what, by conscience, there was no choice but to do. He was never given a hazmat suit as there were not enough. He replaced his mask twice, but the symptoms started upon him just as they did every other volunteer that day. Around him were gasping and spitting colleagues, some walking off balance and stumbling as they continued helping their fellow Syrians. Later, the Assad and Putin propagandists would bolster their claims that these were staged attacks by citing the fact that the White Helmets were not wearing protective gear, not even gloves as they dealt with Sarin. They were correct that the White Helmets wore no protective gear because there was none available. Most would end the day sick with Sarin symptoms, while several other White Helmets, fighting long and hard to save as many as they could, would die of the Sarin gas, themselves.

The regime had brutally massacred its people once again with Sarin gas. American President Trump would soon send missiles to strike select Syrian bases in punishment, but it meant little to the parents burying their dead children. The estimate of the dead was put at 80 people, mostly those under the age of ten. The collateral injuries that remain with so many who did survive, both physical and psychological, as well as the wave of birth defects of the children born to mothers affected that day by the gas, were all just too many to count, and to comprehend.

The horror and grief of the day was encapsulated by one young father's story. This father's excruciating loss broke through the general apathy of the outside world and made headlines. International newspapers and television news broadcasts picked up his story.

Abdul-Hameed al-Youssef, 29, lost everything that mattered in his life the day of the Khan Sheikhoun Sarin attack and very nearly his will to go on living as well. The horror delivered on one man was almost too incredible to fathom. The soon iconic photograph of him holding his cherubic and deceased 11-month-old twins, one in each arm, their perfect angelic faces with their curling light hair and long eyelashes tilted back against their father's arms in eternal repose, could not be ignored, and for a brief moment in time, the conscience of the world shook. The expression on Abdul-Hameed's face as he stares down, regarding his murdered twins, is strangely calm, almost normal. Perhaps it was just shock. Or perhaps he had convinced himself, that in this state of near perfection, his doll-like twins were merely sleeping and nothing more. But the Sarin they had ingested that April morning took their fragile bodies quickly. Then their mother, too - Abdul-Hameed's bride of less than two years. His family, natives of Khan Sheikhoun, would see another twenty members swallowed up by the gas and gone from his life. 23 members of his family in all, countless neighbours and friends besides. Abdul-Hameed insisted on carrying his babies to their graves the following day for burial, just as he carried them about in life, two in both arms. He would be with them until the final moment of separation. The brother and sister were buried side by side, grave markers inscribed with Arabic words sending them to the hands of Allah, as their father could carry them no longer. Their father's last words to his babies were to tell them not to be scared before he collapsed by their little graves. Allahu Akbar was murmured by his friends. *God is greater even than this.* When the funeral was over, Abdul-Hameed nearly lost his balance as he swooned getting to his feet. He was caught up quickly by his friends. They needed support him still so he could walk away from the baby twins' final resting place. Sobbing, the father did not want to leave them alone. He fell to the ground once more and cried like the world was, indeed, coming to an end for him. He would later tell CBS News, *"They were both really smart. I wanted my daughter Aya to be a doctor, and Ahmed was going to be my sidekick."*

Once more, there would be no accountability for the perpetrators. The regime declared the attack a hoax, and worse than this, a false flag attempt by the opposition to draw the West into the fight through sympathy. President Bashar al-Assad would go on interviews hosted by his ally Russia's state television channel, R.T., and declare the dead children seen all over the ground, merely props used by the opposition to further their cause. He went as far as to say the White Helmets killed the children elsewhere and then brought them back for staging in Khan Sheikhoun to make fake videos. Every neutral nation saw the evidence, including the accounts of the people of Khan Sheikhoun, and knew it was once more the work of Assad. Security Council meetings were called by the UN. Russia vetoed their resolutions, as it had countless times in the past. President Bashar al-Assad was in direct contravention of UN Security Council resolutions prohibiting the use of chemical weapons on civilians, including Resolution 2268, which specifically addresses sieges and humanitarian intervention. A ceasefire was called in the days following the Khan Sheikhoun Sarin massacre. Assad responded by gassing Syrians on the second day of the ceasefire with chlorine gas, killing 33 more civilians. In the years following, the OPCW would carry out a full-scale investigation of the attack, and unequivocally put the responsibility fully in the hands of the Syrian regime. For many, there had never been any doubt.

Yet, to the time of this writing, on the twelfth anniversary of the 2013 Ghouta Sarin attack, neither Bashar al-Assad nor Vladimir Putin has ever seen the inside of a courtroom.

CHAPTER SIX

Killer Propaganda

"The truth is incontrovertible. Malice may attack it, ignorance may deride it, but in the end, there it is."

- Winston Churchill, Former Prime Minister of Britain

[Associated Press]

It was convincing. And it was methodically devised to be that way. Behind the Canadian journalist was the United Nations logo – that universal symbol of ultimate humanitarian justice and ethics. Furled U.N. flags stood at attention in two corners of the stage, vigilant reminders of the imperative for impartiality and truth. The journalist, herself, was sitting at a panel of peers giving a briefing about the current state of the Syrian conflict. Seated directly before her were fellow journalists waiting to ask their questions. To the innocent onlooker, this expert had been invited by the United Nations to express her considered viewpoints on the ongoing conflict in Syria. Indeed, without equivocation, the very title of the YouTube video capturing all this is *The United Nations Briefing on Syria Featuring Eva Bartlett, Independent Canadian Journalist.*[9] And surely, as Aleppo, the largest and most ancient province in Syria, rapidly falls to ruin under government siege and ballistic bombardment, this 2016 UN briefing for the world is necessary and timely.

But something here is off. Pull back the camera just a little. Pan the room.

This is not a sanctioned United Nations assembly. It is a back room borrowed by a few Russia-affiliated Assad apologists within the expansive UN building, one chosen specifically for its iconic backdrop covered in United Nations logos to give the veneer of UN respectability. This is not a United Nations briefing by any stretch of the imagination. The Canadian woman, designated as the featured journalist, is not sitting at a panel of varied speakers, neither nationals nor Middle East experts, obliged to give credible and nonpartisan information and insight into the Syrian conflict. She is situated beside a few colleagues who share her pro-Assad agenda, concordantly delivering, via the guise of beseeching help for the Syrian people and calling for an end to the war, a unilateral scathing disdain for Western media and the United States, whom they blame unrelentingly for the current hell that is Syria. This is hardly a full venue of engaged journalists in attendance. In a room with a capacity for 75 chairs at best, there are maybe five journalists within. One for certain, is Western press, a Norwegian reporter who looks more skeptical than invested, as his curious expression would suggest. He wandered in at the last moment, looking slightly uncertain as to what exactly was going on in this room. The other four reporters seated there are of questionable inclination. They may have even been brought along for the ride by the panel as their ready comments and questions seem too prepared, anticipatory even, and wholly sympathetic to the narrative at play at the front of the room. Of the four panelists seated at the long table, their name placards placed neatly before them, the three to the right of the Canadian woman are apparent academics. Yet, a quick perusal into their backgrounds, beyond the obvious that they are all part of the "*Hands Off Syria Coalition*" organization they eagerly represent this day (the imperative in their name decidedly meant for the West), their credentials are somewhat suspect, their agendas more so.

The first of this coalition to be introduced is Sara Flounders. Ms. Flounders, dowdy and maybe sixty-something, is an American socialist writer with unambiguous membership in the Marxist-Leninist Workers World Party.[10] She is an extreme opponent of

American militarism and nationalism and is somewhat notorious for drumming up a rally in support of the construction of the Ground Zero Mosque[11], as it was coined, a highly sensitive proposition for New Yorkers and Americans at large in a time still far too raw for consideration for many after the 9/11 attacks. Unapologetically, in the middle of New York's still broken Downtown, Ms. Flounders loudly championed the placement of the Ground Zero Mosque a mere two blocks away from where the Twin Towers had once been. Despite Ms. Flounders' zeal, the mosque never came to be, as a 70-storey luxury condominium building was determined to be a more profitable use of the land.

Beside Ms. Flounders sits another apparent academic in dramatic, bright red glasses who is introduced as Dr. Donna Nassor, a lawyer and professor at Berkeley. She thanks the speaker for the introduction but never once denies working at the "University of Berkeley" - the prestigious and highly ranked California University, so famous that it is known by just *Berkeley*. Dr. Nassor had for some time been an adjunct professor at Berkeley College in New Jersey, but moreover, she has mainly taught at New Jersey City University, a sadly lackluster institution that has low attendance and budgetary disaster. The dubious "Berkeley" designation is only one of the many non-truths that will be passed off unflinchingly by these speakers, carelessly, cavalierly, as if they themselves were tasked with deciding what is and isn't fact.

On the left of Nassor, and beside the star panelist, the Canadian woman, is Dr. Bahman Azad, the Chairman of this Coalition, which comprises the entire panel of four. He is attributed with having been in the Iranian Air Force as a Second Lieutenant between 1972 and 1973, and immediately afterwards having emigrated to the United States, where he has lived ever since. Dr. Azad is also well known as a proud and extreme socialist with strong anti-American leanings despite the fact that his degrees come, unapologetically, from American universities. He is also the co-chair of the Iran Pledge of Resistance[12], a seemingly now defunct group, whose mission statement had once been to oppose the American military should they ever engage in war with Iran.

Finally, the honoured guest of the panel, described as the independent Canadian Journalist, is Eva Bartlett. Neatly attired with a smart jacket and a long blue scarf trailing down both shoulders, Ms. Bartlett's academic credentials are omitted when she is introduced, presumably, because she has none of note. She is foremost lauded by the panel for her upcoming U.S. tour, where she will go on a variety of American stages, further promoting her pro-Assad Syrian War narrative in small venues through ten cities. The term "journalist" as it applies to Ms. Bartlett, independent or not, is a gross misnomer. She has never worked for any major or mainstream media outlets. Her journalistic feats are limited to an early blog cum diary account she penned while spending some time in Palestine, and more recently, fringe conspiracy media sites and Russian State Television, where she writes or speaks about opposing, often bizarre, accounts of the Syrian war. What will ultimately pull her into the broader public eye is this actual "briefing" at hand, this YouTube-uploaded video right here, but not the entire briefing with all its warts and diversions – no instead, Eva will become famous for a brief extract from this presentation - a five minute out of context clip depicting her as a UN spokesperson, credible for all intents and purposes because of that convenient backdrop. Those wishing for quick conspiratorial sound bites will be fully satisfied as, among other fantastic details of the Syrian war, they will hear her deliberately deride and discredit, along with other Syrian conflict entities, the White Helmets. The YouTube hits on Ms. Bartlett's misleading but viewer-provocative video clip have reached hundreds of thousands of viewers and counting when all iterations of it through various uploads are taken into consideration. However, the veracity of the video's controversial content will never be expounded upon by Ms. Bartlett. She will never take it upon herself to correct any confusion this video may cause, nor elucidate in any discussion or interview that the United Nations did not know her name, never mind having invited her to speak on this particular occasion. Indeed, she seems more than happy with the enormous fame it brings her despite its fraudulence. Transparency has never been a characteristic associated with propaganda, and so it goes with Ms. Bartlett. Opacity, or better yet, "muddied waters", is her vocational mainstay, and her bread and butter. The more uncertainty and confusion she can sow in the minds of her audiences, the murkier the content of her lectures, the better. Ms. Bartlett is American-born, but her acquired Canadian citizenship is what is continually emphasized to the deliberate exclusion of her birthplace, which, in a coalition of anti-American members, makes absolute good sense. Eva Barlett is, indeed, not a journalist by education nor any legitimate affiliation, she is a self-proclaimed activist and writer about "foreign affairs" – all from her skewed and doctored perspective.

Eva speaks confidently about her travels within Syria, about her copious discussions with regular Syrian people, speaking to them in their native Arabic, no less – or so she tells the audience - apparently breaking flatbread as easily as she breaks cultural barriers. When she rolls the names of the Syrian places she has traveled to off her tongue she gives exacting attention to the pronunciation of the Arabic names with affected and overzealous accent, as if to impress upon her listeners her seemingly rich knowledge of the nation entire, not only her familiarity with their language, the richness of their culture, but above all else, the wants and needs of the actual Syrian people. The latter, Eva claims repeatedly, have been generously entrusted to her by the very people, themselves. But have they? With nothing or no one in attendance this day to contradict her claims, she boldly holds herself to a remarkable kinship with the Syrian people. She states emphatically that the ordinary Syrians she has met are far from dissatisfied with their war-torn country. This statement alone, in the context of a country that has endured being blown to bits since the first call for revolution, is outrageous. Yet, perhaps having only visited the regime-occupied regions that have not been completely torn asunder with warfare, the commentary of these particular citizens has been coloured by happenstance or maybe simply enforced by the regime army. For what citizens whose world is encircled by the Syrian Regime would dare speak the truth with the penalty of imprisonment or worse, hanging perpetually over their heads. Bartlett concedes that a few changes made by their beloved President would be desired by the Syrian folk, but all in all the authoritarian dictator they *elected* (and this is a word she actually uses to describe the empowerment of the dictator, Assad) has their best interests at heart, and the citizens are still very much engaged with Bashar al-Assad as well as Aleppo life as it stands this very day. To hear Ms. Bartlett tell it, it is almost as if the revolutionary uprising in 2011 by the Syrian people that was the original catalyst for all the government-inflicted bloodshed that came after never happened at all, as if the Syrian people were so content that there had been no need whatsoever to revolt. Ms. Bartlett does not offer up the fact that in her six alleged trips to Syria, she has never once been inside the liberated areas where rebel faction groups like the Free Syrian Army man the front lines to keep the regime forces away from the civilian population, as they have been doing since 2012. Those hell zones where the Syria Civil Defence, the White Helmets, clean up 24/7 after Assad's and Putin's bombs and bloodshed. Ms. Bartlett doesn't want her audience to know she has never met any legitimate member of the White Helmets, not one. Her misrepresentation of the humanitarian organization does not bode any such intimacy with the real members. How could it? She does not know what the inside of an actual Syria Civil Defence Centre looks like, as one has never been on her agenda, nor the regime's, at least not for any other purposes than destruction. Her tales of White Helmet infamy will be garnered from makeshift theatre that her cameramen followed her with and Syrian actors have performed for, all at the regime's bidding. For certain, she doesn't want it known that she travels only under the protection of the Syrian Army and goes where they direct her, ultimately where Assad permits her to go. Indeed, Ms. Bartlett speaks categorically of having traveled to Aleppo, but it's an odd and unrealistic Aleppo she speaks of, one wholly estranged from the other part of the province, desperately entrenched within the grip of government siege. She brings to this dialogue today little to no mention of the woefully beleaguered Aleppo, from where hundreds of thousands of civilians have already fled, and of how, for those desperate souls left behind, the situation is beyond tragic. Where the children are dying of starvation and the sick are deprived of medicine because their dictator won't allow aid to pass through the blockaded borders, which ally Russia has played a massive role in cutting off from the outside world. An Aleppo where healthy children die needlessly and routinely under the regime and Russian campaign of pain, plunder, and punishment. She has no conversations to offer of having met with the truly broken Syrian people, whose survival is no more than a stroke of luck. She cannot recount in her speeches having ever spoken with the mothers of newborns who are so starved themselves, they can't breastfeed their babies, so instead must watch them waste away on bottles of diluted sugar water. Ms. Bartlett cannot speak to the fact that with the electricity cut by the government, children and adults alike can be found burning toxic plastics and garbage during the raw winter months, in broken houses and flimsy camp tents alike, in a desperate bid to keep warm, and even still, countless besieged children and babies helplessly freeze to death. Miss Bartlett cannot describe the sheer madness of medication and anaesthesia being withheld from Aleppo hospitals for weeks upon weeks, though the few surgeons left must still repair everything from blown-off limbs to cranial injuries amid the hellish screams of the unsedated in this besieged and battered Eastern-most wasteland of a province. Eva has not witnessed the surreal sight of torn skin from barrel bomb shrapnel being sewn up with common sewing thread because surgical sutures were long ago used up.

Ms. Bartlett, through either conviction to her scripted regime narrative or simply unforgivable ignorance, scarcely acknowledges the real brutalized Aleppo - the one walking a tightrope between existence and obliteration as the regime and Russia move in ever closer every hour. As she pays homage to Assad and the "*care*" he takes of his people, she pays no heed to that ancient and history-rich Eastern portion of the province, a once-upon-a-time jewel of the country and of archaeological annals now left to rot. No condolences are paid by her this day to the once- fabled Aleppo, nor the modern industrial capital that provided simple livelihood for many. An Aleppo where at this very moment in time buildings and infrastructure are so blasted away by Assad's Scorched Earth campaign conducted via endless bombardment by Russian MiGs, Sukhois, and GRADs, its very city landscape has become unrecognizable. One, which overnight, became a monochrome cityscape of ashen grey, a skeleton of its former glorious self, where carcasses of buildings hold on precariously to their moorings on desolate ghostly streets, within which the forsaken inhabitants might as well be ghosts, themselves, so estranged from their former lives are they. She cannot convey a staggering, delirious Aleppo where death has everyone marked, either through starvation or barrel bombs. Long gone are the jeweled-toned hues of the souks and the vibrant vitality of the bustling vegetable markets. Long gone are the golden minarets of lofty archaic mosques and the soothing poetic melodies of Call to Prayer from inside those lost towers. Remarkably, Ms. Bartlett does at one point make a fleeting reference to the siege taking place in *parts* of Aleppo, but this brutal act she blames on the West, moreover, America. It is America which, according to her, is deliberately blocking aid from getting beyond the borders of this landlocked nation. Seventy independent nations know differently, however, and have each implored the Syria regime and the Russian front to allow this waiting aid through, and still convoys of life-saving supplies are turned away or criminally redirected to Damascus to be better *appropriated* there. The very issue of aid transfer has been the topic of many a UN Security Council meeting, perhaps second only to their requests for government ceasefires.

Aleppo aside, Ms. Bartlett would likely prefer it not be known that most of her trips inside Syria have been to the capital Damascus and only there – a city with its presidential palace and fierce army control, which again, under regime jurisdiction, is as estranged from the reality of the rest of ravaged Syria as could be possible. A city that features an opulent *Four Seasons* luxury hotel where luxury brand, Molton Brown toiletries, so beloved by Assad's British-born wife, are staples in the guest rooms, and imported Russian Beluga caviar can be found alongside Stolichnaya premium Russian vodka in the dining room. A city where the centralized media boast about putting up festive trees at Christmas and having wonderful religiously-inclusive parties, despite the fact that not so far from the presidential precincts is one of the most brutal and inhumane facilities in current worldly existence – Sednaya Prison. A notorious torture chamber, where anyone deemed in opposition of Assad – men, women, children are sent and barbarically punished for any perceived assent, the majority punished to death, with upwards of fifty corpses leaving its compound daily during its heyday.[13]A type of factory-style Gulags Stalin could have only dreamed about. With a pride of purpose among the sadistic regime henchmen, perhaps rivaled only by the camp guards of Auschwitz. In her copious visits to the capital, Ms. Bartlett has come to know President Assad very well and, for the president, she is most certainly, a public relations catch. The illustrious prospect of a Canadian journalist imparting the regime narrative about the "truth" of the Syrian conflict makes Ms. Bartlett extremely valuable not only to his government's agenda but to his partners in crime, Russia and Iran. Ms. Bartlett, whose optics are nondescript in person and purportedly Canadian in ethics, is the ideal persona for a Russian propagandist. This, combined with Ms. Bartlett's love of Assad, Putin, and the anti-American narrative, matched with her church-mouse features, makes her by far the most dangerous propagandist of the four sitting there in their self-appointed panel. And for the White Helmets, Ms. Bartlett, is one of the two most dangerous Western women currently biting at the bit for Assad and Putin's war propaganda wagon to keep going. The other Assad favourite is absent from the stage this day. Absent, but most assuredly active.

The panel Ms. Bartlett shares the stage with this day presents one homogenous view of the Syrian war. There is a sense of congratulations among this foursome in no small part due to the fact that they served as part of an apparent delegation to Damascus the November past and were entertained by none other than the president, himself, at the

142

Damascene Palace. One of the panelists shares that President Bashar al-Assad was gracious enough to speak to them for two hours, thoroughly explaining the Syrian situation, filling in the "gaps" for them and, consequently, there is no doubt lingering in any of their minds that Assad's version of the destruction and brutality taking place in his nation, is fueled by America, ISIS and other rebel factions, but certainly not his own military aided by Russia's elite warplane arsenal. All those evils that afflict his nation have but one goal in mind, a change in regime, a booting out of Assad, from which President Assad says the foreigners will profit handsomely. President Assad has sent this delegation back home from Syria with one task, to convince the world it is the West, not him, that is creating havoc and heartache in his beautiful nation. Swept neatly under the palace Persian carpet, is the fact that it was the people, themselves, who revolted against the regime in 2011. Nevertheless, getting this constructed narrative to the world is an obligation this panel, here now in this fraudulent UN briefing room, takes very seriously, and with a sense of great pride and purpose, will not stop until it is delivered. What their consequent compensation for their loyalty to Assad is, other than to express their anti-Western dogma, remains unclear to many. Monetary compensation is a valid guess, particularly as many Assad propagandists have ended up living in Russia, with Eva Bartlett going so far as to change her given name to the Russian diminutive on her

Facebook and Instagram pages – both of which have now been removed from social media.

When the briefing has concluded and it is time for questions, the one Western journalist present is the first to put his hand up. He directs his question to Eva Bartlett. The following transcribed exchange occurs:

"Thank you very much, I'm Christopher Renberg with the Norwegian newspaper Aftenposten. A question for-- or two questions -- for Miss Bartlett. Here as a journalist I'm sure you can appreciate getting other impressions and empirical impressions from the ground when you talk about the Syrian people and what the Syrian people want. How can you quantify that? Do you have any independent surveys where you can actually document that and secondly you talk about the corporate media...the Western media the lies and all of this. Could you explain what you think might be the agenda from us in the Western media and why we should lie...why the international organizations on the ground would lie; why we shouldn't believe all these absolutely documented facts that we see from the ground, these hospitals being bombed, these civilians who are talking about the atrocities that they have been experiencing...how can you justify calling all of us liars."

After scribbling down a few notes while the Norwegian is speaking, Ms. Bartlett responds:

"I mean, there are certainly honest journalists amongst the very compromised establishment media...let's start with your second question...so international

144

organizations on the ground -- tell me which ones are on the ground in eastern Aleppo? Yeah, okay I'll tell you - there are none. There are none. These organizations are relying on the Syrian Observatory for Human Rights which is based in Coventry UK which is one man. They're relying on compromised groups like the White Helmets which let's let's talk about the White Helmets...the White Helmets were fun[sic] that were founded in 2013 by a British ex-military officer. They have been fun[sic]funded to the tune of 100 million dollars by the US, UK and Europe and other states. They purport to be rescuing civilians in eastern Aleppo and yet no one in eastern Aleppo has heard of them and I say no one bearing in mind that now ninety-five percent of these areas of eastern Aleppo are liberated."

No one is on the ground to see anything, Ms. Bartlett states conclusively. Full stop. If true, it is essentially a Get Out of Jail Free Card for the Assad regime. If no one is on the ground, no one can tell of the atrocities being committed by the regime. It's a bluff and a wager by Ms. Bartlett that is so categorically easy to debunk, one must gather it is either arrogant carelessness or massive ignorance that provokes her unequivocal statement. A statement which is a manifest lie.

No one is on the ground.

In fact, many organizations stayed on the ground when Aleppo was being ravaged and suffocated. They were not shy about documenting Assad's horrors and reporting them.

Médecins Sans Frontières, French for *Doctors Without Borders*, was on the ground during the Aleppo siege. Established in Paris, France, in 1971, it is a vast organization comprised of doctors from all over the world who work in a volunteer capacity from the irrefutable standpoint of human rights and morality. During the siege of Aleppo, they not only provided what care was possible for Assad's victims, but they also documented everything they could.

From a March 11, 2015 report provided on their MSF website, the medical humanitarian organization underscores the extreme risk in working under a regime-battered Eastern Aleppo.

"You could be sleeping. You could be walking to the shop. At any time, a bomb can happen," says an MSF health worker in one of the hospitals the organisation runs in northern Syria.

This report[14], one of many written during this era of the Aleppo siege, conveys the dreadful humanitarian situation in Aleppo City and the surrounding areas through which their work carried on despite the omnipotent perils. Having been in place in Aleppo since the early days of the Syrian conflict, Médecins Sans Frontières articulates the hell wrought down since mid-December 2013, when the Syrian forces initiated a campaign of aerial bombardments, with one of their bombs of choice being the barrel bomb. One of the more brutal bombs to be dropped on residential areas, it was strategically dropped in the targeted Aleppo, creating massive casualties, economy style. The bomb shell – any durable container with actual barrels being the most commonly used – filled with all manner of available debris - bits and pieces of metal shards, iron bolts and nails combined with TNT impact, causes massive destruction when dropped out of a helicopter and detonated at close range, killing and wounding humans as easily as they devastate civilian homes and surrounding infrastructure in densely populated areas. Sometimes, surviving the savage barrel bomb attack is worse than actually being killed by it, particularly in a country stripped bare of medical aid. A Médecins Sans Frontières physician spoke out about the human casualty toll that he was seeing routinely in an Eastern Aleppo hospital from this indiscriminate brand of barrel bombing:

"Many victims become permanently maimed. Losing a limb in Aleppo city is particularly traumatic, both physically and psychologically, since wheelchairs aren't available and the context of war makes it harder for them to adapt to a new life. Moreover, shortages in medical equipment and poor levels of post-operative care have meant that in many cases doctors carry out amputations when under other circumstances the limb could have been preserved.[15]

Then the doctor speaks to the physician shortage in the same article:

"However, access to healthcare is now virtually impossible due to lack of supplies and qualified medical staff, and medical services for the residents of eastern Aleppo have diminished to alarming levels. From an estimated 2,500 doctors

working in Aleppo at the beginning of the conflict, less than a hundred remain in the medical structures still operating in the city. The rest have fled, become internationally displaced or refugees, or have been kidnapped and killed.

"The aerial bombardments have led to a lack of electricity and destruction of houses and infrastructure. People are now seeking new ways of heating, and the widespread use of home-made combustibles has caused a number of domestic accidents, such as burn cases among children. Treating burnt patients is very challenging in the current scenario of war and lack of medical care in Aleppo.

"....normal daily life has stopped, people are running away, and markets, schools, and any place with presence of civilians are likely to be bombed."

S.A.M.S., short for Syrian American Medical Society, is another not-for-profit medical organization that was hard at work on the ground in besieged Aleppo. Established in 1998, the organization has been in Aleppo since 2012, working in 9 healthcare facilities providing critical and non-critical care. Ultimately, all functioning facilities would be destroyed by regime and Russian aircraft. During the siege's peak, approximately 1700 SAMS staff were at work in the besieged areas. Despite impossible working conditions and at great risk of peril, they continued their mandate, combating needless plights of malnutrition, particularly among the youngest of the population, waterborne diseases, chronic diseases, and of course, the constant war injuries.

Dr. M. Zaher Sahloul[16] was in eastern Aleppo with S.A.M.S., treating the regime and Russia's victims. He speaks about the abhorrent in-hospital experiences and those of the afflicted in an article he wrote, dated November 8, 2015.

"There are only 30 remaining doctors in Aleppo, and they have been describing an unimaginable situation, some of which I have seen firsthand. They have to perform amputations on children on the floor of their rudimentary emergency rooms without anesthesia or proper sterilization. They are running short on blood products, intravenous fluid, antibiotics and pain medications.

The doctors have been struggling to provide health care for a traumatized population of 300,000, while their hospitals are bombed daily and their medical supplies and medications are depleted.

They have been working nonstop for the past three months, dealing with the influx of a large number of polytrauma and crush patients suffering from horrible injuries, pulled from under the rubble.

Hospitals are targeted frequently in Syria, especially in Aleppo, mostly by the Syrian government and lately by Russian jets."

Then there is the famous Sakhour Medical Centre, also known by its Nom de Guerre, "M10". "M10" was an integral and efficient trauma hospital servicing the besieged civilians of eastern Aleppo City. Treating patients since well before the revolution, it was bombarded by Russian and regime aircraft on at least four separate occasions between September 28th and October 14th, 2016. The final blast of airborne munitions by Russia destroyed it completely in October 2016. Comprehensive evidence, in the form of photographs, videos, and satellite imagery, corroborates eyewitness accounts that the hospital was deliberately targeted and ultimately demolished. The destruction was a clear disregard for the Geneva Conventions Act stipulating that no civilian hospitals shall be bombed in war. [17]

Like so many entities fighting the regime offensive, there was something of a warrior sensibility to M10. Perhaps it was in the seemingly indomitable commitment by doctors and staff to stick it out to the end that almost gave the hospital a soul of its own. When that seemingly diehard soul of the building and the living forces within it were ultimately destroyed, an article written like a sort of obituary was composed for it. Dated December 14, 2016, and published in *Time*, the article describes the obliteration of one of the last functioning hospitals in eastern Aleppo with the title:

"Obituary: A Hospital In Aleppo (2013-2016)"[18]

"Medical personnel and facilities have been targeted systematically by the Syrian government and its allies. Physicians for Human Rights (PHR) has documented at least 757 killings of medical personnel since the popular democratic uprisings began in March 2011. The Syrian government, its ally Hezbollah and Russia are responsible for more than 90% of those deaths. The latter half of 2016 has

been the bloodiest stretch for humanitarians in Syria. In November, attacks occurred at a rate of one per 24 hours. In the past 162 days, there have been at least 147 attacks. More than a third of them took place in besieged Aleppo, all perpetrated by Syrian government and Russian forces. Assad has made targeting medics a key component of his military strategy. Killing a doctor ensures that hundreds will bleed to death; bombing a hospital terrorizes an entire neighborhood, driving displacement and forcing surrenders.

M10's story is not unique to this crisis. But in looking at the ongoing government takeover of Aleppo, the destruction of the city's most fortified hospital was the harbinger of the city's collapse, if not its catalyst. There is a reason why the protection of medical personnel in times of war was enshrined in the Geneva Conventions. In Syria, we saw a deeper connection: as go the hospitals, so goes the hope of the people. Perhaps that is why al-Assad never viewed hospitals as neutral."

The writer goes on to describe what is now a commonplace event in Assad's war on civilian hospitals, their physicians, and the patients.

In a medical article *Aleppo Abandoned: A Case Study on Health Care in Syria,*[19] the documentation of medical facilities and the health care workers embattled within them is as daunting as it is disturbing. Again, barrel bombs, precision-guided missiles, and double-taps do the dirty work of the Syrian regime, determined to obliterate the defiant hospitals that are still in the business of saving civilians. The executive summary begins with a brief synopsis that sounds like but one circle of Dante's Hell:

"A barrel bomb falls from the sky, tumbling through the air toward civilians in markets and homes. It shatters when it hits the ground. Shrapnel and nails filling the barrel fly in all directions, causing catastrophic injuries. Minutes later, after the first responders and medics have rushed to the scene to provide emergency aid, another bomb falls – targeting them. This is a double-tap strike. Those left standing transport the injured and dying to a nearby hospital, where doctors race to save lives knowing at any moment they could be bombed. When the last casualty is treated, it is time to count the dead. Doctors and first responders pick up body parts and wonder whose mothers, fathers, and children the mangled limbs belong to.

The doctors, nurses, medics, and other health workers in Syria's opposition-controlled areas have been abandoned by the international community and UN Security Council. They cannot fathom how the world can stand passively by and watch as a quarter of a million people die, millions more are displaced, and civilian homes and workplaces are obliterated. They are left standing in their barren, makeshift hospitals with nothing but sandbags protecting them from the next airstrike, wondering how much longer they have left to live.

They know that as long as the world's indifference continues, the odds are against them.

Welcome to Aleppo."

Oxfam International, founded in Britain in 1942, was initially established with the goal of wiping out famine wherever they could. Oxfam was on the ground in Aleppo during the siege. Andy Baker, Oxfam's leader for the Syria crisis, speaks of the organization's work in besieged Aleppo.[20]

"The two generators that Oxfam has provided should help provide a more consistent supply of clean water to Aleppo's nearly two million residents. But food and medical supplies remain blocked. Clear water is vital, but it won't stop starvation, never mind protect people from indiscriminate aerial attacks."

"The UN announced on 10 November that it was distributing its last food rations in East Aleppo, and warned of mass starvation if aid is not allowed in."

The Big Heart Foundation, TBHF, is a United Arab Emirates organization that was originally started as a fundraising organization in Sharjah, UAE, but expanded its commitment to helping civilians in desperate need in 2015 by becoming a full-fledged NGO.

The Big Heart Foundation was on the ground in Aleppo during the siege.

The senior advocacy officer of the foundation, Abd Alwahab Jessry, outlines the perilous work carried out in Aleppo, including the distribution of food rations to 22, 180 families in East Aleppo since October underscoring this with the caution that distribution will be discontinued if a complete cessation of hostilities and airstrikes for the security of aid convoys cannot be guaranteed.

Also, in Ms. Bartlett's proud gamble to assert there was "no one" on the ground, and consequently no evidence to disprove her Assad-apologist narrative, she forgot the very civilians themselves. Ordinary people were witnessing the horrors up close. In a bid to document the crimes, tech-savvy twenty and thirty-somethings were now recording in real time on their cell phones. These high-quality videos captured on their phones would be hastily exported to the outside world through internet cafes, breaking through the regime government's internet firewalls.

In Syrian author Rania Abouzeid's non-fiction book *No Turning Back*, she articulates the diligence and speed with which the Syrians managed to get the atrocities of the regime onto their phones and then, with the news and media platforms of stations like Orient TV, Al Jazeera, and Al Arabiya, directly out into the world.

Following one such early protest, an affluent young Syrian, given the pseudonym Suleiman in the book, was perhaps one of the first to strike up the courage to defy the government he had been afraid of for two decades and started filming. Later in Suleiman's bedroom at home, he managed to get his evidence to the outside world. Author Rana Abouzeid outlines the process in her book,

"Suleiman opened his Acer laptop, transferred the footage, and activated the proxy he had used to access Facebook before the government unblocked it. He and his cousin searched for Orient TV, Al Jazeera, Al Arabiya, and a slew of other stations they knew of, as well as others they didn't, like Shaam New Network, or SNN, which they came across during their search. They didn't have contacts at these outlets. They found generic e-mail addresses, created a new e-mail account with a fake name, kept the subject line simple – Protests -and started uploading. The Internet often cut out, forcing them to restart. After about three hours, Suleiman hit SEND."

He had made contact with the outside world. Now they knew.

First attempts like this successfully brought the nation's full-scale massacre and atrocities to the eyes of the outside world. It was a risk to those uploading, but it became an operation that would be repeated consistently throughout the Syrian conflict, and certainly well into the Aleppo siege and beyond. The uploads still remained in internet perpetuity. Millions upon millions of uploads.

There is, however, one group that Ms. Barlett concedes was on the ground during Aleppo's siege, the White Helmets. On the ground they were, and experiencing the full extent of the regime and Russia's wrath so that they became the ultimate eyewitnesses. And what they saw and experienced, they carefully saved. Innumerable documents, video recordings, and meticulous record keeping, right down to the name and age of each victim treated or lost by the humanitarian organizations in Aleppo, are a clear testament to the selfless work they carried out there. Physicians in the area add their own body of evidence describing the humanitarian work of the Syria Civil Defence volunteers, when documenting the continual transfer of the bombing victims by the White Helmets to hospitals and field medical centres. Even the civilians were speaking up for the work of the White Helmets, telling anyone who would listen, that they were the only field humanitarians saving them. What will be the most damning evidence of all for the claim of Assad's war crimes and crimes against humanity, is the comprehensive video footage and photographic proof captured extensively and saved on computer drives by the White Helmets from their daily rescues. A collection of evidence vastly greater than for any other conflict in history, including the two world wars combined. It is stored in a building of archives inside an undisclosed location in Amsterdam, Netherlands, awaiting Assad and Putin's day in court.

Continuing her response to the Norwegian journalist, Ms. Bartlett states,

"They're [the outside world] *relying on compromised groups like the white helmets, which let's...let's talk about the white helmets..."*

And so, Ms. Bartlett's slanderous attack on the White Helmets begins. This is where Ms. Bartlett's conviction to her bizarre propaganda, which originated back at the Damascene Palace at teatime with Assad before boarding a flight to the United Nations building in New York City, here, now commences. *" the white helmets purport to be neutral yet they can be found carrying guns and standing in*[sic] *the dead bodies of Syrian soldiers and their video footage actually contains children that have been recycled in different reports so you can find a girl named Aya who turns up in a report in* [sic] *month say August and she turns up in the next month in two different locations so they are not credible. The SOHR* [Syrian Observatory for Human Rights] *is not credible unnamed activists are not credible once or twice maybe but every time not credible. So your sources on the ground you don't have them. As for your agenda - not your but the agenda of some corporate media - it is the agenda of regime change."*

Guns, torture, recycled children, regime change...and her conviction *"no one"* is on the ground to witness and substantiate the overwhelming claims of Assad's murderous campaign. This practiced and procedural telling of the Assad narrative will become Eva Bartlett's vocation for years to come. Indeed, her ultimate mission statement is to discredit the White Helmets to the point that their reputations, tarnished irremediably, the volunteers in hard white hard hats will be neatly rebranded as terrorists. And as per the standards of any good propagandist, she needn't wholly convince anyone of her "facts" but merely plant adequate confusion about the humanitarians to effect the result she needs. Muddy the waters enough, and the White Helmets' essential funding from the international community to continue their life-saving humanitarian efforts could be unilaterally revoked with far-reaching consequences for the very state of the conflict, itself. Ms. Bartlett's ready propaganda imperils not only the lives of innocent civilians and health care workers, but the very lives of the White Helmets, themselves. It is a dark mandate, but one which Eva seems wholly and unscrupulously cooperative in carrying out.

Eva Bartlett is, however, only the tip of the iceberg in this propaganda hell on the Helmets. She is a mere lightweight harbinger of the Assad-apologist yet to come, British-born Vanessa Beeley.

Hand-picked by Assad himself, Ms. Beeley, armed with a full quiver of regime and Russia propaganda arrows so vehement and exacting in their trajectory, would become known as the Syrian conflict's *"Goddess of Propaganda"*. She is, without a doubt, Assad's media golden girl. If Ms. Bartlett was a thorn in the side of truth, her British counterpart, Vanessa Beeley, would become a shot of Russian Plutonium in integrity's teacup. With slick sleight of hand and a vast assortment of bold-faced lies delivered with a lovely British accent, an alternate reality about the White Helmets would come to life.

Ms. Beeley, a 60-year-old former plastics saleswoman turned anti-establishment activist, also designates herself as a journalist. In keeping with her colleague Eva Bartlett, her available vitae reveals no sound journalistic credentials nor educational background. She has never written for an established large news source, much less a Western one. The bulk of her writing is published by fringe news outlets like Mint Press News, Russia Today, The Wall Will Fall, The

Last American Vagabond, Global Research, Sputnik Radio, 21st Century Wire, and other independent media outlets. Outlets that focus on conspiracy theories delivered through sensational tabloid-like content. Both Ms. Beeley and Ms. Bartlett are regular contributors to several of these media organizations, and their audiences are large and growing. On these platforms her articles brandish outrageous, but predictable, theories such as the 9/11 attacks were USA-devised and not orchestrated by al-Qaeda; the 2015 mass shooting on French satirical magazine Charlie Hebdo were "false flags" staged by the authorities[21]; and hitting at the heart of the plight of the Syrian people, she denies the use and efficacy of the dreaded barrel bomb, in a fairly new article she wrote for a media agency called Substack, entitled (apparently facetiously) *"Barrel bombs are back!".*[22]

Ms. Beeley uses provocation, not proof, to promote her stories and their inherent lies. It is a tried-and-true Russian propaganda mechanism. Fact and evidence are equally tenuous in her business, or non-existent. Her modus operandi is killing the truth with bizarre counterargument, but doing it with old-school politeness. The daughter of a British Parliament Lord, her manifest disdain for her home, the United Kingdom, is odd. She regards her native Britain as the real tyrannical regime, not Syria. The *West* to Ms. Beeley is little more than a dirty word, second only in perceived egregiousness to America.

With no formal education nor any real prowess in the world of journalism to which she seemingly always aspired, it is likely Ms. Beeley found unmatched validation in her "journalistic" ability by President Assad, himself. Her visits to Syria have led her invariably to Damascus and to the President on more than one occasion. A voracious social media user, in 2016, she met with Putin's liaison to Syria, the Russian Deputy Foreign Minister Bogdanov, along with the Russian Director of Information Press, Maria Zakharova, as well as the man, himself, Bashar al-Assad, in Damascus. On Facebook, she described her two-hour meeting. She subsequently posted on her Instagram account a picture of her beside President Al-Assad in his Damascene palace, and with the giddiness of a schoolgirl going through a flustered crush, hashtagged this monumental photograph, *"My proudest moment"*. Another Instagram image shows a picture of Assad, the close up of a wry smile on his contemptuous face, for which her quote is *"every inch of Syria will be liberated."* In yet another post, a lone Christmas tree, not real but lighted in gold with a few red balls and some pots of dead flowers anchoring it to the empty street, is hash-tagged with, #DamascusChristmas. Not one but four pictures of the same tree are captured and preserved on her Instagram, clearly the only highlight of the oft-touted festive Christmas in Damascus within miles of Ms. Beeley's camera.

Ms. Beeley has a natural flair for interviews and PowerPoint presentations alike. She is, for all appearances, amiable, well spoken, and confident about what she is talking about. Again, taken at her word alone and its delivery through her demure British accent, she is highly believable. She is a competent storyteller. She has a growing fan base, mostly of conspiracy theorists, and at the time of writing, her Twitter account (now called X) has a follower count of 125,000. Not bad for a previous unknown.

Her Syrian regime narrative reads from the same script as Ms. Bartlett's. It's a simple story, really. President Bashar al-Assad is fighting the evil West and all the various terrorist factions within Syria to win back a country these villains are unlawfully attempting to take from him. She wants her audience to know that Bashar al-Assad is but a simple sovereign leader merely trying to govern his nation during a difficult situation. Accordingly, all Western stories coming out of Syria, demonstrating Assad and Russia's mass destruction of the nation and brutalization of the Syrian people, are abject fiction. Laughable, even, according to Ms. Beeley. It is the rebel terrorist factions who are destroying the country, murdering the people, and starving the children by blocking humanitarian aid. It is the terrorist rebels who have driven 14 million residents to flee their homes. One of these terrorist rebel factions she rhymes off is, of course, the White Helmets. Yet, for Ms. Beeley and Assad, the White Helmets are a breed apart, and they have become the fulcrum of each of her discourses on Syria.

By 2019, at the height of the regime and Russian military assault on the Syrian people, the new Syria Civil Defence had quite literally made a name for itself. White helmeted heads seen in action all over bomb sites easily garnered them their nickname. The preponderance of video documentation of their search and rescues in the demolished country had piqued the attention of the world. There they were shown again and again on videos, the uniform brown jackets with the epaulettes on the shoulders, and on their backs the now familiar circular logos of white safety hats and their humanitarian mission statement, both in English in Arabic, the donated signature safety hats atop their heads. To Assad and his apologists, these grass-roots humanitarians were far more than a fly in their soup. Bobbing white heads scrambling through massive piles of heavy concrete rubble, digging for survivors, or racing through the streets via ambulances en route to find survivors after yet one more bomb drop, putting out fires, picking through rigged fields to take out the mines, risking their own lives to save the very souls Assad and Russia were hell-bent on decimating -this was all truly problematic for the perpetrators. Having first made real headlines back in 2016 in besieged Aleppo when the original team had, against all odds, rescued the "Miracle Baby," a 10-week-old baby who had been trapped for 19 hours under slabs of concrete, the organization's popularity soared again. These ordinary men and women turned rescuers were making the forgotten plight of the Syrian innocents matter to the outside world once more.

Responding to the world's interest, two small-budget, Oscar-nominated documentaries on Netflix would bring them into millions of living rooms. The organization would be nominated for three consecutive Nobel Peace prizes, be honoured with the Eli Weisel Holocaust Museum Humanitarian award, and countless other accolades. By then, they had come under the wing of a seasoned humanitarian director. Consequently, money poured in from sponsor nations, providing them with ambulances, heavy machinery for their endless rescues, stretchers, and medical equipment, all of it to support this organization that was one of the only lifelines in the field the Syrian people had. Indeed, a lifeline and Assad's worst nightmare.

As the White Helmets began drawing worldwide attention, Vanessa Beeley was gaining a sizeable fame and notoriety herself. It was perhaps this understanding of her own growing celebrity which in 2019 prompted her to go "on tour" with her PowerPoint presentations in seven cities across Canada. There was no mincing words about what the true subject of her talks would be, as the title of her tour, *"The Role of the So Called White Helmets in Syria,"* aptly said it all. The Syrian conflict was going to take a back seat to the discussion of these "so-called" humanitarians. Canada was an odd choice for a national tour to defame the organization. Ms. Beeley should have been aware that the Canadian government was a huge supporter of the humanitarian group and that a branch of the White Helmets Administration office manned part-time by the head of the White

Helmets, himself, Raed al-Saleh, was slowly establishing itself in the Canadian province of Quebec, under the French-translated name, *Les Casques Blancs*. In addition, the Canadian government was supporting the women humanitarians of the White Helmets, who primarily worked in northern Syria, providing medical care and counseling in the neglected refugee camps, with millions in aid annually. Undaunted, Ms. Beeley booked speaking venues with the University of Ottawa, the University of Montreal, the University of Winnipeg, as well as other smaller venues in Ontario, including cities, Hamilton, Mississauga and Toronto – seven Canadian cities in all. Indeed, she must have been bolstered by the very idea of walking onto the stages of legitimate Western institutions to spread her message after having lurked in the shadows of fringe tabloids and Russian television and its affiliates for so long. Her schedule for the tour was proudly displayed on her Facebook page. *"I'm so excited to go to Canada,"* Ms. Beeley remarked victoriously beneath the tour advertisement.

For the uninitiated at these proposed venues, her submitted vitae of journalistic accomplishments including her "awards", must have seemed valid on paper as she described herself as an *"internationally-acclaimed British Journalist"*.[23] Universities are, after all, cornerstones for diverse discussion. Canada prides itself on free speech and dialogue, particularly in its academic institutions. However, the backlash was immediate. Her critics came out in full swing. Kareem Shaheen, a Canadian journalist, and foreign correspondent who covered the

Middle East, had this to say on December 2, 2019, on his Twitter account upon hearing Beeley was hitting the university stages:

"Really shameful that @UMontreal is inviting Vanessa Beeley, an apologist for the 21st century's most murderous regime, Bashar al-Assad's, to go give a 'journalism' talk. Pity the state of academia."

His wasn't the only criticism, and soon the University of Montreal found itself in a position where it needed to investigate the "investigative journalist". They discovered enough about Ms. Beeley that they pulled her from the roster immediately. Frederic Merand, director of the Montreal Centre for International Studies, expressed openly in an interview with Radio Canada that he felt uneasy about Beeley's visit to the university, saying the line was very fine since she isn't a researcher but calls herself a "journalist".

Merand remarked, *"All points of view are welcome at the university, but it is not the place to spread lies, fakes news or false truths."*[24]

Shortly after, the University of Winnipeg followed suit and disallowed her from speaking at their institution as well. The University of Ottawa was not far behind. Beeley would once again spin the narrative, bellowing about her rejection, citing the constitutional unfairness and restriction placed on free speech, eventually demonizing Canada[25] for its Western support of the White Helmets. The message to her, however, had been made loud and clear - hate speech would not be tolerated in Canada – not for holocaust-denier

Ernst Zundel of decades past and not for Vanessa Beeley in 2019. Bound and determined that the show would go on, she would replace the cancelled university venues on her tour with much smaller, accommodating venues such as community centres, libraries, and churches. In early December 2019, her tour commenced in Canada.

The University of Ottawa was replaced last minute by the Ottawa Library, and it is unclear whether the library blindly undertook the seminar without properly vetting Ms. Beeley. Notwithstanding, on December 8, 2019, the show went on at 2:30 on the auditorium stage of the main branch of the Ottawa Public Library.

Through an amateur videographer presumably hired by Vanessa Beeley and her team, later uploaded on YouTube, the viewer is taken through a wobbly-captured front foyer of the Ottawa library and then led into the auditorium where this guest speaker is primed to give her lecture. The tour title *"The Role of the So Called White Helmets in Syria"* is already up on the PowerPoint screen, as the few guests take their seats.

Ms. Beeley, pleasant and with a down-to-earth appeal, is standing at a podium on a small stage when she begins her lecture. In her introduction, she announces that she is *"coming clean"* on what she describes as her two biases she would like her audience to know about for the sake of *"complete transparency"*. Her first bias, she states, is that she stands unequivocally for the "Protection of International Law". She is a stickler, she says, for the adherence to that United Nations collective agreement, International Law. The law she refers to is one that binds every participating state through the signing of a treaty with comprehensive stipulations ensuring, perhaps foremost, the protection of human rights. A law, which, when breached, is examined at a tribunal at the Court of International Law and United Nations hearings. If a partner nation defies international treaty requisites, they are automatically in direct violation of them. The United Nations stipulates the following necessary protocol behaviour for being a bound party to this International Law: "*States' legal responsibilities in their conduct with each other, within State's boundaries, and in their treatment of individuals. International law encompasses many areas, including human rights, disarmament, transnational organized crime, refugees, migration, statelessness, the treatment of prisoners, the use of force, the conduct of war, the environment, sustainable development, the oceans, outer space, global communications and world trade*"[26]

That Ms. Beeley should heartily emphasize her devotion to the protection of international law while promulgating the Syrian regime's principles of conduct, is, to say the least, bizarre. No more blatant a contradiction could she have started her speech with. The Syrian government has historically been penalized through the domains of the Geneva Convention and onward through the United Nations and NATO, for the continual transgressions of international law. Following the beginning of the wholesale bloodshed on his people, including every form of violation of human rights imaginable – a

167

campaign of nation-wide bombing, torture, kidnapping, the use of prohibited weapons, including the egregious use of Sarin and other banned chemicals, and the violent impetus for massive migration of the Syrian people out of the nation. This utter lawlessness has resulted in heavy sanctions against the Assad Regime by the United States, the European Union, Australia, the Arab League, and numerous non-EU countries, including Georgia, Croatia, Macedonia, Montenegro, Iceland, Serbia, Albania, Liechtenstein, Norway, and Moldova. In 2022 Syria was the third most sanctioned nation in the world. Preceding these comprehensive global sanctions, was an embargo on Syria's oil sector enacted in August 2011, sought to halt the violence by Assad on his civilians. In 2020, secondary sanctions were enacted through the Caesar Act[27] named for the pseudonym of a former Sednaya Prison employee at the notorious institution in Damascus who revealed the plethora of damning photographic evidence it was his job to capture of the thousands of tortured and murdered inmates.

Her second admitted bias, which she espouses with a bold face and apparent conviction, is that she is against war. For most people, this would go without saying, but Ms. Beeley seems compelled to make sure her audience knows that war offends her to her very core. To point out the glaring contradiction here, of course, is to once again state the obvious. With more collected evidence of Assad's unprovoked war on his civilians, and with a murder toll into the hundreds of thousands, a refugee rate exponentially higher as everyday Syrians flee from the mass-murderer, than for any other conflict in history, her statement is not just patently false, it is brutally ridiculous. For a woman cogently in opposition to war, she is openly, vocally, endorsing one of the most war-hungry and murderous dictators of the 21st century.

Within minutes of starting her lecture, she gets down to brass tacks by describing to her sparse audience the Helmets' organization as being a direct affiliate of no less than four terrorist groups inside Syria, working with them, supporting them, and espousing their principles. It is important to characterize these terrorist groups Ms. Beeley is referring to. They are as follows:

Shabab al Sunna

This militant organization, founded by young men in 2015, is known for its atrocities against civilians, and has made clear through terrorism, its mission for a worldwide Islamic State. They have been established affiliates of ISIS since 2019. Their mission statement declares: *"We want everyone here to apply Islamic law... We don't want a government from unbelievers, we want a government from Allah."* It was designated as a terrorist organization by the United States in 2021.

Al Nusra Front

This faction, also going by the name of Front for the Conquest of the Levant, and formerly Jabhat Al-Nusra, is a jihadist terrorist organization working inside Syria, and in opposition to the imperialist regime in order to establish an Islamic State. It once had ties to Al-

169

Qaeda before declaring independence from that organization. A full armed and highly militant organization, the group's Islamic goals - including the establishment of Sharia Law - make it a particularly dangerous group.

Al-Qaeda

Founded in 1988, this known terrorist organization's agenda is to fulfill what they believe is their Koran mandate of an Islamic State worldwide with the exclusive practice of Sharia Law. They have been described as the vanguard of Jihad, with extensive terrorist attacks around the world, the majority focused on the United States and its allies. A fully armed and well-established militant group, atrocities are carried out against opposing ideologies, perpetrating horrors on civilian populations. Their former leader, Osama bin Laden, was the kingpin for the bombing of the USS Cole naval ship as well as the 9/11 attacks on the Twin Towers in New York City, causing the deaths of well over 3500 civilians.

ISIS [Daesh]

Considered the most violent of all the militant groups, the terrorist organization ISIS (Islamic State of Iraq) during the American military campaign in Iraq and more recently ISIL (Islamic State of the Levant) or "Daesh" in Arabic, has almost earned a league of their own in terms of horror and brutality carried out in their mission to establish an Islamic State and provoke the world into war. They rekindled the world's attention, when they videotaped four decapitations of American journalists in Syria, including James Foley, Steven Sotloff, Peter Kassig, and Kayla Mueller, with the clear message that America was to meet the organization's demands, or more killings would occur.

Kidnappings, torture, beheadings, brutalization, and globally staged terror attacks, and the dream for an Islamic State with its Sharia Law trappings, are what all of these terrorist organizations have in common. They are fearsome and loathed.

But herein lies a critical distinction. If Vanessa Beeley is bound to her conviction that the White Helmets are quite comparable to these terrorist factions – factions, if she must agree are exponentially worse in their terrorism, why is she not focusing on these other groups? Why does Ms. Beeley, the proxy of Assad, hold the White Helmets in the greatest contempt, giving a pass to the other terrorist groups, which she posits the White helmets are *almost* just as bad as?

The answer to this is obvious. ISIS and Al Nusra Front aren't saving regime-targeted civilians and documenting Assad's war crimes.

Beeley has called publicly for the White Helmets to be considered legitimate targets in the conflict countless times, stripping them of the legal protection offered to humanitarians in war by International Law. She even goes so far as to rename the White Helmets Al-Qaeda when she legitimizes the lawful killing of them.

On one of her hundreds of Twitter posts about the White Helmets, she states: "#*AlQaeda Civil Defence is not 'protected' by international law, they are auxiliaries and members of internationally recognized terrorist organizations and as such they are a legitimate target when they support attacks against a sovereign nation and its people. Clear?*"[28]

Ms. Beeley's accusations against the White Helmets defy every piece of cogent evidence that has come out of Syria about them. The crimes she charges them with run the gamut from producing hoaxes and false flag attacks to rape, torture, and summary executions. Five minutes into her Ottawa Library lecture, Ms. Beeley outlines a contrived and outrageous description of the White Helmets:

"*Contrary to their marketing material where they claim they are there to serve all humanity...umm...they are effectively embedded exclusively with the terrorists and armed groups inside Syria. They do not work in the 85% of Syrian territory that is now back under the protection of the Syrian government.*"

"*I will go further into the*[ir] *war crimes committed against the Syrian people.*"

Photographs are put up on her PowerPoint screen depicting individuals she claims to be the White Helmets standing on the bodies of dead regime soldiers, fully armed. The origin of the pictures is never explained. The first glaring contradiction for anyone familiar with the White Helmets is that these counterfeit uniforms don't match the legitimate ones. No context is provided. Her claims that they are terrorists notwithstanding, the White Helmets have never carried arms, nor have they, logically, ever been filmed bearing arms. The photographs are clearly doctored, but they are Ms. Beeley's pretense of visual evidence for her audience. She has two such pieces for her audience this day.

Next, Ms. Beeley speaks with a note of triumph in her voice about having entered an actual functioning White Helmets' Centre in Daraa al Balad on September 20, 2018 - this despite having just stated the fact that there are no White Helmets operating in government-liberated areas. Indeed, the city in question, Daraa, fell to the Assad regime and its army on July 6th, 2018, with all rebel movements and vulnerable humanitarians such as the White Helmets fleeing at peril of death. The discrepancy seems completely lost on Ms. Beeley as she goes on in her presentation to offer up a video of this "centre". As the camera goes through the rooms of this building, a few props meant to represent the White Helmets in one of their actual centres are sparsely spread throughout. The purported "centre" looks more like a theatre stage than it does a functioning base. For good measure three white-coloured helmets, notably not the style of the Petzl-manufactured helmets provided to the actual White Helmets and without any of the attached black operational accoutrement including the regulatory light and ear guards, are set close to the floor and above these are two or three generic safety jackets with reflective striping on them, but no sign of the actual standard and now easily recognizable White Helmet uniforms, coats and pants. And there are no signs of the building being an actively functioning centre. There are no certainly no signs of recent activity in the rooms shown. There are mats on the floor for the volunteers to rest upon and for sleep at night shift, nor the traditional teacups for the ritual Syrian beverage. There, is, however, a large White Helmet logo-emblazoned flag for direct viewing by the camera, as if the volunteers in an actual centre would need a flag to remind them who and what they are. Then, most curiously, there is an orange medical stretcher set up in the corner of one room. It's a strange and ridiculously chosen artifact. Having never been in an authentic White Helmet Centre, Ms. Beeley cannot distinguish the blatant discrepancies in this staged caricature. White Helmet Centres are operated with the same standards, in the 120-plus centres situated, in liberated areas throughout the Syrian nation. Five to seven male volunteers, presided over by a manager, service the centres in 12-hour shifts, waiting for calls to duty. Should the volunteers have a nighttime shift, they have thin mattresses to sleep on. Typically, in the middle of the floor, in between this collection of mattresses, is a small heating mechanism for making tea or simply for warmth in cold temperatures. Their own cell phones and the walkie-talkies provided to them are always set somewhere nearby, as calls and messages to family and friends are a favourite pastime of the humanitarians during free time, and the radios are a necessary piece of equipment. The placement of these standard items may change a little from centre to centre, but what is universal is the placement of the helmets, jackets in each centre. The coats are lined up neatly on hooks side by side in a specific and regimented order, the helmets lined up in the same fashion beneath them. They keep their boots on. As time is of the utmost essence when a call for rescue comes in, the gear must be easily accessible as the volunteers literally run from the building, having grabbed these necessities, putting them on in their ambulances and vans on the way. What you will not find in an actual WH centre is an errant medical stretcher on wheels. These, usually in short supply, are found only in the ambulances again for quick retrieval of victims. There would be absolutely no reason for a stretcher to be in a functioning centre. These items Ms. Beeley ignorantly, or wittingly, parades as genuine articles, are frauds placed there to convince. Perhaps, they actually did convince her.

The other contradiction she discusses in her seminar is the rescue of the White Helmets out of regime-held areas by Israel. At 20 minutes 15 seconds into her speech, she recounts being told about the evacuation: *"...the special evacuation by Israel of the White Helmets in the South...ummm....which, of course, was pretty much orchestrated by Canada...."* Ms. Beeley refers to the emergency evacuation, which was carried out in July 2018 by the UK, the U.S., and Canada with the aid of Israel, allowing transfer through the Golan Heights and into Jordan. The White Helmets and their families had been trapped in Quneitra and Daraa when the regime forces closed in on the city, and they faced certain death if caught.

Going full throttle in her defamation of the humanitarian group, Ms. Beeley unflinchingly accuses the White Helmets of staging the most recent sarin massacre, which was carried out on Douma, Syria, on April 7, 2018, wherein prohibited chemical weapons took the lives of upwards of 50 civilians and injured well over a hundred. Doctors, medics, and the White Helmets recorded ample video for evidence while chemical samples were collected. A two-year-long investigation by the Organisation for the Prohibition of Chemical Weapons (OPCW) concluded in January 2023, determining that the Syrian Air Force perpetrated the chemical attacks. In her predictable counterargument, Ms. Beeley says the OPCS is a compromised organisation paid off by the West – essentially the same description she gives the White Helmets and with the same propaganda counter-argument tactic used to defame them.

To better legitimize her claim of the White Helmets habitually staging false flag or fake chemical attacks, she moves on from Douma to a previous chemical massacre which devastated Khan Sheikhoun, Idlib, on April 4, 2017, just a year earlier. For backup, she introduces to her PowerPoint a former United States Marine and Iraq Weapons Inspector for Operation Desert Storm, Mr. Scott Ritter. Since his departure from the American military, Scott Ritter has given a lot of anti-American and pro-Russian interviews. He has adequate vitriol for the Syria Civil Defence as well. Ms. Beeley shows part of one interview he gave to the host of the Ron Paul Liberty Institution channel shortly after the Khan Sheikhoun Sarin attack. In summary, Mr. Ritter disparages the White Helmets and concurrently the OPCW. He criticizes the collection standards of the Sarin samples conducted by the White Helmets, which were later accepted by the OPCW along with samples obtained by several other independent countries, and confirmed them as valid. Consequently, this proved Sarin was used on the Syrian people and not by the White Helmets or other rebel factions, but by the Syrian regime, itself. Ritter says this lack of adherence to standards, despite the fact he, himself, was not there observing the collection protocol, means the OPCW has *"lost its integrity"*. When referring directly to the White Helmets organization, Ritter says that they co-exist peacefully with Al-Nusra and *"that automatically disqualifies them* [from being legitimate humanitarians]". Ritter and Beeley both mention the fact that the White Helmets were not wearing conventional hazmat suits or gloves despite knowing it was Sarin gas. Previously, Ms. Beeley had produced a photograph of what she claims is an actual White Helmet wearing no gloves and what appeared to be a WW II gas mask. Indeed, the image looked like someone dressed up in a costume. It was a ridiculous submission. Accordingly, the old-fashioned gas mask and the individual wearing it had nothing to do with the White Helmets. The origins of the photo are never properly categorized by Ms. Beeley, other than to state, in the complete absence of proof, that it is a White Helmet holding a child. Apparently, Ms. Beeley believes her word alone is adequate. Full stop.

In reality, the first White Helmets responding to the attack that early morning were not just from the Khan Sheikhoun centre but were volunteers from many nearby centres who received the call that urgent help was needed. The Helmets had no understanding that this attack was anything more than a conventional ballistic attack by the regime. They wore their uniforms. They had no hazmat suits and no gloves as they approached the horrific scene of civilians convulsing on the ground within the radius of the chemical missile drop. The volunteers did not know they were dealing with Sarin. Seeing no injuries on the victims, they initially guessed chlorine gas, one of the regime's chemicals of choice. They had no idea the gas dropped on the civilians that day was far deadlier. It was, in fact, the field hospital physicians who initially guessed the gas used could be Sarin. Dr. Shajul Islam, who was on duty in one of the medical centres on the border of Khan Sheikhoun and another affected area Southern Hama, was receiving a flood of victims that just kept coming. Dr. Islam was immediately suspicious that the patients were contaminated with an entirely different chemical than the regime's routine chlorine.[29] As Dr. Islam takes his cell phone camera around the centre revealing the horrors of the situation, he looks into the camera and speaking with perfect English, says with a measure of desperation in his voice, *"This is not chlorine. We do not smell chlorine on this patient..."* he lifts the motionless hand of a young man on the stretcher to his face and smells it to illustrate his point. Dr. Islam continues walking through the warren of medical tables, each bearing an incapacitated or convulsing victim, "...*this patient has clear, clear pinpoint pupils...*" He lifts an eyelid to show the constriction medically known as miosis. He has already guessed Sarin, though he calls it by its chemical name, "...*these patients have got clear signs of organophosphate.*" As the video reveals the hysteria managed within, Dr. Islam informs that five hospitals have been destroyed that day, and so his centre is overwhelmed to the point they must turn the patients away. They have run out of respirators to counteract the respiratory symptoms that are killing the patients. And the antidote to Sarin, Atropine, is in limited supply. The camera shows a healthcare worker placing the remaining amber vials of Atropine out on the counter before him – there are maybe 10 vials left that will be used up rapidly. As Dr. Islam takes his camera over the body of a fifteen-year-old boy whom another physician is treating, the child dies on the table, and the treating doctor looks outraged at the needless loss of life. What is noteworthy, in light of the accusations of the lack of proper gear worn by the White Helmets that day, is that even the doctors are only wearing surgical gloves and surgical gowns, with some wearing no gloves at all. As for masks, they are using what they are supplied with – standard medical masks. The chemical Sarin affects in degrees. First degree exposure, for instance, those hit with the Sarin, having been in the direct vicinity of the missile drop, are likely to die, secondary and tertiary exposure is typically survivable, though lesser symptoms can last indefinitely. With mitigated anguish, Dr. Islam challenges the

179

world to finally do something in light of this inconceivable massacre of the Syrian people. He says, *"...we're going to collect all the clothes as evidence. We're collecting them in sealed bags as evidence. Anyone that wants this evidence to investigate it, please contact me; we can get this arranged for you to collect this...*[there is] *no doubt this is organophosphate."* His desperate plea to the world is: Please investigate this. Please help us. Please stop the killing of innocents.

The sampling of Sarin residue was one part of the investigation and was found by the experts at the OPCW to be legitimate and acceptable. Ultimately, taking into consideration many factors, the known arsenal of Sarin possessed by the Assad regime, the history of use of Sarin by the Syrian regime, the crater in the ground where the Sarin missile cannister exploded bearing Russian inscription on it, the fact that the rebels had no aircraft to drop the missiles, all pointed to the obvious – Assad and Putin had carried out massacres of their people with Sarin gas. The regime was implicated in both attacks on the people of Khan Sheikhoun and Douma. Any other conclusion was a far-fetched cover-up.

Retribution came on 14 April 2018, when the United States, France, and the United Kingdom carried out a series of military strikes against multiple government sites in Syria. Having once considered negotiating with Bashar al-Assad, when President Donald Trump saw the brutality inflicted by the dictator on his own people, his mind was changed once and for all. The air strikes were minimal and did little to change the brutal Assad campaign already in motion, but they sent a clear message to the dictator.

In deliberately denying all of these crucial and cogent facts, Scott Ritter was evidently just another propagandist with a chip on his shoulder. Having left the army during Operation Desert Storm before the mission had concluded due to disagreement, Ritter now works for Russian State Television and is, in all probability, an employee of Putin. He regularly gives interviews that seek to support the Russian State, whether it be in reference to Syria or now Ukraine. His declared objective, as all propagandists allege, is to investigate and find the truth, to expose lies. However, his criticism of the OPCW and the White Helmets is scripted propaganda - so much like Ms. Beeley's. His declaration that the OPCW has no integrity is a particularly bold statement in light of his very own track record of transgressions.

In June of 2001 Scott Ritter's online sexual exploits with teenagers made him the subject of a sting operation. After his illegal and illicit conduct in front of an undercover police officer online, even after she told him she was a minor, and then agreeing to meeting up with her for the purposes of sex, Ritter was arrested. The original arrest with six counts including unlawful contact with a minor was eventually reduced to a misdemeanor crime of *"attempted endangerment of the welfare of a child"*. [30] He served only six months probation.

In November 2009 he was again caught and arrested for sexual solicitation online with minors. Charges included "unlawful contact with a minor, criminal use of a communications facility, corruption of minors, indecent exposure, possessing instruments of crime, criminal attempt and criminal solicitation".[31] He was sent to Laurel Highlands state prison in Somerset County, Pennsylvania, in March 2012 and paroled in September 2014.

In 2006, his published book *"Target Iran: The Truth About the White House's Plans for Regime Change"* was one clear indication that Ritter had had a change of allegiance. Without mincing words, Ritter argued in the book that Israel was convincing the Bush administration into provoking war with Iran.

In July 2022, the Ukrainian Centre for Countering Disinformation labeled Ritter a Russian Propagandist after he disseminated misinformation on Ukraine, openly stating, *"Russia is winning. The war is over."*[32]

In June 2024, US authorities seized Ritter's passport some hours before he was about to board a flight to Istanbul en route to St. Petersburg, Russia. His fraternity with Russia did him little good. Vladimir Putin's spokesman Dmitry Peskov said that "details" about the situation were not clear. Peskov also said that restricting the travel of former intelligence agents *"is practiced in almost all countries in relation to former intelligence officers"*.

On August 7, 2024, the FBI conducted a raid of Ritter's home near Albany as part of efforts by the Department of Justice to combat Russian election interference.

Having used Ritter as a seemingly valid part of her argument, Vanessa Beeley continues on with the various crimes and machinations of the White Helmets. What Ms. Beeley will purposely not highlight for her audience this day is another Sarin attack, which massacred Ghouta, Syria, on August 21, 2013. Upwards to 1,750 people, the majority children, were gassed to death that day. After an investigation by the United Nations, full responsibility for the gas attack was laid at the feet of the Syrian regime's military under the mandate of Assad. Litigation was proposed in light of the incredible crimes against humanity that were committed. It was the worst chemical attack in Syrian history. The glaring reason Ms. Beeley does not mention this lethal attack is because it cannot help her defamation campaign of the White Helmets for one very simple reason – the White Helmets organization didn't exist then.

Eva Bartlett, Vanessa Beeley, Scott Ritter, and all the other Assad/Russia mouthpieces whose mandated mission was and is to defame the White Helmets for the purpose of eliminating them, have more than just their deliberate attacks on the humanitarian organization in common. They have, each of them, the perfect delivery of propaganda. With most of these individuals having allegiance and fellowship, perhaps even being employees of the Russian State, what they also have in common is their competent ability to deliver propaganda. This, they undoubtedly learned from the greatest propaganda machine in the world – Russia.

According to Muscovite, Anny Turnbull, on her YouTube channel discussing the mechanics of propaganda, she states Russia propaganda can be characterized like a mental pathology. Think of Russian propaganda, she says, as *"If ideology could have a full-blown personality disorder."*

"...the essence of Russian propaganda is gaslighting – but stupid" says Turnbull, *"you just take whatever your critics are saying about you and you say it back to them."*[33]

This propaganda tactic was well illustrated when the White Helmets reported on the Sarin attack in an official release by their organization, dated April 4, 2017, in which they were clear about the perpetrators:

"On Tuesday, 4 April 2017, in the morning, military aircraft conducted multiple airstrikes on the city of Khan Sheikhoun in southern rural Idlib. They targeted residential areas with multiple weapons, one of which contained a chemical agent; this chemical weapon killed more than 50 people, mostly women and children, and caused symptoms of severe chemical weapons exposure in as many as 300 others. Many of those affected are in critical condition. Syria Civil Defence (SCD) teams

from Khan Sheikhoun and al Habeet and ambulance teams responded and provided decontamination, first aid and medical evacuation [of] those affected."[34]

The rebuttal from Vanessa Beeley on her Twitter account presented the exact opposite account, as she points to an interview given in response to the chemical attack with President Assad himself. When asked by the interviewer if he thinks the story of the Sarin attack on Khan Sheikhoun was a fabrication, Assad states,

"Definitely, a hundred percent for us, it's fabrication. We don't have an arsenal; we're not going to use it. And you have many indications if you don't have proof, because no one has concrete information or evidences, but you have indications. For example, less than two weeks, around ten days before that attack, the terrorists were advancing in many fronts, including the suburbs of Damascus and Hama which is not far from Khan Sheikhoun, let's suppose we have this arsenal, and let's suppose that we have the will to use it, why didn't we use it when we were retreating and the terrorists were advancing? Actually, the timing of that attack or alleged attack was when the Syrian Army was advancing very fast, and actually the terrorists were collapsing. So, why use it if you have it and if you have the will, why to use it at that timing, not when you were in a difficult situation, logically? This is first.

Second, if you want to use it, if you have it and if you want to use it – again, this is if we suppose – why to use it against civilians, not to use it against the terrorists that we are fighting? Third, in that area, we don't have army, we don't

have battles, we don't have any, let's say, object in Khan Sheikhoun, and it's not a strategic area. Why to attack it? What's the reason? Militarily, I'm talking from a military point of view. Of course, the foundation for us, morally, we wouldn't do it if we have it, we wouldn't have the will, because morally this is not acceptable. We won't have the support of the public. So, every indication is against the whole story, so you can say that this play that they staged doesn't hold together. The story is not convincing by any means."[35]

In the end, despite the fog of war that Assad and his propaganda minions were intent on creating, the independent and objective evidence would win out.

UN war crimes investigators concluded: *"All evidence available leads the Commission to conclude that there are reasonable grounds to believe Syrian forces dropped an aerial bomb dispersing sarin in Khan Sheikhoun,"* the report said."[36]

In her library speech, Ms. Beeley also addresses the fact that she has been routinely questioned about the reliability of her collected investigations inside Syria due to the fact that she is always being escorted by the Syrian Army, itself, going where they take her. Her response to this is that any professional media company would, of course, be provided regime protection. This is, in true Ms. Beeley fashion, an absurd and false assertion.

It certainly was not the case for Marie Colvin, an American conflict journalist who was afforded no such Syrian military protection as she investigated the country's dire situation. Indeed, Assad did not initially know she was in his country, and to get the real stories out of Syria, that was how it had to be. Going where Ms. Beeley and Ms. Bartlett didn't dare risk their lives to go, to the bloodiest front lines of the conflict, was where Marie Colvin wrote her stories of bloodshed and survival.

Marie, a veteran of war correspondence and journalism, had been to and investigated some of the most extreme war zones in the late 20th and early 21st centuries. Despite her impressive list of war reporting awards, perhaps the most telling badge of honour to her relentless commitment was merely the black pirate patch which concealed the eye she lost in a grenade blast, while covering the war in Sri Lanka. Considered one of the greatest war journalists of all time, she is highly respected and lauded by colleagues in journalism around the world. If there was a story that needed be told, Marie went after it, sank her teeth into every aspect of it. She traveled to places not for the faint of heart, conflict zones that offered up a good chance journalists might never return from them. Those were the Godforsaken places where Marie Colvin had to be. Those were the stories Marie had to write about. And for certain, she needed to see the hell for herself. To bear witness was the only way.

Mike Wallace of the popular news show, *Sixty Minutes*, described the essence of Marie before awarding her the 2000 IWMF Courage In Journalism Award in New York City[37].

"In April of 1999 Marie Colvin was pinned down with some Kosovo Liberation Army regulars on the Albanian border. She wrote,

'The Kosovo Liberation Army held the high ground but little else. KLA regulars armed only with Russian-made rifles and mortar on a spindly tripod huddled together as Serbian artilleries shelled their positions. Shards of hot metal from exploding shells tore into earth, stone and flesh alike.'

She was there. Colvin's stories are vivid because there's no distance between her and those she covers. She eats and sleeps and lives as they do. Marie Colvin is brave but it's bravery with a purpose. She covers headline-making stories, but she covers them from the point of view of those least able to capture media attention. I wonder how many journalists, if we were honest with ourselves, would take the risks that she takes. For most of us, one war, perhaps two, in a lifetime would be enough. But for Marie, covering war is a lifestyle. She has pulled away from journalism to pack, pack. It is her independence that gives her the means to bring us important stories. Obviously, she's a woman of extraordinary courage, and in a strange way, she is also our conscience prodding us always to remember that in every bloody conflict, it's the innocent, the weak, and the powerless who really pay."

In the half-smiling, reflective words of her British conflict photographer and friend, Paul Conroy, Marie was indeed, *"a complete and utter one off"*. He referenced both her courage and her indomitable fighting spirit. In Paul's book, *Under the Wire: Marie Colvin's Final Assignment*, detailing his partner Marie's last war story, he describes the difference between journalists who are granted visas by Assad himself, and those who don't bother getting one or don't need to. The road into Syria as a journalist is much tougher if you don't have that Assad-sponsored Visa. Paul describes his and Marie's clandestine route into Syria in his book, *"Under the Wire, Marie Colvin's Final Assignment"*.

"The no-visa route meant an illegal entry to Syria. The al-Assad regime issued few visas to the press and, even if one were granted, it came with the baggage of state security officials, government-organized trips and close monitoring by the intelligence services. War is never just about bombs and bullets; it's also about media manipulation and propaganda. In short, if you want to get close to the truth, to bear witness, you often have to go 'under the wire'".

No strangers to Syria after months of covering the Arab Spring in 2011, Marie and Paul's last destination together for a story inside the war-plagued nation would be the besieged Province of Homs. It was February 2012. Paul articulates how the process of getting inside Homs, let alone Syria itself, was beset with suspect smugglers, specious "taxi" drivers, questionable translators, and a topography that featured not just the usual rocky Syrian terrain and densely forested countryside, but an aggressively mined route into the city. Every footstep forward whispered impending peril. Yet, accustomed as seasoned journalists to most of this already, they could at least accept these realities if not be entirely happy about them. However, it was a Syrian transmission that added an extra pause to accepting the perils of this particular mission. In his book, Paul Conroy recalls having to tell a fellow journalist a difficult fact he had already informed Marie of:

'J-P, there's something important,' *I began.* 'A few weeks ago a Lebanese intelligence officer passed us some information they'd intercepted over the Syrian communication network. Basically, he told us that there were orders for any Western journalists caught around Homs to be executed on the spot and their bodies thrown onto the battlefield. Statements would be issued by the Assad regime saying they were killed in crossfire.'

This tidbit of news was met with the obvious reaction, but J.P. kept going.

Having managed to finally get inside Homs, and right into the terrorized city of Baba Amr, the twosome eventually hunkered down in a basement overwhelmed with terrified widows and their children, newborns even. Their colleagues in arms were French photographer Remi Ochlik and French Journalist Edith Bouvier, as well as several other Western journalists. The dark, cold cellar packed with pitiful innocents, but devoid of food, was a watershed moment for the journalists. A no-turning-back kind of circle of hell. The feelings he brought away from that time are described by Paul in his book,

"The cellar was a haven for these women and children but it wasn't a bombproof shelter. A direct hit from a 240mm mortar would kill all of them. It was a place of misery, devoid of any hope. All these women and children could do was accept their grim lot and pray that the missiles they heard screeching overhead wouldn't come for them....I felt anger bubble up inside me whenever I thought of the total disregard for innocent life Assad and his military were showing. I understand war; I have seen it many times first hand. But what was happening in Baba Amr could hardly be classified as war. This was the deliberate targeting of women and children. Baba Amr was a slaughterhouse."

This cellar was also the place Marie Colvin would write her last lines on paper and give her last broadcast to the world. Despite the lack of electricity, the ingenuity of some of the other media crew in the basement was able to create a signal to patch Marie through to the almost alien outside world. It was Anderson Cooper from CNN who picked up her last dispatch:

"This is the worst, Anderson, for many reasons..uh, the last one, I mean, I think it was the last time we talked was when I was in Misrata. It's partly personal safety, I guess. There's nowhere to run. The Syria army is, is holding a perimeter and there is just far more ordinances being poured into the city and no way of guessing where it's going to land...It is a complete and utter lie that they are only going after

terrorists. There are rockets, shells – tank shells, um, anti-aircraft being fired in a parallel line into the city. The Syrian Army is shelling a city of cold, starving civilians."

Mere hours later, the basement took a direct bomb hit by regime forces. Marie Colvin and Remi Ochlik would instantly die in the blast. Paul would find Marie's lifeless body amid the debris that had once been the widows' cellar. That was February 12, 2012. Opinions swiftly surfaced that Marie was deliberately targeted after coordinates were picked up by the Syrian regime following her broadcast. In fact, it was later learned that the regime forces had spent days trying to locate Marie and the other journalists' media base. *"This wasn't a stray shell,"* stated American attorney investigating the case, Mr. Gilmore. *"The overwhelming weight of the evidence concluded that this was essentially an assassination."*[38]

Paul Conroy would survive the blast but just barely make it out of Baba Amr alive. It was his diehard conviction to tell the world exactly what had happened in Homs, Syria, to civilians, to innocents, to Marie and Remi. His book and his subsequent documentary *"Under the Wire"* would indeed, do just that.

Marie's family sued for justice against Assad and his regime for the murder of their sister and daughter. Intent on bringing Marie vindication, the family worked exhaustively investigating the crime and speaking with eyewitnesses to gather the truth. With enough evidence in hand, they filed for a wrongful death suit in an American court in July 2016. Through international channels, Assad was formally served with the suit, but he never responded. The President of Syria did, however, issue a statement on Marie's death:

"It's a war and she came illegally to Syria, she worked with the terrorists and because she came illegally, she's responsible of everything that befell her."[39]

On January 31, 2019, a U.S. court found President Bashar al-Assad's government liable for the death of Marie Colvin and the judge ordered Assad to pay $302.5 million U.S. dollars in damages for an *"unconscionable crime"*.[40] The presiding D.C. District Court Judge, Amy Berman Jackson, stated in her ruling, *"By perpetrating a directed attack against the Media Centre, Syria intended to intimidate journalists, inhibit newsgathering and the dissemination of information, and suppress dissent. A targeted murder of an American citizen, whose courageous work was not only important, but vital to our understanding of warzones and of wars generally, is outrageous, and therefore a punitive damages award that multiples the impact on the responsible state is warranted. This is particularly true given that Syria itself carried out the attack – it did not fund a third-party terrorist organization to do so."*[41]

Indeed, to this day, the family has never seen the money.

The list of legitimate war correspondents, journalists and photographers to sneak illegally into Syria, to seek out the truth of the conflict is a lengthy one. The list of those who died in the process is also long. The Doha Centre for Media Freedom has documented 110 journalists who were killed during the Syrian civil war.[42] Add in the civilian journalists, including a vast many Syrians themselves, who were targeted and killed for also bearing witness, and the number is exponentially higher.

***

Lies can be as lethal as ballistics or gas when their trajectory is clear and their target, dedicated. Calculated deception and falsehood can cause irremediable damage. The character assassination campaign that became Vanessa Beeley's cause and vocation and that of so many other propagandists, compelled unmitigated crime and punishment against the White Helmets.

Since 2015, when Russia entered the war on the Syrian people, the White Helmets have known the devastation of the practice of double-taps. The execution of a double-tap was simple. After the initial bombing raid on a neighbourhood, the White Helmets would rush to the site to locate and rescue survivors. It was during this time, that the Russian jets would make a second fly by and drop another bomb on the exact site, a double-tap that would kill far more civilians who gathered to help, and of course, the White Helmets themselves. The Helmets on the ground digging through bomb blast debris, racing after the cries of the voice of a child buried beneath, would often have to make the split-second decision as the jets returned, whether to stay and dig or run for cover. More than one White Helmet, desperate to release a child from her grave of debris and was so close in doing so, stayed too long and lost his life in the double-tap. At the time of this writing, upwards of 390 White Helmets have been killed in the line of duty.

Those are 390 deliberate crimes against humanity that the world, least of all the United Nations, overlooked and never punished, never stopped. At emergency UN tribunal sessions, member countries begged for the investigation and cessation of this known targeting and killing of humanitarians in Syria, but as member states Syria and Russia told their versions of the story, claiming incessantly that the White Helmets were a clear terrorist faction, no UN resolution was ever made to stop the killing.

In early October 2016, a dedicated bomb dropped on a White Helmet Centre in Khan Sheikhoun by Russian aircraft, left many of the volunteers injured. Additional White Helmets resumed the duty for those injured, and although another building was provided for them to work out of, the men in fear stayed outside both day and night under olive trees for better protection.[43]

Seeking out and destroying White Helmets Centres by the regime and Russia was a routine the humanitarians grew accustomed to, and to which they had to adapt. There was, however, no plan in place for what would happen to just one centre in the summer of 2017.

In Sarmin, just outside of Idlib City, a Syria Civil Defence centre was ambushed on the night of August 11, 2017, by armed assailants, clear entities of the regime. Seven on-duty White Helmets were shot point blank in the head while sleeping. When the morning shift of White Helmets came to relieve their team members for duty, they met the monstrous sight of their slaughtered brothers all lying upon a floor covered in blood.[44]

Again, no movement was taken by the UN to address these dedicated attacks on humanitarians, and the fact that they were war crimes was even disputed and debated by some.

The ultimate purpose of the Russian and Syrian regime propaganda was never to convince but to merely sow such confusion in the political discussion, that the outcome was a disoriented audience, one that couldn't tell up from down. This is what Assad wanted for the outside world – to have them witnessing facts through such muddied waters that they couldn't see fact from fiction, or perhaps worse still, they just disengaged from the entire situation.

Early on, the White Helmets understood no real help was coming, and Assad and Russia understood this as well. The volunteers were vulnerable, and they were on their own. They had to continue search and rescue while trying to stay alive in the process. They would move centres occasionally, and they would throw mud and dirt to cover their white ambulances to disguise them from aerial reconnaissance. They had no choice but to run when they saw the second jet circle around for a double-tap. These were their few options of defense and preservation, meager and minuscule.

Their search and rescue operations continued despite all of the known perils and persecution. In fact, they just kept on expanding. Assad and Russia could tell by their heavy equipment and proliferation of ambulances, that the groups were suddenly being heavily funded by sponsor nations. However, even their funding would feel the effects of the heavy campaign of Russian propaganda. The smear tactics were working. Certainly, when dedicated propagandists are disguised as chemical specialists, detracting from the claims of the OPCW and their conclusions about the gas attacks, the waters are so muddied, it becomes harder and harder to discern the truth.

The propaganda being fed online was becoming nearly insurmountable. Everyone from Noam Chomsky to Peter Hitchens to the lead singer of Pink Floyd was weighing in on the white Helmets and designating them as terrorists. The attacks on the organization grew and grew. Doubt set in for those who once believed. Countries began pulling their funding for these humanitarians, their uncertainty about their motives getting the better of their national sensibilities. The inevitable result was that more White Helmets were dying and fewer civilians were being rescued.

It was perfect propaganda at its finest hour. The war on truth was gaining ground.

But there was one more target, Assad and Russia had in their sights to take aim at in order to bring down the White Helmets organization. If the men and women, the Syrian humanitarians of the White Helmets, were perceived by him to be pawns in the game, Assad and Russia were looking now for their ultimate checkmate.

In 2019, the Russian and regime propaganda war would ultimately identify the Achilles tendon of a seemingly impenetrable humanitarian organization that outmaneuvered them for far too long. It was indeed right before their eyes, the golden innermost bullseye on the target coveted by Russia and the regime. In fact, it had never been so in reach. They need only extend a hand and grab it. So, now they looked past the men in white hard hats, directly to the very man at the fulcrum of their cause and the heart of the organization. They were about to strike at the jugular of the man who co-founded this organization and who put the very helmets on the humanitarians' heads.

That man's name was James.

[Photo: Hamid Kutini]
After a brother and friend falls in the field, one
White Helmet comforts a grieving colleague

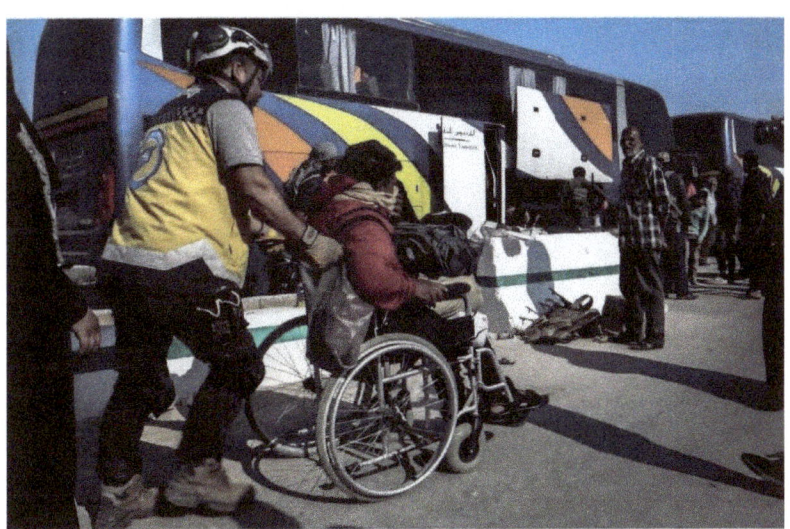

[Photo: Anas Al-Dyab]
One of many White Helmets assisting civilians
who must flee the cities and go north to the camps

[Photo: Anas Al-Dyab]
Daily rescue operations

[Photo: Anas Al-Dyab]
Listening for sounds of life during
search and rescue of a bomb site

[Photo: Anas Al-Dyab/Syria Civil Defense]
A classroom visit from their White Hemet heroes

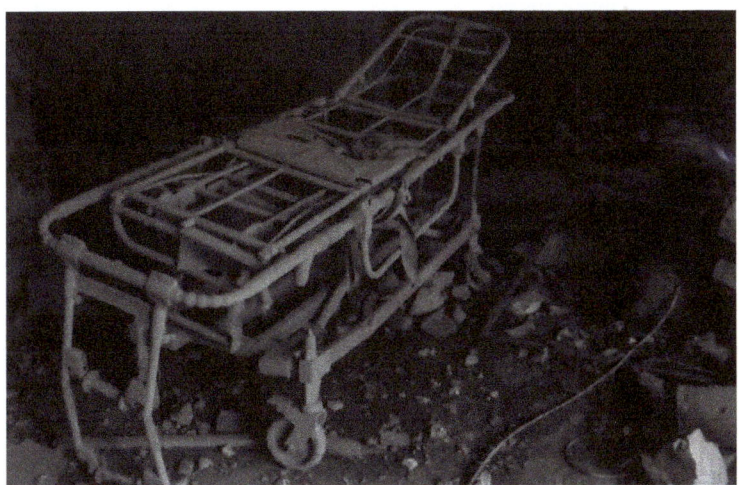

[Photo: Anas Al-Dyab]
A leftover patient bed amid the debris of a deliberate hospital attack by the regime

[Photo: Anas Al-Dyab]
Search and rescue into the late hours of the night

[Photo: Anas Al-Dyab]
Overwhelmed with grief after a day of casualties

[Photo: Anas Al-Dyab/Syria Civil Defense]
A large operation, likely a city block of homes,
calls for all available White Helmets volunteers

[Photo: Anas Al-Dyab]
Covering the white-coloured White Helmets ambulance in mud
so the regime/Russian reconnaissance jets can't spot and target them

[Anas Al-Dyab]
Searching through the bomb fallout for survivors

[Photo: Anas Al-Dyab]
Sharing snacks with the local children during some down time

[Photo: Anas Al-Dyab]
Searching through the night for survivors of a bomb blast

[Photo: Anas Al-Dyab}
Rushing the wounded to an awaiting ambulance

[Photo: Anas Al-Dyab/Syria Civil Defense]
An overwhelming magnitude of damage to work through and locate survivors

[Photo: Associated Press]
White Helmets Co-Founder, James Le Mesurier,
providing training to the recruits in Adana, Turkey

[Photo: Anas Al-Dyab]
A classroom visit from the White Helmets to provide
education on the dangers of the war

[Photo: Anas Al-Dyab]
A White Helmet surveying the wreckage of a neighbourhood
under the blasts of regime and Russian ballistics

[Photo: Anas Al-Dyab]
A father's last goodbye

[Photo: Anas Al-Dyab]
Trying on their heroes' helmets

[Photo: Anas Al-Dyab/Syria Civil Defense]
Saving a little girl

[Syria Civil Defense]
Calling for back up

CHAPTER SEVEN

James

"For James Le Mesurier, right was everything,"

- Sally Armstrong, Journalist

[Associated Press]

James Le Mesurier needed helmets for the search and rescue volunteers he had taken under his humanitarian organization's wing. This ragtag group, the nascent Syria Civil Defence, had for too long been rushing into massacre sites with little to no protection. Durable boots and gloves had been a luxury for them – hard hats were but a dream. Back at his Mayday Rescue headquarters in Istanbul, James scanned hastily through catalogues. He wanted red helmets, thinking it would be a bright beacon atop the heads of these brave volunteers. Pragmatism told him the red would stand out mercifully against the grey debris and dust fallout of a bomb site when visibility was poor. However, this was in a time before double-taps, when the bullseye colour would provide an easy mark for the Russian jets' second strike on the same site – the bomb drop dedicated to killing the rescuers. Ultimately, James couldn't source enough red helmets, so white it was. In quick order, hundreds of white Petzl helmets made in Italy and smuggled across the Turkish border into Syria found their way into the Syria Civil Defence centres, wholeheartedly welcomed by the volunteers. James had no idea that with his luck of the draw, he had quite serendipitously stumbled upon two extraordinary feats – he had unwittingly chosen the very colour that deeply symbolized hope, honour, and justice for the Syrian people, and furthermore, he had just provided the means to these humanitarian warriors' eventual famous nickname – The White Helmets.

James. But not *just* James. He had become something more. *Al-rajl al-ajnabi* rolled off the tongues of the Arab volunteers, or in translation, "*the Foreign Man*". This was the moniker he was given by all Syria Civil Defence volunteers returning from Turkey who had trained with him there. The nickname would be said affectionately and as a matter of habit. Those trained volunteers who returned to their Syrian centres, bringing their newfound skills back to their fellow members, could not stop talking about this extraordinary man they had met. A man who couldn't speak Arabic but had communicated himself, nonetheless, as a brother Syrian from an otherwise indifferent world. With a spark in their eyes, they tried to explain the anomaly that was this British man—a Westerner no less - who had come, seemingly, out of nowhere to take up the Syrian cause with every fiber in his body. In the days following their return, they would show their fellow volunteers everything they had learned with the Foreign Man back in Turkey, each trying to deliver the instruction with the same passion and enthusiasm James had shared. The feeling of respect and deep fondness was mutual for James. For these Syrians, he would pour his heart and soul into this mission.

The moment of his introduction to these nameless souls was a precise and pivotal, if not chaotic, point in time. James had run like hell down yet one more street of skeletal buildings and turned the corner to witness the aftermath of a bomb drop on what had been mere minutes before residential homes, civilian homes. It was then he spotted the flurry of activity on the leftover mountain of rubble, a veritable band of brothers already fast at work doing search and rescue, entirely cohesive and committed in their efforts. Clearly, this was not their first time responding to Assad's fallout. James was as perplexed as he was astounded by what he witnessed. Already in Syria on one of his humanitarian missions, James was no stranger to the otherworldly alien landscape that was now Syria, but to see this spectacle occurring before the fallout of the debris had even settled, he was quite literally stopped in his tracks, his intellect held fast by sheer astonishment at what he observed. Who were these men? As James watched, he recognized they were just ordinary Syrians rushing into the bomb site while everyone else rushed away. Just regular neighbourhood men who had taken on the job of rescuers, yet lacking proper implements while digging through near impenetrable graves of concrete with their bare hands searching for victims and keeping it going endlessly, their shredded skin bleeding, until they unearthed the victims. They worked from morning well into the blackness of Syrian night, with nothing but shared flashlights barely illuminating their rescues. Sometimes neighbours would pull up a car and turn the headlights on for added light. Indeed, they had no stretchers, no collar boards to protect spines, and merely a handful of makeshift ambulances with which to transfer the broken bodies. And for certain, these shopkeepers, butchers, bakers, teachers, thrown into the fray of becoming first responders, had absolutely no experience recovering injured civilians despite their very best intentions. In typical James fashion, even as he watched from his vantage point off a crater-pocked road, he was already devising a plan to aid the rescuers and their rescues. By morning, he had everything laid out on a notepad although only four words were scribbled there. *Training. Equipment. Helmets. Funding.*

James reached out to a contact in Turkey, where there existed a well-established organization of seasoned search and rescuers located in Adana City. He just needed to get the Syrian volunteers across a fiercely guarded border into the northern nation for training. It was merely the first of one of the near-endless obstacles involved in turning these men into trained search and rescuers and maintaining them as such. Scores of recruits made the day-long smuggle into southern Turkey. The training camps in Adana were devised using the full extent of James's military leadership skills and humanitarian works expertise. He was analytical and strategic with what requirements were necessary. First aid, firefighting, and search and rescue techniques were all taught by professionals through an established and highly respected Turkish training organization known as AKUT, a Turkish acronym for *Arama Kurtarma Dernegi* or Search and Rescue Association.

In 2015, as the country plunged deeper into violence, an increased number of enlistments of SCD volunteers applied for training in Turkey. Additional Syria Civil Defence centres sprang up near weekly to combat Assad's growing campaign of civilian terror and infrastructure devastation, his regime wrecking ball swinging across the Syrian nation unchecked by the world. A seasoned military man and leader, the training was effective and inspirational, but there was a different reason James Le Mesurier, or the "Foreign Man", took on near legendary status for his new disciples – he cared deeply, emphatically, about Syrians. More than one volunteer observed that *it was almost as if he wanted to* be *a Syrian.* The volunteers had expected western condescension, an underlying premise of charity that they must fall on their knees in gratitude for. How mistaken they were. James spoke to his groups of trainees with an ingrained kinship for one and all. He restored their misplaced dignity, inspired them with talk of their worth, and motivated them with dreams of a better Syria, one in which each of them could take part.

In between learning new skills at the Turkish facilities, James took the time to sit down with the Syrian men one on one. Individually or with the aid of a translator, he asked about their lives, their children, their former jobs – what life had been like for them before the war...and during. At mealtime, he would drop to a seat on the ground with the others, where the Syrian meals of fresh hummus and chicken and spiced rice, along with the traditional flat breads, were spread out in communal dishes on long tablecloths, as eager for the feast as his Syrian comrades. He shared cigarettes and sipped tea, completely at ease despite the language barrier, compelled to laughter even when the jokes had to be translated to him. He complained teasingly when the Baklava was late to the meal, and the others, seeming to understand from his very gestures if not his words, shared their agreement and applauded emphatically when the platter of sticky sweets was finally delivered. His authenticity was as compelling as his easygoing nature. The sincerity in his lopsided grin and deep blue eyes was worth any number of official signatures on paper to these men. Though they felt forsaken by the world, they believed in James. It was the anodyne the men needed after so much devastation and neglect back home. And so, James managed to do in mere weeks what the world at large, moreover, accomplished the complete opposite of - he made these ordinary Syrian men feel like their lives, and those of all Syrians were truly worth something, and more importantly, that they were, for certain, worth saving.

In the training exercises, James did his best to teach his disciples how to deal with loss, too. He empathized deeply with the bombardment of grief each of these men had experienced though their smiles and jokes deliberately belied their individual heartaches. Syrians, by culture, are known to take disappointment and heartbreak on the chin and keep it their own. The men didn't expect an outsider to understand the loss they had been subjected to for two long years into the conflict. But somehow James did. When the men were drilled extensively on the search and rescue techniques that would recover as many buried victims as possible, James took a "recovered" baby doll used in a practice drill from the hands of a trainee and looked it over. The volunteer who had "saved" the toy said to James in broken English, *"If only they were dolls back at home, trapped in all those rocks."* James nodded, empathizing completely with the inflection of hopelessness in the man's voice. He entered the circle of the men standing there, the doll still in his hand as he addressed them. *"One child or person rescued is one saved. That you could not get them all is by no means defeat. For that one person, you gave everything you could give. Saving that one human being will resonate throughout communities and give hope. Remember that when you leave the site. When you are alone with your thoughts. You remind yourself you risked your life to save a life – a child, a newborn, an old mother – one that likely would have died without your efforts. And that is how the true Syrian story continues. How humanity, itself, continues."* Full stop. A quick translation from a volunteer would follow. Spoken with the conviction and foresight of a prophet, these words resonated deeply within the men. Nods of affirmation came from the circle of men around him, each riveted to the British man's face as he spoke. Most would never forget the words. One day, the White Helmets' motto, inscribed in Arabic on the back of every uniform jacket, would read: *"To save one life is to save all of humanity"*. Words drawn from the Qur'an, yes, but the essence of James' pep talk that day may have been equally instrumental in those particular words being chosen for their singularly profound mission statement.

For James Gustaf Edward Le Mesurier's entire adult life, he had either been a soldier or a humanitarian, and it might be supposed the former eventually turned him into the latter. On May 25, 1971, on the British army base RAF Changi in Singapore, he came honestly into the military life, born the son of a British Lieutenant Colonel of the Royal Marines. His formative education was military-sponsored, as was his time at university, finishing off his degree in International Relations and Strategic Studies at Aberystwyth University. Upon graduation and still a teenager, he would be commissioned in the Royal Green Jackets of the British Army as Second Lieutenant. By 1993, he carried this rank over into the prestigious Royal Military Academy Sandhurst, where he would graduate top of his class and win the Queen's Medal Award recognizing his top achievements in military, practical, and academic standings. By 1993, he was promoted to Lieutenant; a mere three years later, he received the rank of Captain. It was a 23-year-old James who was tasked with top secret work keeping watchful command over particularly important prisoners inside a Jericho prison. The inmates were none other than four members of the Popular Front for the Liberation of Palestine, a militant group which had assassinated Israeli Government Minister, Rehavam Ze'evi at a Hyatt Regency hotel in Jerusalem the previous autumn. The culprits had previously been hunkered down with Palestinian leader, Yasser Arafat, in a compound where he had been placed under house arrest at his Ramallah headquarters. Having been transferred to high security, the streets outside the prison teemed with British and American security, all running the risk of suicide bombers exploding at any moment in retaliation. To hear his friends tell it, James never considered the risk to his own person. He was more concerned with a political solution to the Second Intifada, a hazardous time in Israeli-Palestinian history that constantly put both sides and their civilians in grave danger.

In retrospect, it would seem every phase of his military career equipped him and directed him on a trajectory for what would be his final humanitarian endeavour, the White Helmets. After army work in Northern Ireland, for two years he served as an infantry instructor with the Army Training Regiment in Winchester. He was then called back to his Royal Green Jackets as an Intelligence Officer during the raging genocides in Bosnia and Kosovo. A role in which, with his uncanny power of observation and acuity, he excelled. It was, undoubtedly, in these last places where Le Mesurier had lost his stomach for war and found his true vocation in humanitarian work – in the picking up of pieces for the subjected innocents, and in the putting them back together. The atrocities he bore witness to, and worse yet, was often charged to turn a blind eye to, changed something deep within him, whether he was fully aware of it then or not. He began to question what the hell they were doing, what *he* was doing. In 1999, his military path found him dispatched to the former Yugoslavia where he would work briefly as a Return and Reconstruction Task Force Officer. Scarcely a year later, he quit the military completely, having served for little more than a decade when he retired. The reasons were varied according to friends. James Le Mesurier, a brilliant strategist and tactician, had the formidable skills for the life of a soldier who could only continue climbing the ladder to the highest ranks. But the things he had seen in Kosovo, brutal inhuman things, that the West and himself included were impotent to stop, provoked his exit from the war arena. Still, he was intrigued with high-level intelligence work and was good at it, so he took a shot at a lifelong dream and applied for MI6. Reportedly, he initially got in, but then a quirk in the final vetting process – some small deciding factor that James couldn't guess and that which he was never given an explanation for – dashed his chances and his boyhood dream. His detractors would later say he had, indeed, been a spy with MI6, something Britain categorically denies.

In 2014, James would meet a former salesman from Al-Shighour, Syria, Raed al-Saleh, who trained with him for field duty in Adana, Turkey. With rare smiles but a spirit full of good will and commitment, Raed was a natural kinsman for the Brit. Again, despite the fact that Raed spoke no English and James had acquired perhaps a dozen Arabic words, the two men were able to communicate their mutual respect for each other, and a great friendship evolved in short time. When the Syria Civil Defence officially became an organization, Raed al-Saleh was democratically voted to lead it. It was a role Raed Al-Saleh continued until the organization's last days.

Settling into Istanbul with his new wife, Emma Winchester, a blond Swedish beauty who shared James' humanitarian passions and work ethic, he embraced his new focus at Mayday Rescue with the White Helmets being his primary goal. All at once, he became close friends with the heads of the White Helmets, in particular Raed al-Saleh and another Syria Civil Defence manager, Farouq Habib, whom James had worked with at Mayday and carried over to the White Helmets. It was at James and Emma's wedding in their Turkish island backyard just off the Marmara coast of Istanbul, where James' political and humanitarian savvy triumphed. With best men, Raed and Farouq, at his side, the happy couple had turned their wedding into a necessary fundraiser of sorts. The wedding guests were a comprehensive gathering of family, friends, government officials and statesmen. Syria was on everyone's lips at the reception, as was the complexity of humanitarian work James and the White Helmets were doing for the beleaguered nation. Diplomatic donations poured in as fast as the Champagne flowed into glasses. What James was part of, others instinctively wanted to be part of, too. Charismatic James pleaded the Syrian cause, and his guests, politicians or not, were smitten. Now there was significant money. Now the work within the White Helmets could truly start to make an impact.

Beyond the borders of Turkey, James continued his massive fundraising campaign with urgency and devotion. And as the funding poured in, aided by his gripping PowerPoint presentations and heartfelt discussions about the horrors perpetrated on the Syrian people, while balancing out his talks by demonstrating what these everyday men were able to do in spite of these seemingly insurmountable obstacles, support continued to increase. It is estimated that James raised over $129 million during his time with the White Helmets. More than just hard hats and uniforms could be provided with that budget. Heavy equipment, ambulances, and firetrucks would now aid the volunteers in their search and rescue. There was money to send help into the myriad of refugee camps, which barely housed those who had run from Assad. While Assad sought to murder his people, James and the White Helmets were keeping as many as they could alive. Their popularity soared.

James Le Mesurier was likely as satisfied as he had ever been in his career. Undoubtedly, he found himself at the very pinnacle of personal fulfillment while he watched his White Helmets, under his mentorship, carry out a calling that had only whispered to him back in the ugly days of Kosovo when death was there, too, everywhere he looked. So many lives that Assad had targeted for death were being saved. Surely, that was James Le Mesurier's *fait accompli.* Yet, just when it seemed that James' humanitarian efforts could not be outdone, he managed to accomplish something that would not just benefit his White Helmets volunteers but would make history, itself, stand up and take notice.

Despite all the equipment, machinery, and gear that had been procured for the White Helmets, perhaps the single most important piece of equipment James acquired was a small rectangular box, seemingly innocuous and insubstantial. Upon first glimpse of it, James had quite literally held it in the palm of his hand. It was a GoPro Hero camera. Instantaneously, James envisaged this tiny white box attached to the helmets of the volunteers. The men had been documenting their rescues with handheld camcorders and phones up until then, so that James could see video footage of what was happening in Syria from far away at his office in Istanbul. It did the job, but wasn't always reliable, and the images were often grainy or elliptic due to the impracticality of holding a phone and film while trying to actively do search and rescue.

When the GoPro Hero camera was introduced by a tech expert at a convention, James knew instantly that the teams needed them. The camera was compact, measuring a mere 1.5 x 2.5 inches, easily portable, quickly rechargeable, and mountable to the front of the rescue worker's helmet, keeping the volunteer hands-free. But best of all, the camera would film with an almost surreal accuracy exactly what the White Helmet was seeing, experiencing, and doing all with high resolution and clarity. Accordingly, this little, seemingly insubstantial gadget of a box filmed the daily atrocities the men were dealing with, in almost audacious defiance, revealing all in playback. Originally created for sports fanatics and outdoorsmen to record their adventures and exploits, the tiny GoPro Hero would now record every massacre and search and rescue worked by the White Helmets. James couldn't have known then what would become so obvious later. With the addition of these tiny but exceptional cameras recording every step of the conflict with the White Helmets, he was creating more evidentiary documentation than had been done for any war in history. All in real time. It was a critical turning point in the work of the White Helmets. They were no longer just tasked with search and rescue. They had taken on the role of eyewitnesses to some of the worst atrocities and war crimes in history. The realism was so great and so present, it sometimes recorded the actual injury to or even the death of the White

Helmet wearing it. These videos were immediately uploaded at the Syria Civil Defence Centres upon return from their rescue missions and sent onwards for preservation. Often, they would send reels to news agencies, Al Jazeera, Channel 5, BBC, CNN, who in turn were showing the fields videos on the evening news and reporting them on social media platforms. Finally, the unfathomable war crimes being committed by Assad and later Russia, were being witnessed by the world. Others noticed the ingenuity of this little gadget as footage swept into media outlets. Kristyan Benedict, crisis campaigns manager for Amnesty International UK, remarked on what was a true game changer in the Syrian conflict when she stated,

"The data they collect from the GoPros totally undercuts the Russian and regime narrative that they are only targeting terrorists." [45]

So now through omnipresent capturing of search and rescue footage, the world saw too, what the White Helmets had been seeing for far too long - children being pulled miraculously from what seemed sure deaths out of burials of mountainous rubble and sometimes only their little dead bodies coming out of the ruins, they saw the regime and Russian war jets in the sky dropping the bombs, they saw the killings of teammates just a few dangerous feat ahead of the Helmet behind, who found themselves in the line of fire while carrying out humanitarian duties. They could hear the screams, the cries of terror, the jubilation of souls saved by these men in white helmets.

Observers, from ordinary citizens to government officials, saw what these unarmed neutral volunteers were doing for their people.

Now, with the proper equipment and training in place, the rescues had become exponentially more productive, and significant numbers of lives were saved. News of James and the men in white helmets, responding to the human horrors of the regime's massacres, started making world headlines. It wasn't long before the nickname the White Helmets surfaced and stuck. America's 60 Minutes news show would feature them with that very name and bring them into the homes of millions of viewers. Then Netflix would bring two documentaries on the White Helmets onto television screens, depicting the volunteer underdogs as heroes in simple white hard hats.

The phenomenon that was James Le Mesurier and his commitment to the White Helmets and their rescue efforts became a source of pride and acclaim in his native Britain. He was hosted at Buckingham Palace in 2016 to be honoured by the Queen of England, herself, awarding him with the *"Order of the British Empire"* for *"services to the Syria Civil Defence Group and the protection of civilians in Syria."*

By 2017, six years after Assad's war on his people had begun, the rescue rate of civilians by the White Helmets was no less than 120,000 Syrians and counting. James, Mayday, and the White Helmets had made the impact they had hoped for, yet there was still so much more to be done.

That this should be the legacy of James was an easy wager for anyone from the inside looking out. Friends reflecting on this man's Opus Magnum could only smile and shake their heads, yes, yes, that was James. Every part of his history demonstrated a man who would never be able to look blood-strewn Syria in the eye and just look away. Turning his back on Syria would have been an impossibility for James Le Mesurier.

In James' Mayday office in Istanbul, a painted banner was hung aloft, printed with words that asked him the same question every day: *"What will save more lives?"*

Another of his mantras, a friend recalls, was: *"Whatever we can, whenever we can, for as long as we can"* This second mantra had a certain prescience to it, whether James was aware of it at the time or not.

Principled thoughts, indeed, but one would be hard pressed to find James endeavouring in any other kind. His lifelong behaviour, as recalled by friends and truly anyone who had sat down for a drink or a cigarette with James, spoke of a man with unshakeable good character and good sportsmanship. He had entered the military and war arenas, young and idealistic, but the strange thing about James is that his idealism never faded. He had weathered a lot of extreme and unreasonable, even haunting, situations in his career, but not one, nor the accumulation of them all, could make James any less of a humanitarian.

Although his early days of action in war arenas encompassed a gamut of nations, including Bosnia and Kosovo, Iraq, Lebanon, and Palestine, defining moments in his military career undoubtedly allowed James to discover exactly what type of human being he did and did not want to be. His former army brothers recall James had been burdened with great responsibility as a young soldier, and there were certain places and times, even choices, that turned a malleable kid with a gun into a warrior of a much different sort. Indeed, it was a very young James who was deployed to Kosovo as a Captain with the Royal Green Jackets, where he caught the eye of many in the military arena for his sound strategies, ethics, and his uncanny ability to rouse the morale of his comrades when they were at their lowest. But perhaps his even more formidable attitude, which garnered him recognition by military people and politicians, was that he wasn't a typical soldier merely running the prescribed paces of a war. James observed up close the efforts to reintegrate the Kosovo Liberation Army into civil defense roles and mirrored these sensibilities. It wasn't long before he joined the UN mission in Kosovo as an adviser, creating a great distance between him and his military guns and ammunition. Just as he wanted.

His biting humanitarian questions were exacerbated when, in 2004, he found himself serving in Iraq during the U.S. and British-led occupation phase after the Second Persian Gulf War of 2003, in which Iraq was defeated. By the time James arrived, he saw the nation was a tinderbox of tensions and hostilities, about to burst into an inferno at any given time. It imposed something of a reckoning on James. He realized the people left behind in any conflict needn't so much be lorded over as they needed be cooperated with, worked with, and given a hand up. It was this vision that led him onto a different path in his career, one of exclusive humanitarianism.

But nothing gave James greater pride than his White Helmets. He invoked their heroism that confronted the odds, in a 2014 interview given to BBC Radio[46]:

"The work itself is extremely dangerous. They choose, as volunteers, really to run towards the danger when the rest of the civilian population is trying their very hardest to get away. The indiscriminate nature of the shelling means that the teams never really know where the next bombing is going to come from and a deeply regrettable tactic that the [regime and Russia] use is to bomb a building and then wait for a set time of about thirty minutes and then try to bomb it again and that second bombing's objective is to try to kill those people that are trying to save the lives of those trapped in the first bombing."

James remembered something else as about the White Helmets when he spoke to a BBC Radio 4 reporter in 2015[47], as he described how utterly non-partisan these humanitarian rescuers were: *"the teams are neutral. They are impartial. They will rescue anybody who is in need. And there have been many examples of them doing so and....there are many examples of them having rescued regime soldiers who have been collapsed in buildings and risking their lives to do so...*[there is the story] *of the team in Aleppo City that crawled under sniper fire to recover the corpse of a regime soldier that was left in no man's land and and risking their lives to do so. And when they recovered the body, they found a telephone number on him that they thought was his mother and they rang her and said, you know, we we found your son and he will be given a proper burial."*

It's no surprise friends remember James in sentimental reflection as having far too much charm and panache for the soldier's life, and just the right amount to be a man of the people, winning hearts and championing the downtrodden. In her BBC article, British journalist, Chloe Hadjimatheou writes,

"An old friend, Alistair Harris, describes Le Mesurier as "Lawrence of Arabia-esque" - an image friends say he liked to cultivate. He had a taste for the finer things in life and lived in a series of homes on islands. During several years living in the Gulf, he would regularly travel into town from his home on Futaisi island, Abu Dhabi, standing at the wheel of a boat wearing a suit and brogues, his tie flapping in the wind. But he was never in the Security and Intelligence Services says Harris, a former UK diplomat who worked with Le Mesurier on several projects in the Middle East."

He could often be seen by residents in Marmara, off Istanbul, strolling the streets, walking his dog, typically a cigarette dangling from his lips. He liked people. He loved children and was the father of two young girls who adored him. A video that was posted by a friend shows James stopping in an Istanbul street upon meeting a mother and a toddler, both enchanted with him and his neat slacks, his collared shirt beneath a cashmere sweater, and James out of the blue bowing to the little girl before dancing briefly with her, even turning the laughing toddler about on the pavement, before walking on, smoking his cigarette again. The mother of the child staring after him, evidently charmed.

There are few individuals who have been in the company of James Le Mesurier who have not succumbed to his charm, an attribute likely only to be outdone by his authenticity. A complete stranger, Hollywood actor and documentarian Sean Penn, when interviewed at the behest of BBC journalist Chloe Hadjimatheou for her podcast *"Mayday"*, admits that he was at one point suspicious of the White Helmets and by extension James.[48] Chloe was able to speak to Sean Penn via telephone, and wanted to know what he had learned through his own interactions with both President Assad and James Le Mesurier, as, extraordinarily, he spent the same amount of time with both. Far back during the Arab Spring, Penn's focus had been on Syria for the purpose of producing a documentary of the nation at war. He had even been invited to Damascus to meet with President Assad, and after their meeting, had lunch with the president and his family at their home. He knew all too well the narrative as described to him in Damascus – Assad and regime, good.... White Helmets and Le Mesurier, bad, very bad. And yet, Sean Penn could not reconcile this story told by the Syrian president, himself, with the amount of documented murders and atrocities being carried out on civilians by the government's military. He chose, for reasons not publicly given, to abandon the documentary. It is known, however, that the Syrian President reneged on giving Sean Penn full access to the Syrian story. He was still, however, curious. Had he been told bold-faced lies by Bashar al-Assad? He had spoken to Eva Bartlett in Los Angeles at one point as well, and again was compelled by the narrative she laid out. Her facts weren't impossible, he supposed, and he had heard his own rumours about the White Helmets being terrorists doing the bidding of Western factions. Far-fetched, maybe, but certainly possible, he wagered. That is the beauty of propaganda – if nothing else, it creates doubt and consequentially, often apathy, or even worse. It was some years later, in the summer of 2019, when Sean Penn met up with the man, the myth, the legend, James, himself. Guardian journalist, Martin Chulov, a mutual friend of both Sean and James, would put the meeting together and arrange a dinner in Istanbul, where Sean had been working on another film. Sean admits that despite Chulov's great description of his mate James, he was still skeptical as he sat down to dinner.

In her BBC Podcast, "*Mayday*", Chloe asks Sean the obvious, "What did you think of James?" He didn't hesitate in answering. "*Well, like a lot of people that I've run into over the years with a – you know – strong military background, there is discipline of soul that I appreciate which is to say I had a very good first impression of the human being sitting next to me in the restaurant. I felt he was a very thoughtful person. We did talk about the controversies, about the White Helmets.*"

The next question was equally guaranteed. Chloe asks Sean, "*Having met him, did you feel more convinced that you had a better understanding of the White Helmets?*"

Sean replied, "*I found him very credible. He spoke to – without a pause – each of the controversies that I inquired about in a very convincing way, you know...what does that mean? It means he's very genuine or very good at...at, at, at portraying someone who is very genuine.... I left it very interested in him and I, and I liked him very much. I think if I'm compelled by anything talking about James Le Mesurier it's because I feel it was an unfinished acquaintanceship. You know, I really had intended to fly back to Istanbul to see him.*"

Sadly, that would never come to be.

Indeed, there are likely few to no acquaintances of James who could say a contrary word about him. His schoolmates of the past, as well as life-long colleagues, champion every aspect of their mate as they describe the individual he was. James carried that affability and authenticity into humanitarian works; it was such a big part of his ability to raise significant funds for the White Helmets. The people, the nations, entrusting him with their money, had every confidence that it was getting where it needed to go and doing what James promised it would.

The problem with all this, however, was patently clear.

While the herculean efforts of James Le Mesurier and his White Helmets were applauded by the world and funded by governments, they were also being observed and scrutinized by Assad and his new ally, Russia. For them, the White Helmets were a major problem. Not only were they subverting Assad's intended bloodshed of his people, they were now meticulously documenting it. The Western narrative portrayed the White Helmets as the underdog heroes in the Syrian story, which made it abundantly clear that Assad and Putin were the villains.

Villainy is not an unfamiliar characteristic of the long reigns of either the Assad al-Bashar family regime or the Russian government. It is a role they have taken on historically and too often with great impunity. When people become obstacles to hinder their motives or narratives, they have a long and terrible history of simply eliminating them. As I write this part of the story today, my attention follows a modern day 2021 story of a former Russian spy Alexander Litvinenko turned British citizen who was fatally poisoned with radioactive polonium in 2006 once he became a thorn in the side of the Russian agenda.[49] Litvinenko fled Russia to Britain, and began openly exposing the criminal machinations of Putin and the Russian Government. The Russians have just been formally convicted of his assassination this week in the European Court of Human Rights, with the killing having been approved by Vladimir Putin, himself. As the story goes, Litvinenko was compelled to meet with two Russian henchmen, KGB members Andrei Lugovoi and Dmitry Kovtun, for a cup of tea at a London hotel on November 1, 2006. Just tea, but apparently a particularly potent cup of it. He began feeling sick shortly after teatime and was admitted almost immediately to the hospital. Soon after, bald-headed and a husk of the man he had been from the radiation poisoning, he lay in a hospital bed deteriorating until he died on

November 23, 2006, of multiple organ failure. Nuclear scientists from the Atomic Weapons Establishment at Aldermaston in Berkshire, England, definitively discovered the radioactive substance in the patient's body known as Polonium-210.[50] In typical Russian fashion, the government has denied all allegations and refused to pay the dead man's widow for compensation.

This is the Russia that James Le Mesurier had quickly found himself within the crosshairs of. The growing regime/Russian hatred for James Le Mesurier prompted the obvious question: What to do with a man who was completely undermining their efforts to make the White Helmets out to be terrorists, not saviours, and consequently, shape their own narrative of the Syrian conflict?

James Le Mesurier, growing more powerful day by day, with his work through the White Helmets and his political ties, was thwarting both the Syrian regime and Russia with the momentum of his humanitarian work. But things were about to take a turn. In 2019, he had fallen into a slow burning but highly dangerous plot of character assassination. Poisoned tea would not have worked on James, but the malignant elixir of unending and ferocious lies against a man who prioritized integrity and honour for himself, might be equally potent.

Russia had already labeled James an operative, an undercover spy within MI6, with his intelligence work focusing on the Western bid for regime change in Syria. They threw the accusation out into the media ether with little to no care about how easily this assertion could be disproved. Professional propagandists, Russia knew once a rumour hits the airwaves or print, the very seed of it takes root and flourishes despite its lack of evidence or foundation. They depended on the public to, if not believe full out, to just believe a little. Then the Russians honed in on his time serving in Kosovo during the war there. Caring little for the truth of the matter, that James had actually left the army entire because of the horrific things he had seen in Kosovo, the Russians picked this part of his past with which to paint him as a perpetrator and conspirator with illegal entities. They had no proof to back up their accusations, but they knew, in the long run, none was necessary.

For years, since the inception of the White Helmets, the Syrian regime and Russia pounded away at accusations that James was no more than a British-funded ringleader of a terrorist organization, otherwise known as the White Helmets. Bashar al-Assad, in an interview with his RT Russian Television, referred often to the Helmets as terrorists, his hatred of the humanitarian search and rescuers most evident when his composure sank for the camera and with a fiery spark of rage in his eye, referred to the Helmets as "...*these angels are al-Nusra with a facelift.*" Again, James shirked off the allegations and kept focused, knowing this type of practice was par for the course for the Syrian regime and Russians.

But then there came a bombshell accusation by the regime and Russia that stopped James in his tracks. One that couldn't be as easily overlooked as the others. One that hit this humanitarian and father of two little girls at the core of his soul. They charged James Le Mesurier with organ trafficking of Syrians. It was a blow that sent James reeling.

Amateur journalists and bloggers hired by Russia and the Syrian regime were writing articles and giving interviews about this alleged new ring of terrorist abuse perpetrated by James and his White Helmets. Vanessa Beeley openly accused James in a YouTube video of organ trafficking, just one of many times she sought to defame him. She didn't mince words as in a practiced speech she would repeat over and over again on many stages, she pointed to the screen that flashed a picture of James, and easily attacked a man whose entire life had been spent protecting the most disenfranchised:

"The story that Vanessa Beeley draws on is one of the darkest in European history...and it's to do with the KLA, the Kosova Liberation Army." Chloe Hadjimatheou.[51]

And so, Ms. Beeley takes her Ottawa library audience to Kosovo back to a time when 20-something James Le Mesurier was a soldier there.

"The KLA," she says, *"were running organ trafficking operations, cross-border organ trafficking operations, and they were being whitewashed by James Le Mesurier, a former MI6, who in 2013 set up the White Helmets that are effectively al-Qaeda dressed in humanitarian clothing."*[52]

Ms. Beeley continues, *"We actually -umm- track the blueprints that, in my view, began in Former Yugoslavia, in the Balkans and Kosova, in 1999, and is now being repeated in Syria. Why is this important? Because this is where the harvesting comes in."*[53]

Her horrific claim would be repeated consistently throughout her talks, *"Again, under James Le Mesurier's stewardship of the trafficking of children, of the taking of children for organ trade, of the use of warehouses and hangars as operation chambers for the organ trade."*

She brought the same horrific defamation to her many social media accounts, Twitter and Facebook, blogs, as well as the fringe conspiracy-based news outlets that she worked for. She would go on to bolster her claim by trying to make use of James' military time serving in Kosovo by linking him to the alleged organ trade in practice there by the Kosovo Liberation Army.

Conveniently for Ms. Beeley and her boss, Russia, family members of "victims" were filmed in Russian-created footage claiming their loved ones had been taken by the White Helmets across the border to Turkey to large operating theaters where their vital organs were mined before the dead bodies were stitched back up sternum to pelvis, and returned to their families. Their vulnerability or their gullibility testifying for Russia and Assad is ambivalent at best. And who but James, himself, was responsible for spearheading all of this, according to the Russians and regime. James, the keeper of faith, the would-be saviour of the beleaguered Syrian people, the peacekeeper and life-long humanitarian, was now being depicted as the devil, himself. For months throughout the year of 2019, the slanderous arrows just kept coming, and more than a few were finding their mark.

Continuing with her organ harvesting story, Ms. Beeley tells of family eyewitness testimony of relatives returned with the marks of organ removal. She talks of the vertical incision that is the sign of a body that has been operated upon for the purpose of comprehensive organ harvesting. But she didn't do her research. This is not the incision sign of a body that has been fully harvested. It would have at least three to four flaps, not two. Again, accuracy and verifiable facts were not her goal; accusation and defamation were all that mattered to her, so intent was she on the destruction of James.

Despite himself, James Might have been able to ignore this latest unspeakable slander, but the problem was that the world was not so quick to do so. Skepticism was catching as so many lies abounded, so many alternate stories were being batted about. The truth was covered by the muck of uncertainty.

Dedicated national donors, unsettled by so many accounts of this organ trafficking, pulled their funding, citing national budgetary adjustments, or at best, "delayed" it while the allegations were further investigated. The Dutch government, prior to these sensational and horrific lies, had been a dedicated and generous donor to the Syria Civil Defence. Then, suddenly, they stopped their funding. Other nations would follow. All of a sudden, the money was drying up. Soon, the aid to the Syrian people would too.

Then came further public relations mayhem within the Mayday organization itself. There were problems with the financial books in the Istanbul office. Allegations were made of James misappropriating funds, including $50,000 from petty cash, on the night of the rescue mission of regime-held White Helmets into Jordan with the help of the Canadian government. The money had been taken out for any unforeseen expenses. $8,000 was spent, and James was missing the other $42,000 with no idea where it had gone. He had come home from the mission, exhausted and vulnerable, and could say outright to his wife Emma that he had no idea what had happened to the money. In hindsight, both he and his wife Emma attribute his confusion over the money's whereabouts to weeks of stress and sleepless nights. Notwithstanding, the money was missing, and a public forensic accounting firm was brought in to investigate. When the Russians and the regime got hold of this information, they didn't miss a beat in running with it. James Le Mesurier was a fraud, as suspected all along, came the tweets. In the end, the money was accounted for, and James was wholly exonerated, although too little and too late. But once again, the reputation stuck as it entered the media wires and disseminated into the mainstream. This once glowing and confident man, a leader and defender of the downtrodden, seemed barely able to know himself anymore. This was the crushing blow, to raise skepticism in far too many, that set James reeling. His depression grew as his doubts built about the White Helmet's future and his role within it.

In the first days of November 2019, the Russian propaganda machine annihilated James' reputation. Maria Zakharova, Director of the Information and Press Department of the Ministry of Foreign Affairs for the Russian Federation, took to her Russian State Twitter account on November 8, 2019, asserting the following:

"The White Helmets' co-founder, Jame Le Mesurier, is a former agent of Britain's MI6, who has been spotted all around the world, including in the #Balkans and the #MiddleEast. His connections to terrorist groups were reported back during his mission in #Kosovo."

This claim by Zakharova was categorically debunked on November 11, 2019, in a Reuters article where the remarks of Ambassador Karen Pierce, the UK's United Nations' Representative, responded, *"The Russian charges against him, that came out of the foreign ministry that he was a spy, [are] categorically untrue. He was a British soldier."*[54]

But the Russians knew they had James, and the White Helmets, right where they wanted them. Zakharova continued her barrage of attacks on James day in, day out. And their brutal defamation of a humanitarian whose word and honour meant everything to him, had indeed made a devastating impact on James. He retreated inside his world, trying to make sense of what was left for the White Helmets, if anything at all. He held himself responsible for the entirety of this crisis; moreover, he believed himself responsible for the Syrian people who had depended on him.

The day of November 10th, 2019, James' world was slowly collapsing in on him with seismic effect. He spent it with his wife in Istanbul, the two of them stupefied with the weight of their troubles. Funding had all but dried up, the White Helmets were not getting paid, and support for their work was hurting, and his reputation had taken the ultimate fall from grace. It was the dark night of his soul, and Emma could only support him, but not fix him. A small turn of fortune happened, according to Emma, when James, at one point during late afternoon, started to perk up, and began looking for the bright spot in the clouds.

His friend and colleague, White Helmet Deputy Manager, Farouq Habib, dropped by his place that afternoon, and Emma left the men to chat. She hoped some time spent with a kindred spirit was exactly what James needed to lift his own spirits. But when she returned and Farouq said his goodbyes, James seemed more distraught than ever. Pragmatically, unemotionally, Farouq had spelled out the situation as it currently stood for the White Helmets – and it was far worse than James had imagined. He vocalized as much to Emma, and his mood rapidly deteriorated from there.

Early morning Friday, November 11, 2019, around 4am, Emma woke up to an emphatic knock on her front door by Turkish Police at the Istanbul apartment atop Mayday and White Helmets

Headquarters. James, in Emma's quick purview, was nowhere to be found. Emma noted the balcony door was open, and when she rushed to peer down, she saw amid the commotion, her beloved James. He was lying at the bottom of their 3-storey apartment building, some ways from the balcony in the bushes, with a broken neck and broken limbs, dead. He had been discovered by mosque-goers returning from morning prayers.

Foul play was immediately evident, and the coroner who examined James' body labelled the death "suspicious". Many did suspect the Russians, given their long and wicked history of their foes and antagonists falling conveniently out of high windows to their deaths, over and over again. It was, indeed, one of their methods of choice for the elimination of detractors.

Still others thought that James had committed suicide. That the toll of the slander and lies, the caliber of which the thickest-skinned person would be hard pressed to bear, had finally been too much. That, coupled with his own understanding of how he had let the White Helmets down and, by extension, had let Syria down, was just too much for him to live with. Those who knew James, friends and close colleagues, completely discount this second explanation. They blame the Russians. With their track record, it is a more than reasonable assumption.

When Chloe Hadjimatheou, at the end of her interview with Sean Penn, asked him what he thought when he heard James Le Mesurier was dead, Sean didn't miss a beat in answering, *"I thought he was murdered by the Russians."*

In the end, whether he was physically pushed off his balcony by Russia, or pushed to his death through character assassination, the Russians did, indeed, play a role in killing James Le Mesurier.

Colonel Hamish Stephen de Bretton-Gordon, a British Army officer for 23 years and commanding officer of the UK's Joint Chemical, Biological, Radiological and Nuclear Regiment and NATO's Rapid Reaction CBRN Battalion, was both a close friend and military colleague of James. Hamish, like many others who knew James, questions why James Le Mesurier, a seasoned military man, would choose such a relatively low height to attempt to take his life from. *"In the last probably two years or so, an awful lot of people who've disagreed with the Russians in particular have fallen off balconies. So, I think there is – it is, you know, suspicious."*[55]

James and Hamish met a month before his death. Hamish remembers, *"I didn't leave that meeting thinking, here is somebody, he is really troubled. But having said that, the amount of abuse, the amount of ill-placed propaganda, disinformation that's on social media and the internet coming out of Russian bots and Syria, Syrian regime and others was unbearable."*

In addressing the savage character assassination carried out by Russia and the regime on a man who cherished his character and humanity above all else, Hamish went on to say, *"There must be a decency line, and if you cross that, then something should be done. Some of the* [things] *coming out of these people, I think crosses that decency line. Some of the --- accusing people of being al-Qaeda, of supporting terrorism..."*

In the end, when it was too late for James to see it for himself, the allegations of organ trafficking had been disproved, the missing money from the petty cash was found, and the White Helmets regained much of the sponsorship they had lost from donors. James' ultimate legacy was preserved - the White Helmets continue saving lives.

Overlooking the M40 at Aston Rowant nature reserve, hills near Christmas Common in the heart of the Chilterns, southern England, an art installation was created by artist and sculptor Dan Barton to remember James. The vast field of art, which regularly commemorates war veterans and heroes with 100 permanent full- size metal silhouettes of soldiers, their helmeted heads facing downward, while bright red metal poppies grow, strewn between them all about the field. To pay tribute to James, a decorated soldier who died on Armistice Day, a humanitarian leader whose faith and goodness brought a group of otherwise unremarkable men out of the darkness of the regime shadow and into the spotlight of their life-saving missions, he added 179 soldiers to his installation – 289 in all, marking the very number of White Helmets who were killed in the line of duty. Atop their heads, he placed white helmets in remembrance of James and his murdered Helmets. Drivers who come upon the sight from the road remark what an amazingly poignant sight it is to behold.

The White Helmets volunteers have long since stopped calling James Le Mesurier the "Foreign Man" – though they still smile in memory of that once upon a time nickname which came with the fragile whisper of hope promised for a broken Syria by a man who made it his vocation to help the helpless. On November 11th, 2019, James Le Mesurier, their Syrian brother, their fellow White Helmet volunteer, had been designated by the Syria Civil Defence as the 290th White Helmet to die in the line of duty. The original red helmet -the one he first wore –is kept at the White Helmets headquarters. With every year that marks another anniversary of his death, a new white candle is added, lit in memory of him and his Syrian white heart. Of all the things to be said about James Le Mesurier in his obituary, perhaps the most telling is simply that he wanted to help whomever he could. And that he was a good man.

James Le Mesurier

BORN: May 25, 1971, RAF Changi, Singapore

DIED: November 11, 2019, Istanbul, Turkey

CHAPTER EIGHT

Tom, Dick, and Harry

"Between the devil and the deep blue sea"

- Unknown

[Anas Al-Dyab]

Residents in Daraa and Quneitra were as confounded as they were terrified. What had been days before, relative calm in their cities turned overnight into the most hysterical and ferocious bombing since the Syrian conflict had begun. In late June 2018, the blue skies were all at once growing black with Russian Sukhois and MiGs. The summer sun hid as hospitals and schools were exploding into thin air, their

246

doomed coordinates easily sought out and targeted. Black plumes of smoke from copious leftover fires in every neighbourhood sent their sooty tendrils languorously into the ether, intent on tarnishing even *"Jana"*, the Syrian heavens. A bombardment of nonstop shelling now muted the usual sounds of once bustling marketplaces and local traffic. Troops walked the streets with Kalashnikovs. Hell had descended upon the two southern provinces of Syria, leaving civilians to consider that *Shaitan*, himself, was acting on a personal grudge. But those with a view to the outside world through the internet knew American President Trump had only days before pulled his troops out of Southern Syria, wiping his hands clean of the entire situation, and leaving in its wake one immense vacuum for ultimate bedlam to fill. Not long after defeating and eradicating the rebels in Daraa, Assad's first point of business was installing a national Syrian flag with its traditional two stars smack-dab in the city square, announcing smug victory over a downtrodden people who had been barely hanging on in the first place. The military went door to door looking for civilians on an "informant's list", arresting and killing up to 3000 people in this fashion. It took very little in the way of criminal activity to get yourself on the list. The mere suggestion by a neighbour, coerced or otherwise, that you were a spy was one of the easier ways. Being overheard lamenting your lot in this horrific regime-sponsored war was another. But in their crosshairs first and foremost, were these "so-called" humanitarians who had been cleaning up Assad's carnage for the last seven years, not to mention documenting his war crimes. And so, the White Helmets in these city centres begin scrambling. It was a crisis they were not trained for and for which there could be no preparation. Daraa, birthplace of the revolution, and Quneitra, its neighbouring province, were no longer liberated areas where humanitarian duties could proceed. In fact, in a strange but pointed act, the regime allowed all stationed humanitarians to have free exit north, all except the White Helmets. Their Syria Civil Defence centres were the most coveted targets, with some already leveled to rubble, and so they fled to makeshift buildings and safehouses to recalibrate. Rescue work came to an abrupt halt as every mission ended up in direct missile strikes. Even their ambulances were being targeted. Laying low was not an option either. The regime was searching for them. Surveys went out asking regular civilians if they knew the whereabouts of or had any relationship with White Helmets. The Assad Army was trying to narrow down its hunt. The trapped Helmets were nearby, and it was just a matter of time. And coming for these humanitarians were not only the SAA but the Russian troops, Iran's Quds Force, the Iranian Proxy, Hezbollah, and the elite division of Assad's Special Forces unit named the Qawat Al Nimr. A division of the army notorious for its war crimes and atrocities, including beheadings, summary execution of captives, and the public mutilation of corpses. At the top of each group's Most Wanted List was, of course, the White Helmets.

And there was nowhere to run, as the predators came in for their prey from northern Damascus, pushing the backs of the two provinces right against borders neither the civilians nor humanitarians could cross. Escape was not an option. To the south of Daraa was Jordan. To the south of Quenteira was Israel, worse yet, the contentious Golan Heights. Feeling on borrowed time, some White Helmets were burning their insignia, their uniforms, anything that identified them as Syria Civil Defence. Others capitulated to their fate, making the choice to stay with family and defend until they were captured. And of course, the majority of Helmets looked to the terrified faces of their children and wives and made the decision to get out at any cost. But how? The international community had pulled no punches in letting the humanitarians know the extent of their help was funding, otherwise, they were on their own. Each White Helmet had to consider the notion that their days were numbered.

Internet was poor, but persistence and a patchy signal got one desperate Helmet through to James Le Mesurier in Istanbul as he made his last-ditch plea for rescue to the one man who might be able to come through for them. Help, they needed urgent help, or they were one by one going to be hunted down and slaughtered, came the broken English from a basement just miles beyond a destroyed SCD centre. The plea and the phone call were brief. He had barely disconnected before the co- founder of the White Helmets, James, had begun formulating a plan. Despite the fact that he was supposed to be getting married in a few days, despite the routine chaos of his hectic days governing Mayday Rescue and by extension the White Helmets, all at once, James threw himself into frantic planning and strategy mode, scheming up a way to rescue the rescuers. The former British Army officer, who had just missed the ranks of MI6, was never more in his element.

The first and most critical question was by which route could he get them out. Throwing open a large paper map, he sat for hours surveying and drawing lines that were potential passages and shading in other areas that were completely off limits. His fiancée Emma nearby, who worked alongside him in the Karakoy office and the SCD headquarters in Istanbul, rallying him as well as providing input to the questions he spoke aloud. The most obvious passage was to bring the White Helmets through the Syrian desert and into Iraq, but for a variety of reasons, the route was too dangerous. The Jordanian border would be optimal and most expedient, but Assad's troops had already swept across the border, and Jordan had locked its gates. There was, however, Israel. James circled it on the map, then threw his pen down. Israel. The Golan Heights. The mere consideration caused consternation for James. It was, for certain, the most viable route, but also the most insanely political. He felt a little mad for even putting it into the equation. He needed help with these decisions. He reached out to his right-hand man, Farouq Habib, a Syrian native who formerly worked with him at Mayday and now helped head up the executive board for the White Helmets organization. A meeting was held, and the race was on to find a solution for the worst problem with which the field Helmets had ever been faced. The consensus in the room was that, sadly, in all practicality, there was simply nothing they could do. It was James who persisted in the meeting, resolutely reiterating that there couldn't *not* be a solution. That simply wasn't an option. According to his wife Emma, James asked the room, *"What is the art of the possible?"* The art of the possible. In other words, he wanted every and all options put down on the table, even the most absurd propositions. He had jotted down the number of White Helmets trapped by name, their family members, their current whereabouts, and the positions of the regime army and their cohorts, all pieces of intelligence painstakingly derived. Nearly 1200 people, including the White Helmets and their families, needed rescue. Heaven and earth might need be moved to pull this off, but James was on it.

James even tried to appeal to the Russians themselves, contacting their liaison offer and requesting safe passage for the White Helmets into Jordan. The Russian reply was an absolute no. James recounted, *"They said the White Helmets were vermin who should be eradicated."*[56]

Farouq Habib, empathizing with James' passion but not convinced of a practical strategy being available, knew well the horrors of the regime, and consequently the extreme danger the trapped White Helmets found themselves in. Before leaving Syria, he had spent time in a Syrian prison and had escaped with his life. He knew firsthand what awaited any captured White Helmets.

In an interview Farouq gave to Chloe Hadjimatheou for her BBC podcast on James Le Mesurier and the Helmets, he clearly outlined what was in store for the humanitarians.

"There is a special section, a special unit in the Secret Syrian Intelligence responsible of the files of the White Helmets because they use this file politically." He couldn't stress enough the unspoken bounty on these men and women's heads because of the damage they were doing to the regime by simply rescuing those it massacred and elucidating the government's war crimes in the process.

What became abundantly clear in the meeting was that this was not a mission James and his colleagues could take on alone. They needed help from the international community, and they needed money. And so, the calls began being placed to their donors. James and Farouq spoke to the United Kingdom's representative, outlining the severity of the situation at hand. She was receptive to the crisis and went to work from her office. The next call went to the Canadian government. On the receiving end was the Canadian diplomat to Syria in 2018, Robin Wetlauffer. She reflected on the mission when speaking to journalist, Chloe Hadjimatheou, and with candid words, tacitly underscored by her emotion, she summed up the situation presented to her in those chaotic early days: *"It was only after Daraa fell that we realized holy shit this is moving really fast...excuse my language. We realized then there was really very little time left. I remember writing in bold and underline which is not typically a proper form in diplomatic reporting* [that] *we had an obligation to do something for the White Helmets in the South."* Taking on a huge role in the mission, Robin pulled together other diplomates from various nations like Britain, Germany, Denmark, the Netherlands, all donor countries to the Syria Civil Defence.

All this while in the great multitasking style James and fiancée Emma were legendary for, they also had a wedding to plan. Formal dress attire shopping amid covert operation calculations would most assuredly stress out any potential bride and groom, but not James and Emma. They might have shaken their heads at the madness of the happenings, but on another level altogether, they were a little giddy with the frenetic circumstances and their sudden catapult into their do-or-die fulcrum. Going ahead with the nuptials in the midst of this crisis, was most practical on a number of levels. A backyard party at their lush Island residence just outside Istanbul was the perfect way to gather family, Syria Civil Defence, and donor diplomats all together for a Le Mesurier fete. It was less calculated than it was clever. With the clock ticking, he would mobilize all the help he could. Emma did her part, scrutinizing the seating plan for the guests. At each reception table, she had grouped together a mixture of donors, diplomats, and SCD colleagues. The head of the White Helmets organization and one of James' groomsmen, Raed Al Saleh, was seated strategically with not only some of the most important dignitaries, but a seasoned translator directly at his side who could transform his even-toned but clearly impassioned Arabic into English for those around him. Despite his customarily unsmiling face and perpetually calm demeanor, Raed's boyish, big eyes fired up with gravity and urgency about the situation in Syria, elicited the promises of financial aid from his small audience. Clad in a black bow tie, cummerbund, and grey tails, to which 007 would give a nod, James married Emma in her Gatsby era wedding dress, and for the rest of the evening, they floated around their wedding festivities mingling in triumphant celebration of not only their marriage but the giddy understanding they had worked almost magic there in the garden. A plan, roughshod but ready, had been hammered out to rescue the White Helmets back in their war zone. All this amid the romantic rustling of Princes' Islands' pink bougainvillaea trees shimmering in the moonlit against moist Turkish breezes and the lulling lapping of waves of the Marmara Sea as they caressed the Adalar shoreline in the nearby distance. As the sun set, James and Emma, held their Champagne flutes high in toast to all the possibilities this day and evening of romance and auspicious recruitment had given life to. The trapped White Helmets might just stand a chance. James Le Mesurier had likely never felt so full of purpose and so ready to act.

The honeymoon would need be postponed. Within days, James, carrying little more than his British passport and a substantial wad of cash, some Fifty Thousand Pounds Sterling, hastily withdrawn from the Mayday safe for unforeseen expenses (what those might eventually come to be, he wasn't then sure), James Le Mesurier was on a plane to Jordan. The rescue plan, sound and precarious in equal measures, had been finalized in the days between the wedding and his departure, with calls to Britain's Prime Minister Teresa May, Canada's Prime Minister Justin Trudeau, to President Trump, and ultimately to Israeli Prime Minister, Benjamin Netanyahu. Despite the potential political fallout many, including James and his organization, would encounter from working directly with Israel, there had been no other choice. Without Israel, there could be no rescue. Even the trapped White Helmets had been left in the dark as much for security reasons as to stem the political ire and resentment that might hinder them from proceeding. Israel, the historical enemy of the Syrian people, and a "Zionist" state they considered the thief of their Golan Heights and had occupied since the 1960's, was now going to be their reluctant saviour. It would be a hard pill for anyone to swallow, even the most desperate Arab. Farouq Habib summed this sentiment up in a discussion with BBC Sounds, *"You know, going through Israel cannot be an easy decision for an Arab person especially for Syrians. Our countries are at war for decades and our lands are occupied by the Israelis, so it's not an easy decision. [Sigh] But I had to do it because my colleagues faced death on the other side of the borders."*

Upon arrival in Aman, James was in full operation mode. The first thing he did was set up an ops room in the Mayor's office. Back in Canada, the government was in full swing, doing its part to expedite the mission through daily briefings with James and other contributors to what was nicknamed Operation Magic Carpet. The only problem was with 800 White Helmets to evacuate, there were far too many tasselled flying rugs needed all at once, and little to no available magic. Their plan was hardcore with no Plan B on standby. On paper, the strategy looked great; in reality, the logistics would indeed require a wing and a prayer, if not, indeed, a genie waiting in his lamp for the right hand to give it a rub.

Farouq Habib set into motion liaison with the trapped White Helmets through SCD colleagues out of the Amman headquarters, Nadera Al Sukkar and Jehad Mahameed, who were clandestinely getting information through to them as to where they should mobilize. Running out of time, the escaping White Helmets were haphazardly vetted in Syria. As they left their homes in a dramatic rush, the necessary paperwork, identification, and even phones were left behind or lost. Meanwhile, James was putting together the international logistics. Chain smoking and drinking copious cups of coffee to remedy the fact that he was getting no sleep whatsoever, he was in continuous communication with all players in the rescue, and three escape routes were decided upon. He code-named these crossings, Tom, Dick, and Harry. An auspicious and hopeful nod to the three tunnels used in what has been called the greatest escape in history, when allied prisoners burrowed underground in a Nazi POW prison, digging their way beyond the prison fences and onward to freedom.

The crossings were set up laterally along the border, mere kilometres apart, positioned to be the most efficient rally point for the Syrians, but it would come to pass that war politics, not physical distance, would render the three crossings unrecognizable to each other.

As James and the Amman office were in full operation mode, which included daily nonstop briefings with Canada, America, Britain, and of course, Israel, the huge task of trying to find all the White Helmets on their list back in Syria was proving incredibly difficult for Sukkar and Mahameed. With their every movement requiring clandestine protocol, the mustering of those who were to be rescued, at times, even required the Amman Helmets to go on foot through war zones, physically tracking down the men on the list. The peril of this was unimaginable, but Sukkar and Mahameed knew it had to be done. The potential escapees had been given clear instructions and warned that any departure from those directions could result in the entire mission being aborted, and them being left behind in Syria.

For the White Helmets, the promise of escape, though begged for, brought its own brand of misery to the humanitarians. For their safety and that of their families and friends being left behind, they could tell no one of their departure. They left quietly, secretively, with their spouses and children, packing clothing, blankets, food, and the necessary identification, but only as much as they could carry. A White Helmet who was on Le Mesurier's list, Omar (not his real name), readied his wife, his one-year-old-daughter, and his four-month-old son for a flight into the unknown, and started out on their clandestine journey to the meeting point just beyond Queneitra in the Golan Heights.

The Golan Heights was a formidable but necessary rally point. A mere 30 percent of it still belongs to the Syrians, and it was here that Omar and his family would have to hide out and wait. The Heights or Golan as it is often simply called, is a volcanic plateau where Quneitra is situated neatly within, yet hovering over it is the vaulting and lofty Mount Hermon, controlled by Israel, its rugged grey walls consisting of rock and brush and goats mainly, winter in the snow, runoff water in the spring, and is the perfect vantage point for Israel to "survey" much of Syria. Its steep, rocky, and craggy walls bear gradients of grey and browns, only with the odd bit of green brush sprouting between boulders. It looms as a constant reminder of the smallness Syrians can be made to feel at the hands of Israel. But down in Quneitra, little towns and life go on. The terrain is more fertile, and farmholders have settled in. Trees abound, including oaks, wild plum trees and hawthorne, and of course Eucalyptus. As Omar and his family, exhausted and overwhelmed, walked to the very edge of Quneitra to the heart of the barren Syrian side of the Golan Heights, they saw others in the dark, collecting beneath the protection of trees. Many White Helmet families had already settled in, trying to make something hospitable of the wildness they found themselves in, not knowing for how long they would have to be there. Babies cried, older children babbled, and adults tried to make normal conversations in hushed tones. It had been a long walk, and darkness had just descended as Omar and his wife also settled in under the protective branches of a seedling oak tree tucked in among a stand of much larger trees. And off in the distance, some mere kilometre away, was the sound of the regime's military, their detonations continuing into the night, edging closer and closer. Omar was discouraged, though he put on a brave face. For many of the White Helmets gathered in the grim darkness, this didn't feel anything like rescue; it felt like more broken promises Syrians had become all too accustomed to. Despite the cold and damp that was steadily increasing as their makeshift camp sank deeper into night, they had been cautioned not to make fires. So, it was only the red glowing tips of countless cigarettes flickering like stunned fireflies in the breezy night air. An injured woman cried out occasionally. There was no medicine. No bed in which to convalesce. There was only a modicum of survival here. Come morning, Omar would discover there was a pregnant wife of a White Helmet among them, critically close to giving birth. If they were not Syrians accustomed to enduring the impossible, they might, each of them, consider their situation nothing but a bad joke. But the prayers and thanks to Allah never ceased in those cold, inhospitable nights and days. As one day of brutal waiting rolled into the next, routines began within this new camp under the trees. Habitually, the Helmets glanced at their useless phones despite there being no internet signal. Only one, the leader of the group, Hashem, has been provided with data along with an extended battery and the express warning that he was not to waste it. He must only wait for the text from James or Farouq. The days were hot and petulant with an excess of time lengthened longer still by the residents' ubiquitous uncertainty and fear, by the children's boredom and hunger. Food was running out. It had rained more than one night, and the blankets were damp despite the women's attempts to dry them on tree branches during the day. The pregnant woman hummed as she lay, rubbing her unborn child, singing to it perhaps, providing the only comfort she could, knowing how quickly it could be snatched away. For now, for these moments, her baby was safe inside of her. Omar stared her way sometimes, the feeling biting his thoughts that things would very likely end badly for her, perhaps for all of them. How many days had it been now? At least they still had enough water, though the food now being shared with the most vulnerable, was quickly dwindling. The children were begging their mothers for more food, and would unwittingly take their mothers' meagre portions. Those nursing infants were finding the milk barely coming or not at all. Nighttime was the worst. Surely, they all had thoughts that they had been abandoned...not the first in their lives; abandonment is a fact of Syrian life. Nothing new at all. And then the primal howls of the pregnant woman began, as labour commenced. There were no doctors, no midwives, just more prayers.

Meanwhile, back in Jordan, logistics were becoming a nightmare for James and his team. As White Helmet colleagues on his side of the border had physically gone through the barriers to determine if the 1,202 listed names were at their appropriate meeting sites, there was mayhem and disaster. The regime's elite and merciless Quhm al Nihmr, nicknamed the Tiger Forces, were gaining on them, and their window for flight was steadily narrowing. Netanyahu had made one thing very plain: if there were any deviation from the plan, including advancing regime troops, a rush on the border by Syrians in nearby camps alerted to these happenings, or one more Helmet or family member not on the designated list, the border gate would not open.

And the White Helmets and their families were not mobilizing in real time as they were meticulously detailed to do on paper. Families from rebel zones who had no identification were stuck at village checkpoints; others were afraid to leave aged parents behind; others were slowed by having to make the journey to the rally point by black of night, especially with infants and toddlers in tow. On July 19th, the first prospective date for transfer, James was notified that only five families had made it to "Dick", the Amman crossing point. The crossing would have to be delayed, and all the while, the Regime was hot on their trail. Worse still, ISIS had infiltrated the area of the crossing point "Harry", rendering it defunct, and losing 400 Helmets and their families in the process, as they helplessly retreated from the terrorist group.

Finally, on July 21ˢᵗ, at the break of dawn, the chill of night eclipsed by the excruciating heat of the Amman day, James gave the go-ahead for the commanding White Helmets leader to assemble the remaining two groups for passage across Tom and Dick. James tried, for the time being, not to think about the failure of Harry, about the White Helmets left behind who would eventually be found by the regime forces. He had to focus on what good could come out of an almost impossible situation. James, pacing and nearly out of cigarettes, typically silent but his nerves screaming, had decided on 21:00 hours for the Amman passage, the earliest the night sky would be black over the shared Syrian and Israeli Golan desert. The wait until then was unbearable for both his team and the White Helmets, who awaited a fate, that, in true Syrian fashion, was completely out of their hands.

Back under the trees where Omar waited with his wife and youngsters, the woman had given birth to a healthy baby boy. Clutching her baby, the mother, still exhausted by her labour and delivery, would very shortly have to start out on the long trek on foot to the Israeli border. After days in the ravaging deep cold of night and exasperating heat of days, having run out of food and now nearly water, unslept, the gathering was ragged and hurting. But finally, it was time. The leader got the evacuees to their feet, and repeated instructions. They must walk carefully and noiselessly and as quickly as they could in the direction he would lead them. With the regime shelling closer than ever, they had to, all of them, vanish into the black of night. The scream of one child could be their undoing. A broken ankle from the unforgiving terrain they couldn't see, would mean the end of that person's passage. This, despite the fact that nearly all the children were weakly crying from hunger and cold, and the injured woman was doing her best to keep back muffled sobs of pain.

Like a caravan of ghosts, the group in its entirety, made it to the crossing point, Dick, where Farouq Habib awaited them at 21:30 hours. And suddenly awash in the flood lights of the Israeli Army high atop the endless razor-wired and walled border, the evacuees appeared out of the darkness like phantoms coming back to life. They were now within the reach of hope. Though with the forbidding stage they had emerged upon of rows of watchtowers lording over them with machine guns trained on them by their Israeli enemies, and a still barred and seemingly impassable huge metal gate confronting them, it certainly didn't feel like salvation. Farouq Habib was shocked at their condition as he surveyed the whole. He recounted to Chloe Hadjimatheou of the BBC those moments: *"It was cold, it was dark.... [the gate] is guarded by the Israeli Army and there are a lot of cameras, yeah, and a lot of officers were there. It was gloomy."*

Canada's diplomat, Wettlaufer, recalled in an interview with journalist, Hadjimatheou, the horrifying gap of time losing contact with Farouq for nearly an hour that night, causing her and James helplessly, to consider the worst. *"At one point the phone went silent and we couldn't reach him anymore so it was very worrying. There was I think a period of about forty-five minutes where we had no idea what was going on.... My greatest fear...the worst thing that could have happened would have been that the Assad regime or the Russians got wind of the operation and decided to bring a violent halt to it. That, in trying to bring White Helmets across the border, we would, in the end, put them in harm's way and that they would be bombed. The other thing we were concerned about is that if other Syrians in the vicinity got wind of the operation that they would try to make a rush on the border, and that as a result the Israelis would close the border and no one would get through."*

Finally gathered together and coming into view of crossing, the White Helmets and their families waited for their names to be checked off the list by an Israeli soldier. Time stood still. Then, an uneasy stillness came over the group as the soldier's hand suddenly ceased moving its pen, and a furrowed brow crossed his expression as he looked up from the document and then back at those eager and vulnerable souls in front of him. There were seven evacuees too many in the lineup, six of them children, and none of their names were on the list. The group froze, as did the White Helmet leaders, as they realized what this meant. Those unaccounted for on the list would be left behind, or perhaps worse, none of those waiting would be allowed entry because of this foul-up. The leaders scrambled and made contact with James. With incredible haste, the answer was found. The printed sheets of names had lost the final page in the printing. The missing names were discovered and hurried through. Parents burst into tears when the error was corrected. Holding tight to their children's hands, they prayed that it was the last hurdle. At 27:45 hours, the final blockage to freedom confronting them - the massive metal gate - was cranked open by the Israeli military. The leader signalled to his group, and in single file, the White Helmets and their families, walked wordlessly across the threshold into Israel. Even the children were dead silent. Farouq Habib remembers the sight of them, in absolutely miserable condition, emaciated, speechless, almost stunned by the happenings.

Between the two viable crossings, Tom and Dick, the last person crossed over from Syria at approximately 3 am. Buses waited in Israel to take the evacuees to Jordan. Most collapsed into sleep instantly.

James Le Mesurier had done all he could. But for a man whose heart and passion were with the White Helmets, the understanding that nearly half of the intended evacuees had failed to make it through, cut off at the crossing point, Harry, which was effectively under ISIS control. It had not been the great escape he had hoped for. He said little, but those around him sensed his deep anguish and his abject sense of failure to the men he had abandoned. James, like everyone else on the team, knew what the fate was of those White Helmets left behind to the regime. In the end, 98 White Helmets and their families got through, 422 evacuees in all. They would be settled in donor nations such as Canada, Britain, France, and Germany. Their days as

White Helmets are over. Syria, for now, being merely a shade of their history.

***

Settled in host countries, the White Helmets and their families would start over and learn a new normal. Integration into a completely different culture was challenging. In a steel town in Hamilton, Ontario in Canada, Omar, his wife, and two children were given a home and a new beginning. In 2023, Omar, having learned the language and passed the immigration test, became a Canadian citizen. His helmet is long gone, but he proudly displays two flags in his small apartment – one bears three stars of the revolution of his past, and the other a red maple leaf hailing the freedom of his future.

CHAPTER NINE

Through the Lens of Anas

"He was a brave hero who sacrificed his soul for the sake of the innocent. He never sought fame, but it was his sincerity in his work that made him famous."

- Amjad al-Dyab

[Hamid Kutini/Syria Civil Defence]

Anas was 19 years old when he first put on the White Helmets jacket. A mere four years later, his teammates took it off him for the last time. He was just 23. He was, in the blink of an eye, impossibly, gone.

To his older brother, Amjad, sometimes it feels like he is not gone. That that day he fell under the blow of a Russian blast was just another illogical bad dream in a long list of Syrian nightmares. He thinks that if he messages him on WhatsApp, he will reply. He will be at home with the family in Khan Sheikhoun or at the White Helmets' centre on duty, laughing like always with his best friend, White Helmet Hamid, making the best of those moments until the next bomb drop. Or perhaps he will be out with his camera in tow, looking for the perfect shot. Amjad is still waiting to see the next photograph captured by his younger brother's camera. What will it be, Anas? What does your eye see today that needs preservation in the quick snap of your shutter? A simple blade of grass balancing raindrops, or a toothless old woman laughing gleefully as she shows off her freshly baked bread? Perhaps a confused cat, dirty and pregnant, begging food before the grey brokenness of the bombed-out family home where she used to live? Or maybe the local children playing on the rusty playground equipment, this quiet and sunny Khan Sheikhoun day, their infectious laughter and glee easily translated onto film. Anas saw the stories everywhere. He was never without his camera. Like everyone in his world, he was living through the horrors of a dictator's wanton wholesale destruction of his nation, so not a day, not a moment passed, that there wasn't an image waiting for him to preserve for posterity, for history, and maybe even for eventual justice. Though he likely would have chuckled sadly at the latter. Justice was a word struck out of the Syrian dictionary. He knew that. But still he hoped.

Anas al-Dyab was something very good during very bad times. He had kept hope alive and well in the safety of his gentle boyish eyes and his crooked-toothed smile that seemed ever-present for anyone who needed it. He thrives in the memory of his White Helmet teammate and best friend, Hamid Kutini. In a world where Syrian came face to face routinely with brutal privation, the loss of Anas for Hamid, remains to this day, unbearable. The two had been much more like brothers than mere colleagues. *"Anas was a young man, who was loved by everyone, who had zero enemies, his only goal was to show the world what is truly happening in Syria,"* Hamid Kutini told CNN.[57]

Everyone who knew Anas has their own memories and stories to tell about him. A friend and fellow White Helmet, Hassan (not his real name), recounted how he first met Anas in the small village of Khan Sheikhoun in the aftermath of one of the most ferocious attacks on the country to date, 2017, late March. There was no apparent rhyme or reason for why it was Khan Sheikhoun's turn that spring night. The randomness and ferocity of Assad's attacks seemed at times completely arbitrary. What was becoming apparent in recent weeks, was that the Syrian and Russian planes had conducted upwards of a hundred airstrikes in the province at large, leading the people to believe a large-scale military campaign to take back Idlib was looming. At around 9:30

pm, surface-to-surface missiles, Russian "Grads", hissed through the air, determined to blow the harmless village off the planet. Artillery shelling backed it up without missing a beat. Hassan left his Kafranbel centre and headed the few kilometers to help with the fallout. Young and perhaps proportionately foolish, if volunteers were needed as extras, Hassan and his partner were always the first to run to the vehicle and go. The sense of invincibility among young White Helmets has always been both a blessing and a curse. The aerial bombardment was in full force as they drove into the village. Hassan had never seen anything like it in his life. It was the worst blitz he had been confronted with. It sounded and looked like what hell must be. Darkness saturated with fire. Again and again, the same sequence of horror was playing out, like a movie scene stuck on repeat. The shells and cluster bombs bursting through the atmosphere, giving hideous light to the dark, the helpless heavens, then exchanging their bomb blasts for craters in the earth, demolishing buildings, homes, forests, killing and destroying with random but acute ferocity. And the maelstrom not once stopping to catch its breath. As the two Kafranbel White Helmets drove directly into it, in short order, they realized things were at an intensity that they too were now targets, as random and as dedicated as anything else in the village. It occurred to Hassan that, they, the rescuers, may actually need rescuing. There were, indeed, moments of halting terror for them. Out of their vehicles and into the heart of the fray, heat and horror engulfed them while the screeching, deafening noise tested their courage. Indeed, it seemed to the young men a surreal taste of the fires of eternal damnation in all their Russian and regime glory.

Settings on Hassan's camera adjusted to combat darkness and smoke, as well as the blistering flares of rocket and artillery fire, he captured all he could, his finger hardly hesitating at all on the shutter. In those moments, everything within range was documented. Each image was staggering in its wicked reality. No search and rescue could be done under such heavy bombardment. It went on all night. Hassan hunkered down until first light, somewhere around 5 am, when the munitions gradually became a sputter, and then eventually halted altogether. Assad was, for the time being, done with Khan Sheikhoun. There was little left to destroy. A sulfurous haze, yellow and defiant, wrapped itself around the air and sullied the emerging Khan Sheikhoun dawn. The village, as it came gradually into focus in the light of day, was little more than a graveyard, gray and severe. The countless dead not yet relegated to their graves, however. He caught sight of the Khan Sheikhoun White Helmets and aided them for hours. Then he continued documenting the doom. He picked his way through the wreckage to a building that was still standing. Others were gathered there. Some journalists and civilians milled about. And that's where he met Anas. He was standing just outside the front door, leaning against the concrete wall, looking out ahead of him pensively as if surveying the vast devastation with renewed shock in the light of day. Anas must have taken a thousand photographs that now, Hassan noticed the telltale camera around his neck, a 300mm lens, not unlike the one around his own. They shared another similarity. Anas was wearing a Syria Civil Defence jacket, the yellow panels of it filthy with the soot and dirt of the long night. Hassan approached him, the kinship seemingly already created through their mutual vocation, and for a moment Hassan just stood there before him, breaking his concentration. Hassan remembers they must have said hello. Immediately, Anas sized up his camera, identifying its make and model out of habit. Then Anas looked in the face of the other man, before darting his glance back out at the destroyed city ahead of them, taking another wide-eyed and incredulous survey. His eyes switched immediately back to Hassan's face. The two men stared at each other, their glances oddly questioning the actions of the other. And then, as if on cue, they both started laughing. Yes, ridiculously, they laughed. They stood in a destroyed city, they had risked their lives taking pictures like madmen, both of them, all night long. No food, no sleep, just photographs. So now they laughed at that madness. There was nothing else to be done. And Hassan saw in Anas, indescribably, safety. In his soft brown eyes, in his wide, easy smile, in every part of his gentle composure. Hassan liked him immediately. He got that a lot. People gravitated to Anas.

The two young White Helmets talked mostly about what they were able to capture, compared notes, and tried to make sense of the stories they would tell the world. They were instant friends. Good thing too, because Hassan very much wanted to be his friend. He sensed virtue and dedication. He sensed a partner in crime in this abandoned and plundered universe they had found themselves journeymen in.

After that attack on Khan Sheikhoun, Hassan spoke to him briefly on the phone and through messaging about media work. Hassan would learn from others that this photographer and White Helmet was a force to be reckoned with despite his unassuming and disarming boyish charm. His name was known among many major news outlets – Al Jazeera, Channel Four, CNN, The Guardian, The New York Times. He was the ultimate conflict photographer. He took the images that made headlines, the ones that made people stop and stare when very little could anymore – especially anything coming out of Syria. At the best of times now, Syrian horrors were relegated to the back pages of newspapers, receiving brief mentions. Yet, Anas knew which captured image mattered most when he snapped that shutter each and every time. He would win awards for his images and videos, some posthumously. But really, all that mattered to Anas was that he should get the truth out at a time when truth was a rare commodity, particularly as it pertained to Syria.

Anas was 9 years old when he first picked up a camera. His older brother, Amjad, remembers his obsession with photography even then. Something cheap, no doubt, a hand-me-down, that he was able to make extraordinary use of despite its limitations. His astute eye was the real lens; the camera was only ever the apparatus to do his bidding. His keen brain also delved into computer science. He wanted to be a software engineer. So, it was no surprise to his family when, at 13, a program designed entirely by himself for PowerPoint calculations caught the eye of his teacher, and then his nation. The program created in one quick month of constant work by a teenager, garnered him a win in a science competition. The grand prize was a trip to India, sponsored by the State. The family remembers he was inwardly jubilant about it, but in his humble and reserved way, he modestly took it in stride. His first time packing for a trip, his first airplane ride, his first time away from home. For a young boy from Khan Sheikhoun, Syria, living in a family of limited means, this trip was a veritable Elysium. Likely, he pinched himself, in private, testing whether it was all just a dream. And so, for two weeks, this budding photographer with the artist's eye was able to soak up the exotic delights of New Delhi. He would bring home captured memories of golden saffron, and the indigo Ganges, and, of course, the opalescent Taj Mahal. This was the sight which encapsulated India for him, so otherworldly and majestic, so structurally and culturally different from the grey stone-walled buildings of his Syria. Such strange and unspeakable extravagance that didn't exist in his Syrian world. And he explained with uncanny thrall to his mother, as he showed the miniature version given to him there by the Ambassador of Syria to India, himself, that this palace had been a gift from a king to his sweetheart. And eventually he would reveal with deep pleasure all of the photographs, he, himself, had taken, while his mother and father inwardly reveled that their boy already had seen so much of the world. All this at just 13, almost as if he were in a race for time. Secretly, his mother wanted him to slow down.

Anas Al-Dyab's mother also wanted him to get married. So, when he entered his early twenties, she found no shortage of local girls' names and descriptions to offer him, in order to broker a marriage. As was the Syrian way, the mother would look after all the details and necessities; the son needed only say yes. With his characteristic grin and shy eyes, he would hold his mother off, tell her he wasn't ready, or that there was plenty of time for a wife.

Besides, their country was by that time gripped in war, the punishment for an innocent revolution. Nothing was stable. The future, in and of itself, was a pipe dream. Anas was busy taking pictures of the surreal happenings all around him. Things so stunningly treacherous and unfathomable, that people barely talked about them, they just lived through them, if they were lucky. Come dawn every day, the harbingers of hell would revisit the city, Russian Sukhoi fighter jets slicing the air like clockwork, announcing with this horrific regularity the wrath of Bashar al-Assad, as payloads were dropped, effortlessly exploding the centuries-old homes of families, obliterating everything in their path with what seemed supernatural ease. And then the dusty fallout, and the debris, and the screams, and the blood and the gore. Anas was capturing it all on film. But by then, photography was no longer a hobby, or even a vocation for him; it was his indefatigable humanitarian duty. The world had not answered Syria's call for help. Maybe they hesitated through disbelief. Anas had the proof that it was happening. He had proof that his beloved Khan Sheikhoun was not exempt from the hell the rest of Syria was living.

He had, of his own accord, been racing to the massacre sites with his camera, arriving usually mere moments after the newly-founded Syria Civil Defence first responders had arrived on the scene, already in the thick of their rescue. And as Anas snapped away, the story evolved through each capture. The bomb would break the atmosphere with its incendiary cloud, the massive mountain of grey dusty rubble where once his neighbour's home had been. Next, he captured the White Helmets methodically picking through the ruins seeking out the survivors and dead alike, gingerly but vigorously heaving the rocks out of the way. Then the inevitable graveyard was revealed, the victims already buried in shallow graves. Anas would hold his breath as the bloodied arm of a child would finally peek through, motionless, out from her stony burial spot, the pink knitted arm of her sweater revealing it was a little girl, deposited carelessly in Assad's hell. Then one Helmet would call for silence, listening for the locations of more living bodies. Sometimes, a half day later, hours of digging and meticulous searching with as much caution as they could muster, an entire family, all deceased, would be revealed, and ultimately caught in the shutter of Anas's camera. Of course, in a village as small as Khan Sheikhoun, he was sure to know the family. It didn't matter even if he didn't; they were innocent Syrians whom he had no doubt seen at mosque or passed in the village streets, and they were all his family.

What Anas also captured, beyond the abject horror of the scene, were the actions of the White Helmets, themselves. Not just the fluster of the digging and searching, their white helmets on their heads bobbing up and down as they dislodged rubble, and moved as quickly as they could. He noted them. These men, just like him. Some were his age, but mostly all were older. Their reactions to the reality at their feet varied. While one would lose himself to helpless sobs as a toddler was covered in a blanket and transferred lifeless to a stretcher; another would be beside him, stoic through his grief, a hand on his teammate's shoulder, or rubbing his back, trying to bring his colleague back from his wicked sorrow, just to keep going. Other helmets would survey the scene after the work was done, as if seeing it in disbelief for the first time. That Helmet might shake his head, look to the ground, and move his lips in a whisper of *Allahu Akbar*. All of these human, living, moments, Anas also caught and preserved. But even better imprinted on his psyche than on his film, was the understanding that what these men were doing, volunteering to do, he had to do too. There was no other choice in the matter.

The training to become a White Helmet took 1 week. He crossed the border to Gaziantep, Turkey, and went through the rigours of learning first aid, search and rescue, scaling walls, and even ziplining. It was the first time in a long time that he put his camera down. He then joined the latest round of graduates. He was a White Helmet, just 19 years old.

Returning to Syria from Turkey, he was assigned to the centre at Khan Sheikhoun in 2015, four years after the start of the revolution, and two years after the White Helmets were officially formed. He entered the centre that first day of duty with his usual shy and unobtrusive manner. According to a White Helmet at that centre, Hamid Kutini, he was friendly but reserved in his shyness. They welcomed him in and joined his new teammates. They gave him his uniform and white helmet with the GoPro on top. The usual boisterous ribbing went out from the others once he was dressed anew and standing before his new teammates.

Anas learned the ropes quickly. He had an indisputable finesse for first response. In a week's time, he was invaluable to the team and centre, not just as one more first responder, but as a brother who made them laugh and made them think. Hamid Kutini remembers when they were working or waiting at the centre during their shift, the two men were seldom apart. Not only was Anas filling the empty space that Hamid's recently martyred cousin, Muhammed, had once occupied, but Anas was also, quite simply, the most unique soul - one you could laugh or cry with. And so, White Helmets, Hamid Kutini and Anas Al-Diab bonded as few others did. The remaining photographs of the two are plentiful on Hamid's social media pages. The deep friendship speaks easily and clearly from the countless images and videos. They made the job look easy. No photograph encapsulated their bond better, perhaps, than the one of the two men returning to the centre from a rescue, sitting in the back seat of a vehicle, both sound asleep from exhaustion, Anas sitting upright cradling his camera unconsciously, and Hamid lying down asleep, his weary head in his teammate's lap. Their usual lighthearted grins temporarily absent.

Hamid also recalls that in an organization of dedicated and tirelessly men whose diehard spirits had them work ferociously in the field, even there Anas stood out. His work ethic was uncanny and had a certain live and work hard or die sentiment about it. He never wanted to waste time. The more he did, the more he took on. Photographing the attacks was only one part of his job. He was doing search and rescue, managing the teams, communicating with superiors, and getting the news out. "*He was like a machine*", Hamid recalls. "*And he was almost always the last to leave the rescue site.*" Following a 17-hour shift of physically and emotionally exhaustive search and rescue, while the other White Helmets packed up to go, Anas would be standing precariously balancing himself on intrepid house balconies, taking still more pictures. Looking for every possible vantage point to document the crimes against innocents. Hamid remembers walking back to the centre on foot with Anas because the last vehicle had departed and the camera still hadn't been put away. Just the click, click, click of Anas' camera shutter in the grief-laden air of the desolate leftovers of a now grimly silent place of massacre. Anas needed proof of the horrors. He would not leave without it. And in that way, he perhaps came to terms with what he saw, if such a thing were actually possible.

It was this same devoted documentarian and first responder, who made time for the forgotten and broken children of Syria. In those rare days of ceasefire or retreat by the regime, the White Helmets would hold schoolyard celebrations for the children, doing their utmost to bring some happiness and frivolity into young lives that were filled with incessant fear and loss, particularly the loss of childhood. While some White Helmets would sit hopping on bouncy balls, racing to the finish line with their competitors, the laughing children, always allowed to win, others handed out presents and sweets. In true form, Anas – the one who cheered up everyone and turned sadness into laughter - was assigned the clown costume. Eagerly, he donned it, even having his face painted, and wearing a big bulbous nose. He would delight the children, performing silly dances, and scooping the smaller children up in his arms to throw playfully into the air, hearing them squeal with laughter as they landed safely in his outstretched arms over and over again. Very few remember Anas not smiling. He was always making the best of whatever situation he found himself in. The young Helmet from Khan Sheikhoun knew life, whatever God gave him, was meant to be lived, meant to be shared.

Anas took thousands of photos of the victims of airstrikes, each riveting and shocking in their own right. There was, however, even in his vast body of extraordinary works, a series of photographs shot of one family's horrific story that caught the attention of the world and fixed Anas' place as an honoured and respected conflict photographer. On February 26, 2019, Khan Sheikhoun suffered through another regime and Russia bomb attack. A family home with three young children in it, took a punishing hit, and the White Helmets were immediately in search and rescue mode. The surviving father, Abdul Razzak Qatran, horrified and planted at their side, desperately tried to guide the rescuers to the location in the rubble where the children would most likely have been when the house went down. Somewhere inside were a six-year-old girl, her three-year-old sister, and her one-year-old baby brother. Some hours into the rescue, the White Helmets had managed to find the older girl, alive and wide-eyed but not speaking. Her situation was as heartbreaking as it was critical. As the White Helmets soothed the still trapped child, Anas captured the photograph that would scream the horror of the Syrian story to the world. The six-year-old, with her doll-like face completely covered in blood, her bloodied hands under her cheek providing a resting place for it against all the rocky debris, her little body tucked up like a shocked turtle, as if merely patiently waiting to be found. Yet, just under her knee, the tiny hand of her three-year-old sister poking out from the jagged rubble of their destroyed home, a lifeless hand and nothing more. The BBC- award-winning photograph would stop everyone in its tracks who viewed it. Yet, it was only the first of many stunning and heartbreaking pictures Anas captured that day.[58] The father, waiting for his children to be found, would soon learn only this little girl, his oldest had survived. As the two bodies of the younger children were recovered in full sight of the father, his wicked grief let loose in sobs. He walked alongside the White Helmet who carried his little girl, Elaf, away, and in a photograph captured by Anas, the father is seen bringing the tiny little bare foot to his lips, while he holds the other foot, not wanting to let go. In yet another photograph taken by Anas, the broken father, covered in both dust and blood, clutches his dead daughter in his cradling arms. Each of these images captured, every click of the shutter, undoubtedly took another piece of Anas' soul, but he knew it was his obligation to humanity to shine a light on the perpetual evils carried out in Syria by bringing a spotlight to the worst afflicted, the children. Through the lens of Anas' camera, the world would be subjected to the raw and painful truth of life in Syria for the innocents. It had become his obligation not only as a photographer but as a human being.

When interviewed about the happenings of the day, Anas Al-Dyab reported, *"The rocket hit several residential buildings that led to deaths and injuries among two different families....The girl who was rescued Tuesday is*

Hasna'a Qatran and it took nearly two hours for the White Helmets to pull her out of the rubble. She was released from the hospital on Thursday."[59]

Indeed, the little girl in the blue sweater and pink pants nearby her baby sister's lifeless hands, caused a sensation in the world of media. Later, cameras followed her to her home and to Anas, and a short documentary was made. His brother Anas forwarded that video for the telling of his brother's story in this book.

*** *** ***

In the sarin gas attack of April 4, 2017, on his hometown of Khan Sheikhoun, Anas was not on designated centre duty but, along with Hamid, joined the desperate call for help. The attack occurred just after 5 am, and the helmets were at the epicentre of it within minutes. They charged into it with little to no understanding of what the actual weapon had been. Gas, yes, but not like any they had witnessed before. This was the most unthinkable horror to ever meet their eyes. Though there had been minimal bombing, children were lying all over the ground foaming at their mouths and convulsing to death, their hearts arresting. Adults, too, but their throws of death lasting longer. Bodies were piling up all over the place. It was already a graveyard of the unburied at their feet. Anas and Hamid frantically tried to stem the silent tide of death, hosing off the victims and rushing the most critical to the nearest medical centre until it was too full to take more. Whatever had been unleashed on them, was beyond evil even for

Assad. Completely unprepared, neither the first responders nor the village were ready with hazmat suits, nor even gloves for most of the White Helmets. And the guys were by no means immune to the gas while they handled body after body. Heavy, the sarin gas dropped to the ground, and now, in puddles of yellow poison, they walked through it. It was the first victims doused with the initial onslaught of colourless sarin clouds who were the worst affected. Most had still been asleep in their beds and never woke up. Yet, the secondary effect of the gas, was that Anas was feeling his hands burning, his eyes going blurry, and worst yet, his lungs filling up tight like balloons with the residual secondary stage of the gas, so that he was finding it hard to breathe. The exact symptoms were being exhibited by so many of the first responders. Stubbornly, Anas ignored his own sickness. Every time Hamid or someone else tried to pull him in for emergency care, he would see another child or adult who needed help and would refuse to come in from the field. Time after time, he would forgo medical care for himself, to save yet one more. Eventually, they got him inside the field hospital and stripped him of his contaminated White Helmets uniform, hosed him down. They clasped an oxygen mask to his face and literally needed to force him to sit still until he was properly revived. Then they found him something of a protective suit to wear, and back out he went again. He popped into the centre periodically to fill up on oxygen, taking it methodically and hastily, like a car almost completely drained of gas. Then, in a flash, he was back out in the field to save more children. There were many photographs taken of Anas that horrific day. Likely the most compelling was one of Anas directly behind Hamid as they carried lifeless yet perfect children, rosy-cheeked and without any blemishes, to medical centres that could no longer be of any help to them, the devastation most apparent in the dark eyes of the men. For nearly two weeks after that day, Anas was unable to see clearly out of his eyes. The same for Hamid. The same for many, many of the exposed Helmets.

Not long after the Sarin attack of 2017, Anas was hit in a double attack in Khan Sheikhoun. The regime and Russia were making a massive push on one of the last liberated provinces in the nation, the rebel-held stronghold of Idlib. Anas and his team were on duty during a day of heavy bombing. In the aftermath of the initial strikes, Anas was photographing the massive toll of death and destruction, including a leveled potato chip factory. Suddenly the strikes flared up again, with Anas being struck. His Go Pro camera attached to his helmet captured his hit and continued filming his subsequent fall to the ground, and frame his severely injured legs, blood immediately covering them.[60] The footage is telling of the Anas everyone knew. Though his legs are both broken, his pain likely unbearable, there is urgency yet relative calm in his voice as he calls out to his teammates, including Hamid Kutini, that he can't get up and needs their help. Two White Helmets rush to his side, and one yells out to his colleague and brother, "*I know you, I know you! My dear Anas!*" Then another strike hits, and in an extraordinary act of love and commitment, the Helmet rapidly covers Anas' body with his own to shelter him. There is no stretcher, so the men must drag wounded Anas to safety. Yet, in their attempt to do so, another blast hits, pinning them in place on the ground, then another and another. It was a miracle that the targeted men made it out alive, dragging Anas along with them. That graphic footage was aired by major media networks such as CNN and BBC, revealing yet again the targeted onslaught on the men and their nation by the regime. The media caught up with Anas while he was convalescing in a Turkish hospital, his legs both in casts – femurs shattered, and his brother Amjad sitting in a chair at his side. In an interview with CNN, Anas speaks not of his own situation but wants the world to know something more important. Sitting up in his hospital bed, he tells the reporter in Arabic, "They are targeting innocent civilians. They are trying to kill as many of us as possible."[61] It was a message that made it to the outside world, but ultimately was ignored or forgotten. Still Anas convalesced just enough to get back to Syria and to duty. Like a cat landing on its feet no matter the height, although using up yet another of his lives, it wasn't long before Anas was right back in the field again, picking up exactly where he had left off. The problem was, Anas had been attacked and beat Death so many times, he had lost count, and what he didn't know then was that he was on his ninth and final life.

They may not have known his name, but to the Regime, Anas al-Dyab (the young man who took all those damning photographs of war crimes) was an insurmountable threat to their agenda. The terrorists they claimed to be chasing were not even in his league. For what Anas was doing was not only documenting war crimes of Assad against children, but he was doing it in such a fashion that the world was actually taking notice. He, as with all White Helmets, was the thorn in Assad's criminal thigh. And they this young man was from Khan Sheikhoun.

The final liquidation of Khan Sheikhoun came in 2019. Using the same tried and true campaign he had first employed on Daraa and Aleppo and then each and every other Syrian City in turn, for weeks, Assad would massacre and terrorize the civilians of the small village with the help of Russia, jets, and barrel bombs. When Khan Sheikhoun had been veritably mowed down, and all semblance of structure had fallen making it unlivable, the inhabitants would move out in desperation. Khan Sheikhoun fell easily and predictably. Assad's list of Syrian cities to be destroyed was almost at its completion.

As the last shelling and bombing rained down on an empty town, its only purpose to destroy all homes and infrastructure so Syrians would not be able to return, Anas was there photographing and documenting. A town that had once been vibrant with life in all its colours, with children playing in the streets, and women's washing strung drying on clothes lines, flowers in gardens, and fig trees everywhere, was now a grey carcass of cement and stone. The town had long since given up the ghost, and yet Assad was not done.

Hamid Kutini carefully recounted the day he has never been able to forget. On July 21, 2019, bombardments by the regime and Russia were heavy. Almost as if he were afraid of goodbyes, Anas told no one, not his family, not even Hamid, that he was headed back into Khan Sheikhoun and ultimately right into the arms of the regime and Russia. Hamid recounts waking up that morning, somehow having the feeling in his stomach that Anas had gone there. He was agitated and unnerved. Hamid had to attend the funeral of his brother's wife that day, and despite wanting to go find out if his gut feeling was correct, he couldn't go. Hamid remembers, *"He was trying to take as many photos and videos as possible of the city for the world to see how it is destroyed."*

Hamid managed to radio to Anas and learned he was, indeed, in the death zone and had narrowly escaped being hit by barrel bombs. Hamid was sick with fear, though Anas assured him he was okay. Hamid told him to get out of there, and to comfort his best friend and brother Anas could only reply that he was leaving, just packing up his equipment to go. Relief filled Hamid instantly, and the two disconnected.

And from all reports, Anas had intended to leave. But as he looked around at the atrocity, at the scope of it that was utterly incomprehensible by any means other than photographs for those who weren't there, he put his camera back in action. He would leave shortly. There were just a few more shots he had to secure. The building in front of him, framed perfectly in his viewfinder, had been a children's centre, still standing but barely. It was his last shot with his camera, and he began to gather up his equipment to go. In those same moments Russia sent a double-tap of bombs targeting Anas directly and the building he stood before. It was 11 am, almost exactly one hour after Anas promised Hamid he was leaving when the double-tap came. A wall of concrete was sheared off in the blast, landing directly on Anas and killing him instantly. And off to his side, amazingly, was his faithful camera and all of his equipment, covered in debris but intact. His friend, who was with him, a civilian, survived, having borne witness to the entire event.

Despite countless attempts to get Anas back on the radio for an update, Hamid had heard nothing from him for well over an hour since they had last spoken. He knew instantly what it meant, but prayed on his knees for a different outcome than his intuition provided. He told the team that Anas was in Khan Sheikhoun. They went to search for him. They found him dead under the concrete. It took the entire team to remove the concrete slap that was on top of him – a side wall of the children's centre that had been his last photograph.

They retrieved his camera equipment, grey with thick debris and grit, and put it beside him on the stretcher upon which they transported his body in the ambulance. Later, they would find on his camera, Anas' final documentation of the Syrian conflict, his last testament of the village he knew so well. Image upon image of an obliterated Khan Sheikhoun, the place of his birth, within which were his friends and family and all the people he had fought for, the village, in truth, he had never wanted to leave. Anas al-Dyab, the gentle-eyed boy from Khan Sheikhoun, had finished taking pictures. His days as a White Helmet, protecting and defending his fellow Syrians, were over. In a statement by Raed al-Saleh, the head of the White Helmets, Al-Saleh said Dyab *"was killed while trying to show the world what's going on in Syria. It's a great loss."*[62]

Anas needed to be buried in Idlib City, outside of Khan Sheikhoun, as the heavy bombardment on his home village would not cease for many days to come. The grief and mourning that followed from family and friends alike was insurmountable and has barely abated to this day. Anas had been on a mission since the revolution in Syria began - to get the story out, to tell the world that innocents were being slaughtered whether the world chose to do anything about it or not. He had the proof. Thousands of photographs for evidence. Young Anas had been a beacon of hope for so many. His greatest goal was that his photographs of a genocidal war would be placed close to the courtroom dock at the Hague, where Bashar al-Assad, Syrian dictator and butcher of the Syrian people, would one day be seated as he was tried for countless crimes against humanity. His best friend Hamid Kutini, continues as a White Helmet, doing his best along with his fellow White Helmets to make this a reality. If it is in the name of his hero and brother, Anas, so much the better.

And, indeed, to his old brother, Amjad, Anas is not gone. He is reflected easily in every photograph he snapped, in every life he saved, and mostly in the smiles that form as the bittersweet memories of him are spoken by friends about what Syria was like with Anas in it. Through the lens of Anas, the world came to know Syria so much better. *"Things like that never go away,"* says Amjad, *"How could they?"*

CHAPTER TEN

War Children

"During my work with the White Helmets, I saved many lives from death, but death this time was faster than me. It kidnapped my daughters."

- Omar Muhammed Khair al-Omar, White Helmet

The wounds

[Associated Press]

I'm going to tell Allah everything!

The little boy dying on the surgeon's table understood little about the politics of war, but somehow, he understood about justice. At just three-years-old, he had lived his entire life in Aleppo, Syria, knowing only brutal hardship. Hunger, cold, the screech of missiles falling from the sky, and the thunder of explosions striking neighbourhoods– this was Syrian childhood. And he had been given the ending to his life that countless other children had, death by massacre. He succumbed to his injuries not long after his tearful pledge to God.

The broken and war-battered children of Syria have often been called *"The Lost Generation"*. Either born into the Syrian Conflict after 2011 or already a child or teenager when the war began, life has been an unyielding and horrific existence either way. The only difference is that some children knew of a time before the war, and too many know only life *as* war. For hundreds of thousands of children, life is lived in refugee camps, impoverished and densely populated places that only give the bare semblance of life, and where the bombs still religiously rain down.

Since 2011, the nation of Syria has known a maniacal tyrant's full-scale war on the people, without distinction of whom the bombs hit; vulnerable children have too often been the victims. With tenuous "ceasefires" in place or not, the shelling and bombs have not stopped raining down or blasting away everything in their paths, daily and without cessation, year after year, since Bashar al-Assad turned on his people, seeking to teach young and old a lesson they wouldn't forget. Barrel bombs have ripped apart and maimed small bodies. Sarin and chlorine gas have suffocated their young lungs and stopped up their hearts. Invisible landmines sharing the same ground where children tried to play have exploded their bodies instantly. When the pleas and protestations to the outside world to save the Syrian children were outright ignored, the parents knew they had only to accept this horrific lot in life and deal with it. Parents live perpetually with the understanding that today, tonight, or tomorrow, could be the day their child or children are murdered by their leader. They practice semblances of normalcy despite the raging skies and the uncertain moments of silence. Dinners must still be prepared. Clothes must still be washed. And sometimes, if the child is very fortunate, they can still go to a makeshift school built underground. While the future is a pipe dream at best, the parents understand the importance of education for their children when the war is one day over. There are emergency excavation plans designed by the fathers for when the bombs and shelling come. The problem is there are few places to run to for cover. And should they survive the blast that devastated their home and those homes of a block of neighbours, where on earth do they go to keep up their routine of living? The answer is pitiful. There is nowhere to go.

In 2014, only three years into the war, UNICEF summed up the tragic reality of childhood there. *"After three years of conflict and turmoil, Syria is now one of the most dangerous places on earth to be a child,"* said the UNICEF report. *"In their thousands, children have lost lives and limbs, along with virtually every aspect of their childhood."*[63] Fourteen years on, Syria is a nation of murdered, maimed, and psychologically-devastated children.

Upwards of 55,000 children have been killed during the Syrian conflict, according to the Syrian Centre for Policy Research. It's a 2020 statistic, and the number has grown exponentially since then. UNICEF breaks down the count further, reporting that on average, 1 child has been killed every 10 hours [*since the beginning of the conflict*].[64] These statistics don't account for the children who were ravaged by permanent physical injury or emotional trauma. It does not account for the infinite number of orphans Bashar al-Assad created. Children who lost everything except their lives, older children sometimes need step into the role of parent for younger siblings who have no one and nothing. This indiscriminate taking of innocent life of children by a leader is incomprehensible. Sadly, however, the numbers don't lie. It is the hope of every humanitarian organization working inside Syria, that one day those numbers will be glaring evidence of war crimes. That one day the name of each murdered child will be read allowed as their killers sit in the dock, having no choice but to listen. Or so this is the dedicated goal.

Meticulous record keeping by the Syria Civil Defence documents the death of every child killed by war, from newborn to teenager. Looking at just one year's data, 2021, a chart has names and stats compiled in different columns. Specifics are compiled in deceivingly cheerful colours - one column for the child's name, one for the age, one for the area (city and province) where the child was killed, one for the date of death, one for the verification status of the death (which in one long bright green column are all written up as VERIFIED), another column for the mechanism(s) which caused the death which are unanimously - except for three children - categorized as REGIME FORCES – ARTILLERY SHELLING, and then one final column with a file link shows pictures of each young victim. It may be the saddest column of all. Most of the photographs were provided by the parents, taken antemortem of the child, healthy and full of life. Still others are brutally raw, taken often off a doctor's table as the dead body is examined. The youngest one I have seen in the documentation of the Syria Civil Defence is an infant with the umbilical cord still attached. A child who never stood a chance at life, not even safe in the mother's womb.

It is the loss of children during search and rescue or through disease or malnutrition that emotionally affects the White Helmets more than any other aspect of their work. Their stories are horrendous. It is probably the single most soul-crushing experience for a White Helmet to pull from the rubble a destroyed baby, lifeless and gone, who was born into a war that he never stood a chance of living through. If asked, each Helmet will tell you, no other single event will bring them to their knees quicker.

Sometimes the pain hits so close to home, the White Helmet in question is nearly crippled by the tragedy. Sometimes the victim is their own child.

On July 3, 2021, White Helmet, Omar Muhammad Khair Al-Omar's, world came crashing down around him in every way imaginable. A seasoned Syria Civil Defence volunteer, he was accustomed to bombings and the consequent search and rescue. He just never really believed the reality of the horror he was rushing to, near daily, through his work as a rescuer, could ever really touch so close to home. In Balyun Village, Ariha District of the province of Idlib, Omar was off duty. He and his young pregnant wife were outside enjoying the balm of the cool early morning hours of a summer morning, sipping tea while their three children slept inside their home, a son and two daughters. Surviving a bombing is often the luck of the draw for civilians, but this summer day Omar's family's number had come up. Although the sounds of bombing and destruction in the distance was a normalized fact of life for civilians, the sound of bombs ripping through the sky dangerously close to their street was gripping enough to wake their young son and he ran outside to where his parents were, for safety. Indeed, instantaneously, the bombs seemed on a trajectory too close for comfort. By now, Omar and his wife were on their feet on high alert. But missiles were headed his way. His house literally exploded in the moments just before he grabbed his son and ran with his wife. Before the debris had settled, Omar raced back to his flattened home. The roof was now at his feet. Mightily, with the strength of a terrified father, he began lifting rock and debris away with his bare hands, searching for his two daughters who were inside. He was like a madman as he clawed at the near impenetrable slab of roof, and he barely recognized when a team of White Helmets arrived. He had found his older daughter, 14-year-old Iman, motionless and covered head to toe in grey debris under the roof. She was lifeless, gone. He moaned his grief long and loud into the soot-filled heavens. The volunteers moved their brother and teammate out of the way as they went to work with their tools, digging. They managed to excavate the body of Omar's daughter just before another bomb ripped into the house. Everyone ran for cover. Then Omar ran back through the dust, knowing his other daughter was inside. Somehow, the younger girl had made it outside of the house only to be killed in yet another blast. Omar saw his younger daughter, Noor, only seven years old, also taken by the bomb, still and lifeless, and not answering her father's hysterical calls. Indeed, Assad had *"kidnapped"* his daughters, as Omar was quoted saying later, right off the face of the earth. Kidnapped them with no intention of returning them ever again.

In the days following the deaths of his daughters, Omar had a near desperate need to return to his demolished home, just to go back, back to where he had, mere days before, had a family that was whole. Just to go back and be near the memories of his girls, near the places where they had played and done their homework. Just to go home again no matter its condition now. All of the local White Helmets went with him for both support and to document this horrific crime. Photographs taken by the White Helmets show a devastated father – Omar – sitting in the rubble of his home, stoically surveying the devastation of what had been so few days ago, the place he and his young family called home. Now, grey debris, rocky and jagged and unyielding, had settled everywhere with only the odd spark of bright colour contrasting the gloom. It was these defiant bits of colour which stole Omar's focus and he went to them, understanding immediately their significance. He searched through those colourful places with his hands, knowing they were mementos of his two lost daughters, of things they once played with and held in their hands. Indeed, it was the younger daughter's pink knapsack. Not far from that a bright blue schoolbook that had belonged to Amal. When Omar eventually left the bomb site, he took these things with him, holding them tight to his chest, as he staggered away, supported by his brother White Helmets.

A fundraiser was started through social media platforms in order to somehow help this father, who had suffered the ultimate loss of half of his family, as well as the very roof over their heads, to try to put his life back together again. This usual method of crowd-sourcing for donations was restricted in the case of Omar and his family, as I had made the naïve error of honestly stating the recipients were Syrian. Not only was the funding page revoked, but I was also disallowed from using the platforms thereafter and haven't since. Apparently, they translated the request for donations for a Syrian man and his pregnant wife, who had just suffered the loss of two children and everything they owned in the world, as a request for funds for Syrian terrorists to buy ammunition. That's how it felt. One more shocking piece of disregard from the outside world for the Syrian victims. Eventually, through available routes, $1300 Canadian dollars were raised and delivered to Omar. In true Syrian fashion, he was embarrassed to take the money and at first refused. We wouldn't take no for an answer. Few months later, Omar sent pictures of his newborn daughter. A bittersweet moment.

The summer Omar lost his girls was a particularly deadly one for the Syrian people in general. The Syria Civil Defence documented that during June and part of July 2021, the Syrian Regime launched 192 attacks, killing 54 civilians, 11 of whom, were children.

Children are sacred to the White Helmets. They have come face to face with so many maimed and murdered young lives, that their hearts and minds are deeply impacted by the innocence and precious nature of little kids. It is, bar none, the cruelest punishment from Assad to throw bombs on neighbourhoods dense with children. The White Helmets have a specific protocol for the recovery of babies and children, a very dignified and respectful protocol. When a child is found lifeless during their searches, all onlookers who are not SCD or family members must move away from the recovery site. They never ask for the bulky and cold black body bags. Instead, the Helmet will call out for a ready blanket to cover the innocence of someone's child, nestling them in something befitting that innocent soul, something warm and soft, usually made by a mother. The Helmet will carry the dead baby or child carefully in his arms away from the scene of hell, delicately, gingerly, close to the chest and heart, almost as if the child were still alive and needed protection and comfort. Usually the dirt-stained face and cheeks of the White Helmet tasked with carrying off the child, streaked with long trails of tears.

Sometimes it takes the unimaginable to gain the attention of the world. Dead and dying children are a plight that happens elsewhere, and the world regards them as sad vestiges of a nation that they believe "is always at war" or for which "nothing can be done". It takes a lot to stir the conscience of the madding crowd on the other side of the world or even in a nation next door. For Syrian children to make world headlines, to stand out, they must be noteworthy. In their innocence, they must do something sensational or the world simply does not have time for one more malnourished or bomb-blasted child.

There was, of course, 13-year-old Hamza, referenced in the first chapter of this book, who made just such headlines, who stirred – ever briefly - the consciences of the West. Having lived his whole life in the birthplace of the Revolution, Daraa, Syria, he would eventually become the childish face of the revolution after being abducted and tortured to death by the Regime military police. The unfathomable brutality inflicted on a mere child garnered the attention of American President Obama and then U.S. Secretary, Hilary Clinton. The world, however, has a short attention span. And although Hamza would stay indebted in the hearts of all Syrians, he and all Syrian children would once more be forgotten by the world. Until the Boy in the Ambulance made his way onto their television screens, and once more, the plight of Syrian children was back in media focus.

The photograph of rescued five-year-old Omran Daqneesh sitting in an ambulance is likely one of the most famous images of the Syrian Revolution children, and perhaps the revolution, itself. He was rescued by the Bab al Nayrab White Helmets Centre in Aleppo, following a Regime/Russian airstrike that brought down his house and buried his entire family in it. Having been transferred from his bomb site into the ambulance, the boy, in the chaos of the moments, was left momentarily all by himself in the vehicle seat. Covered in dust and dried, crusted blood, he sat wide-eyed and obediently, still and visibly shocked by his situation. Photographs and video capture the moments for the world. His behaviour during the video is riveting and heartbreaking all at once. The little boy asks nothing of anyone, doesn't cry out for a parent, but at one point brushes his hand up to his face, where he feels something odd stuck to his cheek. He looks at it on his hand. He sees it is blood. He makes no reaction to this fact and simply continues sitting perfectly still again. No words. No other movements. No questions. No crying. It is perhaps this very un-child-like reaction from a child that has just experienced the unimaginable, that makes the world gasp. The child seems to accept his awful circumstances without any thought of protest. Omran moves the world to tears and anger, and even questions. And once again, Syria is back on the international radar. It is a brutal reality that the thousands of other injured and dead children victimized by the regime and Russia before Omran, for whatever reason, did not make the grade.

Famously, a CNN anchorwoman telling Omran's story in international news on her station, loses her composure and comes close to tears as she tells the story about the so-called "Ambulance Boy" to the camera and about how the United Nations has requested 48 hours of relief in the fighting in Syria. As his image reappears on the TV, the anchorwoman says what she feels, "*...what strikes me is we shed tears but there are no tears here,*" and she gestures toward the picture of Omran again with her hand, "*he doesn't cry once. That little boy is in total shock. He is stunned. Inside his home one moment and the next lost in the flurry...in the fury of war and chaos...*"

Omran and his older sister, who was also sitting in the ambulance now, were transferred to hospital, where doctors who attended to him gave a full account of his state and confirmed there were no brain injuries. They did tell of him crying from pain later when the shock wore off. However, after a visit from President Assad, himself, to the Dagneesh family, the story of the Ambulance Boy took a major but not unsurprising regime revamping. Indeed, after Assad's visit, the father was encouraged to tell the "real" story on TRT Television[65], as well as other Pro-Regime channels. The coerced father explained that the rescue had been a complete hoax and the White Helmets had never rescued his son (despite extensive video footage of them unearthing the child and his sister from their bomb-blasted home in Aleppo), but instead his child had been kidnapped by his home by gunned men for purposes of staging a scene just as President Assad had earlier reported

303

in yet another interview with Turkish Media [TRT World][66]. In damage control yet again, President Al-Assad, spun the Omran story in typical regime fashion. It was all a hoax he tells the interviewer, despite the countless eyewitnesses including White Helmets and hospital doctors and nurses who rescued and tended to him. He says Omran was a child actor in a staged bit put on by, of course, the White Helmets.[67] The interviewer asks Assad if he may show him a picture, which he begins to pull out of his vest pocket.

Reporter: This young boy has become the symbol of the war.

Assad: uh-hem

Reporter: Do you know this picture?

Assad: Of course I saw it.

Reporter: His name is Omran. Five years old...

Assad: Yes...

Reporter: ...covered with blood, scared, traumatized...

Assad: uh-hem

Reporter: Is there anything you would like to say to Omran and his family?

Assad: Go to the internet to see the same picture of the same child with his sister both were rescued by what they call them in the West White Helmets they were rescued twice each one in a different incident and just as part of the publicity of those White Helmets. This is a forged picture not a real one.

Assad: ...we as government are killing the civilians. Who can believe that story? No one.

Who can believe that story? Well, for certain, the doctors on duty receiving the children and also being bombed by the regime as they provided care for them. For certain, the parents who were offering eyewitness testimony and mourning the loss of their children.

Then there were the Sarin Twins. On April 4, 2017, the Russian air force threw a canister of deadly Sarin out of its fighter jet and into the city centre of Khan Sheikhoun in the Province of Idlib. When the canister had been filled and loaded into the aircraft, there had been no care whatsoever for the age of the victims to be targeted by the deadly gas, despite the fact the bullseye coordinates were a residential neighbourhood. Two of those victims were nine-month-old siblings, twins Ahmed and Aya. The surviving father, 29-year-old Abdel Hameed al Yousef, was with his wife and twins in their home, in the epicentre of the sarin bomb drop. His wife and babies immediately showed signs of the sarin poisoning, and he took them outside, hoping the fresh air would alleviate their acute illness. Instead, helplessly, hysterically, he saw his wife and babies perish brutally and swiftly, by something odorless and invisible. It had taken mere minutes for his entire young family to simply die. The father couldn't believe his babies were actually dead, until the doctor said the words.

Friends who came to comfort the young father also took photographs of the horrific crime, but it is surely within these images that the sinister and surreal horror of the entire event truly becomes apparent. The photographs of Abdul sitting cradling one seemingly sleeping baby in each arm are gut-wrenching to observe – not because their bodies have been brutally battered by death but, indeed, because they bear no marks at all. Little Aya and Ahmed, as perfect in this deathly repose as the blond curly-haired cherubs of fables. Indeed, without a so much as mark of any kind on their hands or faces, the children look perfect. They look alive. But they are not. They are dead from Sarin gas.

The father walked supported to the place of burial with his two babies in his arms, his friends holding him at the arms, keeping his gait steady so he didn't fall. He had only momentarily released his children from his arms in order to help dig their small graves with his own hands. When it was time to place the children within their eternal resting places, the father foundered and grew unstable, shook his head no, defiantly wailed that he will not do it. He seemed confused about what was going on as he regarded his children again. Then the confusion cleared and he remembered they are dead. Indeed, he must lay them down now in graves, his baby twins, just babies. But just yesterday, they were healthy and playing, babbling to their parents in their home, crawling at his feet. No disease. No fall. No lack of food. They were so perfect and so innocent and so little. They look nothing at all like the terrorists Assad tells the world he is hunting down and eradicating.

Regime sieges were a swift and brutally pragmatic way of taking the children too.

As the regime besieged so many cities and whole provinces during the Syrian conflict, Assad ensured that no food or medicine could get to the people. It was, once again, the children who suffered most from this. After ballistics, starvation was the biggest killer of children during the Syrian conflict. No one was more aware of this than the Syrian mothers. Sieges killed the most vulnerable easily and en masse.

There is a story, perhaps more of a fable, of the Syrian mother who cooked "rock soup". She had put her young, hungry children to bed, their bellies empty, and then went to the nearby stove. While the children lay in their beds, fighting the pain in their empty stomachs which their mother could not stave off, they heard her putting a pot on the stove and filling it with water. Then, after a while, she would add small pea-sized rocks to the water and set her spoon stirring them so the hungry children could fall to sleep believing their mother was preparing food for the next day. It was the only comfort she could give them.

Even countless cities that were not under the stronghold of Assad's sieges, were starving. So little food aid was getting through the regime's border blockades despite it being shipped by humanitarian organizations like UNICEF and World Vision and waiting for distribution. Had it only been allowed through, so many children would still be alive. Yet, in their typical stoic fashion, the lack of food for babies no longer causes the moral outrage among the mothers it once had. There was no point in screaming at the walls of the houses or tents. Emergency UN security sessions had addressed the desperate food shortage, calling it a catastrophic humanitarian crisis, yet nothing was done. Starvation had threaded its killing tendrils into the new fabric of Syrian culture. They could not take blood from stones. Syrian mothers endured while their children slowly wasted away.

Such was the case with Baby Muhammad. A common Syrian name, but a unique, beautiful little baby boy, whose eyes the size of saucers in his skeletal, thin head, too large now for his body, reached directly into your soul.

The staff of S.A.M.S. was responsible for the care of baby Muhammad, and released this information on their website:

"Our staff at Ibn Sina Hospital in Idlib have been treating Muhammad Habab since July 18th. He was suffering from severe malnutrition, combined with severe dehydration shock and protein deficiency! Muhammad is currently under observation in the pediatric intensive care unit. He is expected to recover and improve, but unfortunately, the effects will remain with him for the rest of his life."

In a July 23, 2020, White Helmet Facebook post, the organization wrote about Muhammad:

"Currently, baby Muhammad is in intensive care in hospital receiving treatment. His situation is extremely critical. His pain levels at least seem to be controlled. Let us keep this precious baby in our prayers and demand the international community protect millions of other Syrian children sharing his fate."

Then again, in a July 30, 2020, White Helmet post, more encouraging words:

"Good news in the case of Muhammad, as his vital signs improved, he was graduated from the pediatric intensive care department, after spending 11 days there, and he was monitoring [sic] by SAMS staff. When our cadres were greeted at IBN Sina Hospital, Muhammad [SIC], he weighed 3kg, suffering from severe and acute malnutrition. And severe dehydration shock! During his treatment, he weighed 4.9 kg due to the abnormalities in his body in response to malnutrition. After intensive follow-up, the baby gained actual weight, reached 3.2 kg, and his vital signs improved."

A follow-up White Helmets Facebook post on July 30th read:

"Baby Muhammed continues to flourish under the careful attention S.A.M.S. medical team. They report that his condition is very good and he is gaining weight. He has graduated out of the Pediatric Intensive Care Unit at Ibn Sina Hospital. He is now nursing with mom and will continue to improve."

On August 4, 2020, I received a message from a White Helmet that baby Muhammed now weighed 4kg (8.8 lbs).

Yet on August 10th, while I was at the WH Office in Istanbul, meeting with Raed, the White Helmet sitting beside me received the sad message Baby Muhammed had died. The White Helmet waited until we were leaving the WH office to inform me. We walked away sober and solemn, both of us tearfully remembering the little baby boy with the big eyes and the determined will to live that he demonstrated by habitually stretching out his skinny little arms and legs, as if wordlessly telling us all he wanted to be saved; he wanted to grow. A fighter to the end, Muhammad is a little baby boy we will never forget.

In Syria, there were so many ways for a child to die. With this understanding, early on into the conflict, educational programs were devised by the Syria Civil Defence Organization to provide information on the best way for children to carry out their days and survive despite the dangerous and various aspects of war. Delivered in a child-friendly narrative by local White Helmets teams, they used printed animated pamphlets brought along by the Helmets into the classrooms on their routine visits to educate the children on protocol for survival in the least scary way possible. The children would be educated on the proper steps to take during air strikes, fires, and what to do if remnants of war (mines) were discovered by them. The visits also gave the children an opportunity to get to know the White Helmets and understand they were safe during the conflict and someone was indeed looking out for them. They would pass around their helmets and let the children try them. There would be laughter by the children and Helmets alike as the too-large hard hats eclipsed the small heads.

After the educational demonstration, a party would often ensue in the courtyard of the school, where games were set up amid brightly decorated and festooned backdrops. Sometimes even the children were invited ahead of time to practice and rehearse a song or play presentation to be acted out at this same ceremony or event. Parents were also invited to the festivities. A perfect opportunity for them to see their children having fun and feeling safe under the wings of the humanitarians.

Indeed, the White Helmets have taken on many important jobs to make the way of life better for the Syrian children of war. When there was the opportunity between air strikes and during days of clear skies, they would rebuild playgrounds and schools, cleaning and restoring, and painting. In particularly hot weather, building makeshift swimming pools were constructed and filled by firetrucks with cold water to thwart the heat. The children are beyond giddy and gleeful in the water after the consistent days of heat during Syrian summers.

White Helmets and parents alike do their utmost to mitigate the damage being done to young brains and nervous systems by the impacts of non-stop conflict. However, it is hard to combat the effects on children of hearing explosions at all hours of the day, of witnessing blocks of neighbourhood homes instantly collapsing and gone in moments, of experiencing the horrific loss of neighbours, parents, and siblings wounded or killed. The daily routine of this for children can all but guarantee Syrian children develop mindsets of fear, anxiety, and instability, and the understanding that life can be snatched away in a moment.

An Idlib father became famous for a video that went viral showing how he had taught his three-year-old daughter to laugh instead of being afraid when the bombs rained down. In the video, Salwa, the little girl, is standing alert on the sofa, clad in a pink dress, as the twosome listen to the latest wave of strikes and the father films it. Mohammed asks his daughter: *"Is that a plane or a shell?"*[68] *"A shell,"* she answers. *"And when it falls we will laugh!"* The anticipated laughter ensues. It is a coping method that works well with Salwa, but likely would be ineffectual with most children of war, so terrified of bombs they instinctively are.

The psychological effects on the Syrian children are profound and often last a lifetime. A UNICEF short documentary outlines the rationale behind the development of a healthy child's brain versus one that develops to be unhealthy. The documentary states[69], *"...a child's early experiences are crucial in how their brains develop. Children who feel safe and nurtured have the best chance of growing into healthy, happy and resilient adults. Those who do not are at greater risk of developmental delay [,] mental health and behavioural conditions [and] even health problems like cardiovascular disease and cancer and these impacts can last throughout their lifetime [.] Children exposed to war are among the most vulnerable....their earliest years have become marred by conflict [,] displacement [,] violence and loss [.] When highly distressing or potentially traumatic events occur a child's nervous system is flooded with the stress hormone cortisol....if it happens repeatedly and if there is no safe space to rest to recover it can wire [,] indeed it can rewire the brain."*

Common psychological disorders in many children who have sustained long-term war and conflict include heightened stress, anxiety, depression, and PTSD (Post-Traumatic Stress Disorder). Research shows that the greatest traumatic experience that can perpetrate psychological disorder in a child is the separation from a loved one, specifically a parent or sibling.[70]

Psychiatrist, Dr Mattar, explained *"that children who are struggling with trauma often exhibit specific behaviors, including emotional withdrawal and self-imposed isolation. Children may have their anxiety, fear, and elevated stress levels manifest through physical symptoms, like jumping at loud noises and nearby sounds.[10] For younger children, chronic bed wetting can be a common sign of disrupted mental health while adolescents often display more aggressive behavior. In more extreme cases, children may turn to self-harm, substance abuse, or even suicide as a means of escaping the reality of their experiences."[71]*

It is imperative that the Syrian children who endured the 14 year conflict, many now teenagers, be provided with psychological therapy and treatment in order to survive in the aftermath of the war as well.

With so many children psychologically impaired from years of neglect from the hell of war raging within their worlds, it is incumbent upon for the international community to now step up, from any moral perspective, to provide them with the help they need.

In the outskirts of a neighbourhood of the Province of Aleppo, there is a remarkable and near daily occurrence – children at play on defunct war tanks. While children may be born amid a rocket-filled sky and blasted neighbourhoods or perhaps within the desolate conditions of mostly neglected refugee camps, their instinct is still to behave like children. The dichotomy of being born into war yet still showing an unshakable desire to play as kids do is astonishingly demonstrated at the *"Graveyard for Syrian Regime Tanks"* or just simply the *"Graveyard of Tanks"* in the Province of Aleppo. Nicknamed such, after the early rebel strikes back in 2011 gained momentum and countless victories over the Syrian Arab Army allowed the rebels to capture the regime tanks and then dumped them broken here when they became useless. Accordingly, the tanks are older than the children who gravitate to them. It is a striking scene to see so many children using this tank graveyard as a veritable playground, playing hide and seek among the T-72 Mahmia or the T-72 Shafrah – the main battle tanks of the regime, or climbing out of turret holes playing at being rebel fighters, themselves. So young are some of these children, they have no inclination of the brutality and destruction the ghostly vehicles once were capable of. They know only that adventure abounds where reality is put on hold and their imaginations reign supreme.

The hard facts:

As of March 2024, more than **650,000** children under the age of five [in Syria] are chronically malnourished[72]

By mid-March 2024, opposition activist group the Syrian Observatory for Human Rights (SOHR) reported the number of children killed in the conflict had risen to **26,282**[73]

CHAPTER ELEVEN
7.8 on the Richter Scale

"This is bigger than us, this is beyond our capacity."

- Ismael Alabdullah, White Helmet

[Rendering]

If injury ever knew insult, it was at 17 minutes past 4 o'clock on the morning of February 6, 2023, in northern Syria. A clock in the rubble peered face upwards at the rescuers, its lifeless hands stunned

316

into submission by the 7.8 earthquake that tore down the wall it had hung on. Despite the absent tick-tock, the White Helmets knew the clock had started counting down on finding survivors. A shocking survey of the wasteland of wreckage stretching as far as the eye could see meant the race against time was already on. Countless thousands of people were trapped in this latest onslaught of incomprehensible brutality to hit Syria. After 10 years of search and rescue from Assad and Russia's bombs, the White Helmets knew well how to cope in the face of disaster and despair, yet this was something entirely different.

But why them? Why now? There was no time to ask why, although everyone was thinking it. Even the most devout were perhaps questioning God. How could they not? After 12 years of horror and destruction, why had Providence picked out their sad, broken nation for still more?

The epicentre of the earthquake was in the country bordering their north, slamming into and cracking open Gaziantep, Turkey, then spreading out instantly, a swift and determined geological wave of destruction with Northwestern Syria right in its path. The Syrian cities of Jarabulus and Afrin on the Turkish border were decimated, and then the northern parts of Aleppo and Idlib provinces were swallowed up as well. The grounds cracked open, the roads split apart, forming treacherous abysses, and the buildings collapsed like sandcastles at high tide. At shortly past 4 o'clock in the morning, most people were one moment asleep in their beds and the next buried helplessly in the ruins of their homes and apartments.

Then, as if mimicking the cruelty of the notorious Russian double-tap, nature unleashed a massive aftershock wave registering 7.2 magnitude which struck the same regions not long after the first. What buildings and infrastructure had barely survived the first quake easily succumbed to the powerful second one. There would be several consecutive large tremors on the initial day, and for many days following, although, for a brief moment in time, people thought it had to be over. Security video footage released from a remarkably intact mosque, revealed that just as devout followers of Allah returned to their temple, believing the worst of the quake was done and praying prostrate that they were right, the mosque itself shook in defiant response with a shockwave tremor. The footage shows the worshippers running from the building, leaving both their prayers and their prayer rugs behind, fleeing for their lives. Once again, for those survivors above ground, nowhere was safe. Even after the shock waves ceased. People, children, now homeless in the severe cold and grit of a Syrian winter, hunkered down in whatever covered crevice they could find, hungry and desolate, their terror of what was to come next, unimaginable. But they were the lucky ones.

The Syrian people were not strangers to earthquakes. It was a part of their lives to regularly feel the slight angry rumbles that barely ever surpassed a 2.0 on the Richter Scale. When the rumblings had ceased, they simply went on about their business, perhaps straightening a picture on the wall, or picking up an upended teacup off the floor. With approximately 102 earthquakes hitting Syria annually, there is, on average, a quake every 3 days. But nothing like this. This earthquake had struck at this already battered and beleaguered people with a near apocalyptic punch.

Despite the prevalence of small quakes in the region, seismologists knew Syria was overdue for a big one. The scientists in Kandilli Observatory and Earthquake Research Institute at Boğaziçi University in Istanbul, had been formulating models depicting a massive quake was brewing restlessly beneath the earth's surface.[74] They just didn't know with any real precision when it would come. They had been watching a particularly critical load of stress building along the East Anatolian Fault, a major strike-slip fault zone. This particularly expansive fault, some 700km long, created 5000 years ago when Turkey was squeezed westwards through the European continent, is situated precariously against both the Arabic and African plates. The pressure on the Anatolian plate had been threatening collision for decades when it finally ferociously collided with its bordering plates on February 6, 2023, heaving their weight over each other and bringing inevitable upheaval on the largest scale, violently buckling the stability of upwards of 20 cities throughout southern Turkey and northwestern Syria.

As the White Helmets scrambled to the affected regions, the destruction and devastation were an entirely new beast set before their eyes. Even as they mobilized at 5am in the dark, the scene was clear. The region had been leveled. The dead and dying were nearby but unseen. There was no protocol for this type of disaster, and no machinery in their arsenal to combat the destruction left in the earthquake's wake. They knew immediately they needed help from the outside world to even attempt to tackle what lay ahead of them. And they needed it fast. The very lives of thousands of people desperately depended on expedience. Way down below the destruction, with every tick of the clock, another breath could be lost or taken.

The White Helmet teams merged instantly, every functioning centre sent volunteers, the majority of them entering into the devastation zones from safer, more southern Syrian areas. Of the Syria Civil Defence centres within the quake zones, several White Helmets died with their families in the pre-dawn earthquake. Organization between the teams was headed by Syrian White Helmet Manager, Ismael Alabdullah, who also became the prominent spokesperson to media outlets around the world for the state of the rescue. As they inventoried their heavy-grade equipment – donated excavators, backhoes, and bulldozers – they recognized immediately, they were desperately lacking in excavation machinery that could manage this disaster, let alone enough fuel to fill and refill the engines. With the ground, having become a buckled topography of concrete piles of insurmountable wreckage, they most certainly needed more advanced technological equipment to scope into the wreckage for life. Nor did they have near enough White Helmets to carry out the time-sensitive work. This vast expanse of devastation across their cities warranted more than a 20- hour shift of post-bombing excavation. Left without international aid, it would take days to weeks to recover the civilians inside the mountains near-insurmountable rubble. 1-2 days, they knew from experience would be the maximum allowable time to possibly keep babies and children alive, the elderly, the most vulnerable, 3-4 days might just barely keep the average human being alive; however, the lack of water by then would become the second biggest threat after their injuries. Beyond that time frame, it would become a search and recovery mission for bodies. And despite them facing a 10-year humanitarian conflict alone without any international intervention, the White Helmets knew the West and other international communities could not turn a blind eye to this formidable natural disaster that had befallen Syria. Politics and its resultant excuses were one thing – but this wasn't politics, this was an act of nature that had rendered them helpless. Surely the West would come to help. Or so they thought. But they had thought help had been coming 10 years before, too.

In the days before the earthquake, there had been a brief moment in Syria where the clouds were finally clearing, when the regime and Russia, with few provinces left to blast to bits, had reduced their campaign of destruction and death. There had been respite for the Syrian people in rebel-controlled regions. They had dared to hope things could, if not entirely, in some reasonable way, go back to normal. Hospitals were being restored, children were going back to school, and the bombs in the heavens had ceased for some time raining down 24/7. People were returning from camps to houses, which, although badly damaged and fragile, at least had a roof and four walls to prove they were homes. The White Helmets had even managed to reconstruct playgrounds. There had been Syrian children back on slides and swings just yesterday.

Obadah Alwan, a media manager for the Syria Civil Defence headquarters located in Istanbul, Turkey, was alerted to the disaster by the persistent ringing of his cell phone by friends and colleagues barely more than a half hour after the earthquake occurred. *Alwan said: "I had colleagues calling me. I was barely awake and one of my colleagues was already waiting for me outside. We went straight to the office and started getting in touch with people who are on the ground."*[75]

From the headquarters in Istanbul, he and the team worked on plans to bring international aid, international media, and his colleague White Helmets, on the ground in the fallout, together for the most expedient way of saving as many lives as possible.

The pleas went out. The calls for urgent and lifesaving help were not answered. The White Helmets and the Syrian people were baffled, confused. Across the border in Turkey, mere miles away, help had already arrived from countless nations, all mobilizing to save as many human beings as possible. The response was....deadly.

Manpower and lifesaving aid went urgently to Turkey from numerous international nations.

The United Kingdom had sent 76 search and rescue specialists with equipment and working dogs, emergency medical teams, and a field hospital, along with a C-130 Hercules Critical Care Air Support Team.

The United States sent two 79-person search and rescue teams, 100 Los Angeles County firefighters, and structural engineers.

Italy sent a firefighting team from Pisa, as well as transport flights carrying health equipment and health workers.

France sent 71 search and rescue workers and 65 firefighters.

Spain sent two urban search and rescue teams with 85 personnel, along with volunteer firefighters.

Austria dispatched 84 soldiers from their military disaster relief units, including doctors, firefighters, and search and rescue dogs.

Many other nations sent whatever means they could.

As for Syria, nothing and no one came to their aid. Other than a few minor local relief resources, the White Helmets stood alone on the precipice of the ultimate humanitarian disasters. They would not have enough body bags to confront what was coming for them and Syria.

72 hours was quoted by the United Nations as the maximum time of survival for a human being trapped in rubble before extrication. They knew this just as the White Helmets knew it, but they spent those crucial hours bogging themselves down in the red tape of politics. Worse than this, they asked for Bashar al-Assad's approval to cross into Syria to help the earthquake victims, and were willing to come to Syria's aid, but were halted by the UN. It took one week for the UN to get Assad's approval. One week before Assad granted access to the earthquake zone by opening extra border crossings.[76]

Legal experts have told the BBC that this bureaucratic blunder, which cost the lives of thousands of Syrians, could have been prevented. They said the UN never needed any such permission from Assad or the Security Council, for that matter, they needed only apply a broader interpretation of international law as it governs humanitarian disasters. International human rights lawyer, Sarah Kayalli, berates the United Nations' slow response:

"What matters in terms of responding to an earthquake is time and the immediacy of the response. And the UN just stood there completely paralysed."[77]

Another criticism delivered firmly to the UN was by a former senior UN official, Andrew Gilmour:

"If a UN lawyer tries to interpret it [the international law to deliver cross-border aid] *as meaning you somehow can't provide mild power to a starving baby, then he is making an obscene and illegitimate farce of international law."*[78]

Despite the plethora of legal voices that condemned the decisions of the United Nations, they stood their ground that they had acted within the legal parameters prescribed by international law. UN spokesperson Stephane Dujarric defended the organization:

"To deliver humanitarian aid across an international border, we need either the consent or the government or in the case that we have in Syria, a binding Security Council resolution....we can have academic discussions for weeks, months, and years about international law. Our position is that international law has not delayed our work."[79]

Dujarric would go on to cite security concerns and political concerns. Realistically, the only concern he did not address was that they knowingly allowed Syrian human beings who might have survived if rescued in a timely fashion to die needlessly.

To further validate the lawyers' professional disagreement with the actions the UN took (or didn't take) Marcos Sassoli, special advisor to the prosecutor at the International Criminal Court, outlined that the Geneva Conventions – the very foundation set out for international humanitarian law – prescribes all the necessary framework needed by the United Nations to deliver aid without the permission of a government. Sassoli stated, *"The Geneva conventions, to which Syria is a party, has a provision stating that an impartial humanitarian body....may offer its services* [to all sides of a conflict]*"*.[80]

The sad reality of the time wasted by the United Nations was summed up when, a week after the earthquake, Martin Griffiths, the UN's head of emergency relief, visited the Bab al-Hawa bordering crossing. He commented on his Twitter account, "[The UN has] *so far failed the people of north-west Syria. They rightly feel abandoned, looking for international help that hasn't arrived."*

The news to the White Helmets that the United Nations had denied help to their nation was no surprise. They had witnessed over a decade of "emergency" UN Security Council meetings, allowing Russia veto power over every decision to help the beleaguered nation. The process, although farcical, left bewilderment, if not anger, in the hearts of the volunteers.

In Syria, the White Helmets were on their own, and as every moment slipped by, as every day turned to night and then morning again, they lamented the lives that were being needlessly lost. So many children, had they just been gotten to sooner, would likely be alive and playing today. But the White Helmets had never been so overwhelmed. There were so many obstacles to getting to the lives they wanted to save. White Helmets Manager, Ismail Abdullah, recalls one year on from those horrific days of February 2023, the helplessness every volunteer felt having to leave people to die because they didn't have the resources or manpower to save them.

"A year on and I still feel the pain of every life we lost on that day. The situation required a response far beyond our means. We needed heavy machinery, advanced technology, and specialized crews. We needed open borders to transfer those in critical conditions to get urgent medical care. Perhaps we could have saved ten more lives, even one more life. But instead, we were almost completely isolated from the outside world, and the international systems that had failed the Syrian people for over 12 years continued to fail us in the aftermath of the earthquake."[81]

Indeed, in those early critical days no one came to help. The White Helmets were on their own. There were 3,000 White Helmets volunteers trying to navigate through a death zone of about four million Syrian people, a great many of them buried underground, waiting and dying.

Drone footage shows the destroyed neighbourhoods from a sobering perspective. Everywhere, the ground is ashen and gray from the earthquake detritus. The Syria Civil Defence white ambulances are scattered diffusely at different wreckage sites as the volunteers work away, their large machinery employed digging and excavating like peculiar and helpful giants roaming through the wreckage, the brilliance of the machines' bright colours in stark contrast to the wasteland gray. The volunteers move as fast as they can. There are no breaks. There is barely time for sips of water. Every hour lost is a life taken.

Amid the dark days of search and rescue, there are buoying moments of jubilation and celebration. As the White Helmets brought forth life out of what had seemed sure death from collapsed buildings, both the rescuers and the awaiting families broke out in cries of hysterical relief and happiness. There are stories that stand out for the White Helmets, miraculous moments of survival, particularly, among the children.

During one rescue in Aleppo, a terrified father watches ceaselessly every movement of the White Helmets as they unearth the area of concrete where his young child is buried. When the young boy, crying and caked in dust and debris, is raised into the light of day, the Syrian father weeps and nearly collapses.

Another very young boy uncovered from copious slabs of concrete in Aleppo, is wide-eyed and shockingly coherent, as his little face peeks up curiously at his rescuers as they lift away the last heavy pieces of his encasement. His state of health after so many hours is beyond extraordinary. The maybe-six-year- old swats playfully at the White Helmet, who has gathered him up in his arms and says, *"I waited a long time for you Guys"*. The rescuers don't know whether to laugh or cry.

Then in Jenderes, Aleppo, there is astonished celebration mitigated by sadness, as a newborn girl with her umbilical cord still attached to her deceased mother, is recovered from under the rubble. Born inside the hell of the earthquake, it is a somber task to separate the infant from her mother. The baby girl was immediately transferred to a hospital in Afrin, and named Afra after her mother. Upon complete recovery, the child was adopted by her sole living relative.

The survival of the most vulnerable such as newborn, Afra, and all children, who survived not just the earthquake but also made it beyond the first week, is a miracle unto itself. The horrible reality of crush injures, a medical term describing the impact limbs and organs take from persistent impaction and squeeze, was responsible for taking countless lives in the hours and days after their rescue.

After near-endless digging and scouring the site of a collapsed home, an entire family is brought back to the light of day alive. Five members in all – each and every one breathing and moving. It is an unparalleled victory, this saving of five joined lives.

After an impossible three days, death is again defeated when a little girl named Noura is pulled from the rubble following the loss of all of her family members. She is orphaned, but she is alive.

But how long could the miracles continue?

The answer is they couldn't.

A family of a White Helmet in Idlib was known to be under the deep rubble of their family apartment. The poor construction had crumbled like a house of cards that early morning of February 6th.

Inside, together were a grandfather, grandmother, a dad and brother, his wife, and their four children, including a nine-month-old baby boy. The excavation of so many collapsed apartments, one right on top of the other, is a difficult one. In agony, the White Helmet and his colleagues waited out the excavation, limited in its capacity due to a lack of proper machinery and tools. A painstaking 160 hours – or nearly six days past – as the rescuers worked as fast as they could, but realistically had lost all hope that the family could still be alive. On February 12th, 2023, the lifeless bodies of the entire family were finally brought forth from the rubble. It was a great loss that had in all likelihood been needless. If only they had gotten to them sooner, they might still be alive, every one of them. If only the United Nations had allowed help in. It filled the rescuers and the remaining family with unimaginable sorrow and brutal disappointment at the outside world.

As days turned to weeks, some aid eventually arrived via the United Nations distribution, but it had come only in time to help recover hundreds upon hundreds of bodies. The wait had been too long. The delay had caused the senseless deaths of so many people who, in all likelihood, would have been saved.

The White Helmets searched for the dead for a long time, for weeks after the earthquake. Eventually, their duties changed course. White Helmet Manager, Ismail Abdullah, reported,

"Beyond the immediate search for survivors, our teams conducted safety assessments on homes and public buildings, removed 442,000 cubic meters of rubble, enough to fill 177 Olympic-sized swimming pools, leveled 887,000 square meters of land, the size of 124 soccer pitches, including areas for camps and collective shelters for those displaced by the earthquake, reopened roads that are a vital lifeline for communities of 800,000 people, and rehabilitated water supplies and sewage networks."[82]

The other duty for the White Helmets, aided by grieving family members and neighbours, was the construction of more and more graves. As innumerable black body bags were set spread out on a morgue floor and further still beyond the doors into the outside, graves were being readied for the bodies within. In the countryside of Afrin, a vast swath of land became a cemetery for the victims of Jeneres City. An aerial view shows a configuration of thousands of rectangles side by side, row after row, each grave made of stacked cinder blocks after the earth had been dug by shovels. The Muslim custom is to clean the body three times – the *"ghusl"*, fragrance it, protect it in a white shroud known as a *"kafan"*, and then lay the body to rest within three days. The graves are unmarked, typically with only a number written by hand on the headstone. Prayers are said during the actual interment. In Syrian tradition, women and children do not attend funerals, only men. Many of these rituals were left to the surviving family members or neighbours to carry out. A responsibility and a duty known all too well in a country having sustained 12 years of bloodshed. Saying untimely goodbyes was a familiar but cruel part of being Syrian.

The final tally of the earthquake victims was 53,000 dead in Turkey and 6,000 dead in Syria, with an additional 3.7 million children, already living in unbearable conditions, impacted heavily by the humanitarian crisis.

It is an unbearable irony that thousands of Syrians who had managed to escape 12 years of wholesale murder and bloodshed by their president, incredibly with their lives intact, only to perish in an "Act of God". But religious faith is great in Syria. For the most part, even if Syrians attribute the earthquake as sent by God, there is seldom blame apportioned to their Almighty God for the event. As with the endless hardship sent by their government, the vast majority are religious enough to accept it as yet another test. Many believe there is no better coping mechanism during a tragedy than to accept it as part of Allah's will, which is deemed unquestionable. Indeed, for those looking in from the outside, into the nation of Syria that has suffered perhaps worse than any other nation in the 21st century, there is amazement about the strength, stoicism, and perseverance of the Syrian people. Against the most brutal odds, they rise again and again, and they walk on.

CHAPTER TWELVE

Checkmate

"In life, unlike in chess, the game continues after checkmate."

- Isaac Asimov, Writer

[Rendering]

With one desperate move in the dead of night, it was over. Bashar al-Assad had fled Syria. The reign of the Assad family, five decades long, existed now only in history books. On December 8, 2024, the Syrian people were, after nearly 13 brutal years, free.

For years, the Syrian revolutionaries had been carefully playing their chess pieces, moving about pawns that Assad paid little attention to, forfeiting a martyr rook, situating horses ever and ever closer to the last row of their opponent's board. Tiny movements. Little by little. *Schuway schuway.* Until the black king opened his palace doors, and the opponents in white were directly outside them.

For more than a decade, the mantra among the people had been "Revolution until victory!". In 2015, the rebels had almost brought that battle cry to fruition. They had been so close. Assad and his fighters had grown weary, while the rebels had grown stronger. In the spring of 2015, rebels were taking city after city in province after province, with the Syrian Army on the run. A crucial border crossing with Jordan, an integral trade route, the Nassib border was taken. Then the rebels pushed forward through the northern province of Idlib. By April, they had taken the provincial capital, Idlib City, a jewel in the Syrian crown. Military bases were being scooped up by the opposition while the Syrian Army gave the pretense of defending them, before all but surrendering them to the more powerful forces they were being confronted with. Assad's army was diminishing as soldiers continued abandoning it in the face of the sturdy rebel advances. The loss of numbers prompted Assad to withdraw his troops from certain areas and place them in others in order to increase the defense of more important regime locations. But the rebel advance and the morale of its fighters just continued growing. While the motivation of the Syrian Arab Army was a paycheque, the impetus that kept the rebels going was the hope of getting their land back, of freedom, of victory against the tyrant Assad. The two carrots dangling in front of the respective horses were surely not equal.

But as if with any foundering dictator, Bashar al-Assad gave the right speeches to try and rouse his fading army. In one rallying speech, he announced, *"Defeat does not exist in the dictionary of the Syrian Arab army,"* he said, vowing: *"We will resist and we will win."*[83]

It wasn't until August 2015 that Assad came true on his promise. With the onslaught of Russian Air power aiding the Syrian Regime indefinitely, the rebels, so close to their prize, were on the back foot again. Once again, the mantra *"Revolution until Victory"* seemed like little more than a pipe dream. Though the Rebels had no inclination of giving up. They simply had to recalibrate.

Another nine years would pass with Russia aiding and abetting the wholesale slaughter of the Syrian people, and the razing to the ground of a once beautiful nation. Then, in early autumn of 2024, the state of Assad's war on his people, had given off a vibe the Rebel forces were acutely aware of. It was no coincidence that Putin's ongoing war in Ukraine had caused these changes in Syria. Significantly less bombing, less troop advancement, less activity altogether. It became very clear that Putin was no longer helping the Syrian president. Nor was Iran. Once more, the dictator was on his own with a degraded army that had few weapons and even less morale. Indeed, many soldiers refused to fight, and desertion rates climbed again.

The Rebels took this opportunity to make their victory push once again. Recalibrating in Idlib, the province they had helped control for almost a decade, they started their march southwest into the regime-held Aleppo. Pandemonium rocked the inhabitants. A lengthy trail of panicked students at Aleppo University is captured on video footage fleeing the school, as long lines of armored trucks and vehicles driven by the opposition pull in to the city. On November 29th, 2024, with virtually no resistance from the Syrian Arab Army, the Rebels took Aleppo, the first major city on their road to Damascus. Their first order of business was to remove all two-star Syrian flags and banners. Government forces would announce their withdrawal from the city the next day. With this significant victory accomplished, the Rebels moved their troops onward to Hama. Slight defense was waged by the Syrian Army, but the Rebels quickly overwhelmed them. Long lines of Hama inhabitants are seen streaming out of Hama in their vehicles and urgently away from the new control of the rebels. On December 5th, 2025, Hama was taken by the Rebels. Their first order of business was to free the prisoners in the notorious Hama Prison. Next was to topple the prominent and once permanent statue of Hafez Assad. The effigy fell from its platform in one piece, before shattering in cement pieces on the ground beneath. It is the obvious portent that the regime of the Assad family, 54 years long, is over. The ruling dynasty is done. But the rebels weren't through yet. Next is the once great city of Homs, through which the rebels entered confidently in their long densely-packed caravans, their fighters standing in the backs of the vehicles armed and ready; the procession of their fighters never-ending as it entered the city. It was lost on none of the rebels that this was the birthplace of Syria's great defender and martyr, Baset al-Sarout, their rebel hero. At the age of 19 years old, a successful soccer goalie with curly black hair and a boyish grin, fought against all odds back in 2017 to keep the Syrian Army out of his hometown of Homs for as long as he could. Sarout, a natural leader and fighter (though he'd never held a gun in his hands before the war), led a ragtag team of recruits to keep the regime out of Homs for an astounding 8 months, gaining the respect of every revolutionary who knew his name. In 2019, Basset Abdel al-Sarout would return to the front lines of battle, famously wishing righteous martyrdom over defeat, and was killed on June 8, 2019, defending his beloved Syria to his last breath. He would become the face and champion of the Syrian Revolution. On December 7th, the Rebels took the city of Homs, exchanging the stony countenances of regime leaders on buildings with posters of the face of the legendary Sarout. Settling their necessary forces in place, the next day, December 8th, in the early mornings, the rebels forces were on the road to Damascus. A short trip, less than 2 hours, saw them streaming into the capital. Although Assad, his wife, and teenaged children were long gone by this point. The first order of business here was to free the innocent detainees in the slaughterhouse that is Sednaya Prison, not far from the presidential palace. To their shock and horror, the find the detainees they had been so desperate to set free and return to their families, vanished. Later, in their place, they will find a lengthy paper log of the names of the dead, executed at Sednaya. Next, the rebels stormed the palace itself, ransacking the political point of power, in which the demise of thousands upon thousands of Syrian Civilians (particularly the children) was devised without a shred of conscience by the Assad Family. That is all over now, however. At this point, the world at large had seen the headlines that the regime had been toppled and Syria now belonged to the Syrian people. As the Rebels and the people entered Umayyad Mosque, there were cries and songs of victory and praise afforded Allah. Revolution has at last brought victory.

The main Rebel group responsible for putting Bashar Al-Assad and his family on the run and taking back the nation is the well-known Hay'at Tahrir al-Sham, or HTS, with rebel leader Ahmed al-Sharaa at its helm.

From this rebel faction group, HTS, came the interim leader of the new Syrian nation, Ahmed al-Sharaa. The 42-year-old al-Sharaa had worn many different hats throughout his life - civilian, military man, rebel, even terrorist affiliate, some of the titles blackening his past as he looked forward to the one title he might never have dreamed of –

President of Syria. So it is of little surprise that while the vast majority of the liberated people of this new Syria celebrated the leader who took the place of their butcher dictator Assad, there were many on the outside of the country looking in who were skeptical. Even some Syrians, themselves, didn't know what to expect. From experience, they knew government could not be trusted. Yet, others say he was born for the role. Although his birthplace was Saudi Arabia, he grew up in an upper-middle-class family in Syria. He excelled at school and was intelligent, strategic, and political in his mindset. In an interview back in March 2025 in the Damascus Palace, al-Sharaa reveals his understanding of the evils of the Syrian regime and President Bashar al-Assad came to him when he was 19 years old. Still a teenager, and with little experience in life, let alone any political savvy, he recognized the overwhelming problems in his nation but had no clue how to deal with them. His father had been a major figure in the origins of the Syrian Revolution of 2011, but he knew nothing of had to create effective opposition. No regular Syrian civilians had any interaction with the government or politics in general. Fast forward, and al-Sharaa is an al-Qaeda fighter in Iraq battling against the Americans and British. The jump from an ambitious dreamer walking the streets of history-rich Damascus to Islamic radicalism is difficult for many to digest in the context of a future world leader. He explained this transition to his two British interviewers from *"The Rest is Politics"* podcast, by discussing his deep unrest with not only the decades-long brutality wrought down on his fellow Syrians, but in addition, describes how the *"....the Palestinian Intifada had a big impact on me psychologically. I felt the need to learn and I read a lot about Damascus and Syria, the incredible depth of its history and the great civilization it represents. I could see the state of the country and the appalling way that the former government was running the country. I felt pain for the burden that Damascus carried and how the regime was abusing Syrian society and this ancient city. I believed that this regime should fall."*[84] He segues into his time in Iraq, explaining, *"... so I had two reasons for going there* [Iraq]. *First, I saw it as an opportunity to learn and gain valuable experience by witnessing a total war so that I could return to Syria and benefit from the knowledge I would gain. Secondly, I was driven by the passion and youthful spirit I had to defend the people of Iraq from occupation."*[85] Al-Sharaa downplays his role involved with al-Qaeda but specifying many smaller factions, one of which he was part of, which eventually amalgamated into the new al-Qaeda, and to this end, he seems to accept responsibility for being a part of one of the biggest terrorist threats to Western nations. Three years into his tour in Iraq, he would be arrested by Americans and put in prison for five years. He claimed that within that time of incarceration, having moved about between at least three different prisons in Baghdad, he came to know many prisoners and their ideologies, and immediately recognized his ideology was different than so many others he had encountered. Al-Sharaa says he was criticized for his difference in opinions, taking a less radical stance from a very common radical mentality that would later form the foundation of ISIS. Al-Sharaa spent his days in prison planning his return to Syria and thinking of government opposition, strategizing, and preparing. Two days before the Syrian Revolution began in Daraa, al-Sharaa was released from prison. He returned directly to Syria. He went back with a group of like-minded Syrians, maybe five or six, he recalled, whose mission would be exclusively to take down the regime. The handful of loyal rebels within the first year, according to al-Sharaa, climbed in numbers to 5,000 rebels. The number would fluctuate, increasing and decreasing, through fighting, but from 2021 to 2024, HTS was the most powerful military faction in the Syrian Opposition. Throughout its revolutionary tenure, the HTS, a derivative of the terrorist faction Al-Nusra Front, would also be branded a radical terrorist faction by the United Nations through the UN Security Council Resolution 2254. After the fall of Damascus in December 2024, a transitional government was installed. By January 2025, the newly created Syrian Revolution Victory Conference held in Damascus, announced the dissolution of HTS. The former HTS and several armed factions pledged allegiance to the interim government and declared that they would become part of "state institutions". The dawn of a new Damascus, a new Syria, had finally come after 14 years.

Despite the celebration among the people of the fall of Assad and the regime, a potential crisis for the Syrian people stood out notably as too long a duration without a dedicated government in place. Should an interim government with its parliament prove one more instability in the nation's trials, the vacuum for power this could create could be dangerous and almost promised.

Less than three months into the advent of the new Syria, a familiar string of horrors from days gone bone broke out: persecution, terror, death. On March 8th, a massacre of approximately 1000 people in the Idlib city of Latakia brought new horrors, causing the victory celebrations to pause. Latakia, home to the Assad family and dense with the Alawite religious sect still loyal to the former dictator and family densely populating the region, saw an outburst of fighting. At this point in writing, with ongoing investigations into the deadly three spring days in March, descriptions are alleged and as reported. A White Helmet I spoke to described, via translation from his Arabic to English, a cover-up of truth of actual events that needed much more investigation. The current report is that loyalist fighters of Assad in the region struck out militarily in protest against the new government. In retaliation, the pro-government fighters struck back. The origins and execution described are murky. What is known by the Syrian Observatory of Human Rights is that at least 1000 people were killed in the three-day massacre, with at least 750 of those executed being unarmed civilians. Indeed, it had become a free-for-all style of killing, as Alawites, Christians, among other religious sects report being attacked out of the blue. Houses were burnt to the ground. People in the street were shot point-blank. This was the horrendous but perhaps expected fallout of what many perceived as one dictatorship replacing another. It would be the first huge test for the new interim president of Syria.

The de facto President, Ahmed al-Sharaa, outlined his plan for making the government transition and the power shift. The Syrian Salvation Government (SSG), which had been founded on November 2, 2017, in Idlib as an opposition government, if only in ideal, to the Syrian regime, would be the temporary government within Syria, working out of Damascus. President al-Sharaa stated this will continue for three months before the next phase, involving a constitutional declaration took place, the National Congress, and then ultimately the appointment of the President of Syria. Al-Sharaa set out the steps with seamless articulation, but as with everything in the new Syria, only time will tell how seamless the facility of these concepts will come to be.

Bashar al-Assad's destiny as a person of asylum in Moscow is surely not the one he had hoped would come to be for the family dynasty. Certainly, not the one the inflexible and cruel father, Hafez al-Assad, had charged him with. But, perhaps it is the exact ending to the nightmare perpetrated by Bashar al-Assad on "his" people. He was never supposed to be President of Syria. His father, Hafez, likely knew he was incapable of being the leader of the nation, let alone keeping the country together. And so, in shame, the default heir to the throne had run away from his people, his duties, his destructive legacy, and perhaps any claim to his family name. In true fashion, he had not even prepared his Syrian Army for the days of his abandonment, let alone his people. The colours he had shown while dictator of Syria, all bled into a massive black defeat. Worse than his father could have ever imagined.

As for the leader of Russia, Putin's narcissism had spread himself too thin. As the world wordlessly condoned his bloody crippling of Syria, he invaded Ukraine a few years later, thinking the world was his for the taking. When Putin and Russia could no longer support Syria and threw their hands up, they left behind critical air and navy bases that had once given them a foothold in the Middle East. If the new president of Syria has anything to say about it, he won't be getting those back any time soon.

As for the White Helmets, the double-taps and persecution have ceased. The only humanitarian organization to stand with the Syrian people throughout the entire revolution has been embraced by the interim government and by the Syrian people, even those who had spent the duration of the 14-year-conflict in regime areas and consequently, didn't know the men in white hard hats existed.

The president of the Syria Civil Defence, Raed al-Saleh, and his Deputy General, Farouq Habib, were called immediately from their headquarters in Canada to Syria to meet with the interim government. A major briefing was undoubtedly provided by Raed and Farouq to President al-Sharaa pertaining to their part in maintaining safety and rebuilding infrastructure in Syria through their humanitarian organization.

On March 29, 2025, Mr. Raed al-Saleh officially resigned as the head of the White Helmets, in order to accept a ministerial position in the new Syrian government. Mr. al-Saleh is now the Syrian Minister of the newly established Ministry of Environment, Emergencies, and Disaster Management. A position for which his significant experience and dedication within the Syria Civil Defence make him the ideal person.

With search and rescue for the White Helmets fundamentally done, the volunteers will turn their attention to not only the old matters of providing aid and relief to those in need, particularly in the still-languishing camps, but also the enormous project of rebuilding Syria, through the clearing of the vestiges of war, and the rebuilding of infrastructure. The sooner the better.

In this new, free Syria, there is also time for the odd vacation for the White Helmets and their families, who have dedicated so much of their lives to rescuing and putting back together what Bashar al-Assad and his regime wantonly yet systematically destroyed. Their cameras snap a lot of pictures still, not for the purpose of proving crimes against humanity, but because the sky is somehow so much bluer in a free Syria, the horizon and the few clouds that linger above it, the whitest white. There is not a war plane to be seen.

EPILOGUE

White is Not the Colour of Surrender

From Damascus, jasmine begins its whiteness. And fragrances perfume themselves with her scent. From Damascus, water begins ... for wherever. You lean your head, a stream flows. And poetry is a sparrow spreading its wings. Over Sham ... and a poet is a voyager. From Damascus, love begins ... for our ancestors. Worshipped beauty, they dissolved it, and they melted away. From Damascus, horses begin their journey. And the stirrups are tightened for the great conquest. From Damascus, eternity begins ...

From *A Damascene Rose* by Nizar Qabbani, Syrian Poet

[Syria Civil Defence]

347

Come the month of April in Syria, white Jasmine flowers are faithfully celebrated with romantic and sumptuous festivals. For close to a week, the capital Damascus, known as *Sham* to the people, is festooned in wedding white, honouring the sweet nectar blossom that is said to reflect the heart and virtue of the Syrian people. The national flower, bright in colour and fragile in appearance, is deceivingly strong and resilient. It flourishes ubiquitously in the spring and early summer, winding gracefully through gardens and climbing languorously over the walls of neighbourhood homes. A hardier variety also grows profusely on bushes, sturdy enough to bear the raw cold of Syrian winters. No one can quite remember when exactly the Persian specimen arrived in the Arab land, but as with generation upon generation of Syrians, they laid seed, took root, and thrived. Jasmine's wafting aroma, simultaneously sweet and musky, is often tapped for perfumes and oils. Its tenacious perfume needs only the slightest breeze to carry it from flower across the land for what seems forever. Great poets, like the regime-exiled Nizar Qabbani, composed many a rhapsodic love letter to the virtuous flower, comparing its distilled aroma to the spirit of the Syrian people and then later to the capricious and daring whispers of political dissent that swiftly entered the early conversations of the revolutionaries. In the first days of the Syrian protest rallies, children advanced to the unflinching barricade of regime henchmen, naively carrying the delicate petals gingerly in the palms of their hands to present to the soldiers as offerings of peace.

Perhaps, so great was the ideal of the promise and goodness of these white blooms, that the young innocents thought they could persuade men bearing guns to treat people with dignity and kindness. Sadly, the black Kalashnikovs won out, and the white petals scattered helplessly to the ground, were trampled underfoot.

One needn't look hard to find the colour white deeply embedded, both symbolically and philosophically, in the generous tapestry of the Syrian culture.

The crescent moon, starkly white in its heavens, atop every mosque dome, has, since the time of the Ottomans, gathered up the people of Allah under His mercy.

While the Christian churches are adorned with white crosses promising salvation from the holiest of saints, his garments coloured like the fleece of lambs.

If mercy and holiness were colours, they would probably be white.

For the most admired and loved friends, they are told by Syrians that they have white hearts. It is the highest compliment one can be paid by a Syrian.

White has always represented not only virtue and innocence but the absence of blemish or malice. A colour which is at once all colours and no colour

In deep and honest retrospection, the helmets crowning the heads of the search and rescue volunteers could only have been white. These common men and women – saints to the Syrian people – knew to look for the white helmets for safety, protection, and perseverance. But perhaps more to the point, these White Helmets, gauntlet bearers of all things good and decent, would find themselves battling blackness far too often. Whether it be the accusation that they stood with the black flag of ISIS and al-Qaeda, the black ballistics deliberately targeting them at all hours of duty, or the defaming narratives pronounced on their humanitarian beings that were black fonts on the pages of fraud stories about them, they stayed the course, adjusted their helmets, and walked on.

The double-taps are done now. There are no more Russian Sukhois fighter jets in the sky. The smear campaigns and character assassinations no longer matter. Long gone are the mountains of Assad's rubble through which to search for broken children. That time is done now, merely black print on the white pages of history books.

The volunteers of the White Helmets often stood alone in the world, but they always stood together, with or without the helmets on their heads. Amid the debris of bombed-out neighbourhoods, they were brilliant beacons for the terrorized Syrian people. A touchstone with virtue and compassion in a time of horrific betrayal. No matter what Assad stole from the people, the White Helmets always managed to give something back to replace it.

When hell rained down, the White Helmets soldiered through, warriors who battled the regime and Russia, unarmed, yet from the winning vantage point of their true, selfless beings, from their altruistic souls. Under the helmets, and behind the SCD uniforms, their hearts – white as Syrian Jasmine, were always their true armour.

The white flag has universally been known as a sign of surrender. With a piece of white scrap found on the ground or a patch of white clothing, the more beleaguered side has always been able to wave high this request for pardon when it was losing, and capitulation was the only hope. Surrender, despite everything, was easy enough if you waved a swath of the colour white.

In Syria during the years of genocidal campaign by Assad on his people, the men and women of the White Helmets found themselves many times in the crosshairs of defeat and destruction, whether through bombing, or dedicated assassination of their characters, both weapons meant to take them out for good. Yet, what unfailingly bobbed over the horizon to confront their enemies were simple white hard hats atop the heads of humanitarians, and the declaration through their continued work saving human beings, that there would be no surrender. These men, fortified by their pledge to save as many people as they could, would not back down. Not ever. As with their legendary motto inscribed on every jacket, the impetus to keep going, leapt by bounds over the usual war fodder like land and monetary gain, they kept going, because with every life they saved, they saved humanity.

There could be no greater motivation, and for them, no sacrifice was too great.

Anas al-Dyab, the young White Helmet photographer and rescuer who won the trip to India and not much later died in the line of duty in a Russian double-tap, was, of course, a prolific photographer. His vast body of photographs, award-winning and provocative as they are, is quite simply the story of the Syrian people as much as they are of the actual Syrian conflict. Anas loved colour in his photos, but he also gravitated to the starkness of black and white photography time and time again. Some of his most poignant images were captured on colourless canvases. Looking them over, one wonders if there was reason to his rhyme. If the competing black and white presented a unique sort of neutrality, an equality of all things, wherein the brightness of white could shine through like the sun shines through the black clouds of broken buildings and devastated landscapes. Where the simple square window frame painted in white and picked up in the camera as such, could redeem the cracked and hurting dark building it looked out of. Where the close-up of the leathery wrinkled face of an old man, black beard, and black and white scarf of bound Keffiyeh on his head, could, through this contrasting black and white, draw the viewer's attention to the smiling white teeth and the lucid whites of his happy old eyes. Maybe Anas understood exactly that the effect of the bright on the dark is what creates the brilliance of the moment. Maybe that is why he injected so much bright white into his work.

In the same way, the volunteers were mere impartial canvases of white, walking through but never projecting darkness, and never allegiant to the colours of any one particular side. The White Helmets' neutrality, their desire to care for all sides of the conflict, formed their essence and their mission. And no matter the circumstances, the peril, the prejudice, they were faced with, they would never back down. Their white was not ever going to be the colour of surrender.

AFTERWORD

In the month of May 2025, I woke up to the announcement on social media that the White Helmets organization, officially known as the Syria Civil Defence, was going to dissolve. They would now fall under the auspices of the new three-starred government, taking their search and rescue role forward under the new nation's Ministry of Natural Disasters and Emergencies. Despite their duties simply evolving to perhaps something bigger, something national, spreading out now to defend all of Syria as they had always wanted to do, it still felt to me like it was so much the end of an era. I wondered immediately what the new uniforms would look like. I knew the old logo might be replaced; I wondered if the colour of their helmets would change too. Maybe James would finally get the red helmets he always wanted. I don't think so, though. I think it is a memento of their past, of their journey from revolution to freedom, a reminder of all the lives they saved, that the colour white will be preserved atop their heads. Well, that's what I hope anyway.

It will take about a month or so for the White Helmets to transition to their new roles. They have, however, never stopped carrying out their duties.

Four days ago, June 20th, 2025, while Christians were in Sunday prayers in a church, in Damascus, an ISIS member stormed through the doors of the church full to its brim with worshippers and began shooting at the congregation. When young men sprang in defense to the door, the terrorist blew himself up, killing scores of worshippers, at least twenty children, and injuring upwards of 60 more. It was fresh hell for a nation trying so hard to heal. In the initial photographs and videos coming out of Damascus, the White Helmets were prevalent, coordinating the clean-up after their rescue and recovery duties were finished. In their yellow summer jackets and their white helmets, they were, strangely, an incomparably comforting vision among the broken church pews and the pools of blood on the floor, even the holy pictures slipping down the stony church walls. My eyes lingered on one Helmet who just stood there in the mess of that broken church, unfolding a body bag and looking off in the far direction of the church. Perhaps that is where the bag was needed.

In the days after the attack, the people of Syria came together, all sects, all religions, all ages, men and women alike, and mourned the loss of their brothers and sisters, so brutally struck down. President al-Sharaa made a public speech of heartfelt condolences for the Syrian people whom the nation, entire, had lost. People, en masse, lined up to give blood for the critically injured. A photograph of a woman in a niqab lying on a hospital bed, giving blood while another Muslim woman stood waiting her turn beside her, captivated me. In the streets outside the church, Muslim clerics hugged Christian priests. I wish the terrorist heathen who had stormed the church, could see what he had, ultimately, accomplished. That would be but a pittance of compensation for all he took in the name of nothing.

Today, June 24th, was the funeral for the dead. Somewhere in Damascus, local carpenters made dozens of wooden coffins, affixed wooden crosses to the boxes, and painted them white. The Syrian people, came out in the thousands, bigger than any protest rally I'd seen, to pay tribute to the victims and honour them.

A lengthy line of White Helmets ambulances, holding the coffins of the dead within, made its funeral procession to the church where the funeral would be held. The White Helmets removed the coffins from their vehicles, and they were handed off, the crowd lifting them, one by one, up and over their heads, as they passed them along, and person after person participated in getting the deceased to the church. Indeed, the people had in this mournful union, become as one. The image of the coffins, white and perfect, floating over the chanting people was heart-wrenching, but somehow beautiful too. When the church's capacity for mourners was filled, thousands more waited outside, crying and praying. They honoured their dead and assigned them no creed or religion as they did so.

Those June days of horror and grief are some of the last days the humanitarian volunteers will ever carry out as *White Helmets*. And yes, the colour of their helmets may change in the days and years to come, but their hearts will always be as white as Sham Jasmine. Having answered the call, each of them, to the most unimaginable of vocations, they stayed the course for the Syrian people. They stay it still.

Citations

Books & Documentary Films

Last Men in Aleppo. Larm Film and Aleppo Media Centre. Documentary Film, January 23, 2017.

Articles, Reports & Online Sources

"14th Anniversary of Syrian Revolution | Nearly 657,000 Persons Killed Since the Onset of the Revolution in March 2011." SOHR, March 20, 2024.

"'Barrel Bombs Are Back!'" Vanessa Beeley. *Substack Media*, January 15, 2025.

Beeley, Vanessa. "Charlie Hebdo Provocation." *The Wall Will Fall*, September 14, 2015.

Beeley, Vanessa. "Vanessa Beeley Lecture in Ottawa – The Role of the So Called White Helmets." YouTube, December 17, 2019.

Brabant, Malcolm. "Mysterious Death of White Helmets Co-Founder Spotlights Toxic Propaganda." *PBS News Hour*, December 24, 2019.

CBC News. "Dead Syrian Children's Images Fuel Opposition Fury." June 1, 2011.

Clavel, Emilie. "Pro-Syrian Regime 'Conspiracy Theorist' On A Canada Speaking Tour." *HuffPost*, December 5, 2019.

Daily Freeman. "Film, Lecture Examines Potential War with Iran." July 21, 2021.

Day, Joel. "One Tragedy, Four Stories: How the Earthquake in Syria Played Out Around the World." *Express.co.uk*, February 13, 2023.

English, Joe. UNICEF Media, March 15, 2020.

Farthwaite, Rosie. "BBC News Arabic." *BBC.com*, March 7, 2023.

Hadjimatheou, Chloe. "Intrigue Podcast – Mayday." *BBC Radio 4*, November 9, 2020.

Havis, Richard James. "European Cinema Post Mag." September 21, 2018.

Hernandez, Joe, and Geoff Brumfiel. "NPR Science." *NPR.org*, February 7, 2023.

Human Rights Watch. "Syria: Crimes Against Humanity in Daraa." News Release, June 1, 2011.

Islam, Shajul. "First Footage from the Khan Shaykhun Chemical Attack." YouTube, April 4, 2017.

Karimi, Faith, and Jomana Karadsheh. "Syria War: White Helmets Group Says Aid Centre Hit by Barrel Bomb." *CNN*, October 6, 2016.

Kucukgocmen, Ali. "Key Backer of Syrian 'White Helmets' Found Dead in Istanbul." *Reuters*, November 11, 2019.

Martynyuk, Leonid. "Russia Uses Ex-UN Weapons Inspector's Ukraine Misinformation for Domestic Propaganda." *VOA*, April 24, 2023.

Medecins Sans Frontieres. "Aleppo's Reality – Daily Life Under Barrel Bombs." Report, March 11, 2015.

Middle East Eye. "Seven White Helmet Members Shot Dead in Northwest Syria." August 12, 2017.

MiddleEastEye.net. "Citizen Journalist among 11 Civilians Killed by Air Raids in Northwest Syria." July 21, 2019.

Neuman, Scott. "The Two-Way Podcast." *NPR*, July 26, 2015.

Oxfam International. "Aleppo Crisis." Oxfam.org, November 17, 2016.

Reuter, Christoph. "The Story of the Destruction of an Aid Organization." *Spiegel International*, September 12, 2021.

Reuters.com. "This Syrian Father Helps His 3-Year-Old Daughter Face the Fear of Bombings with Laughter." February 18, 2020.

Sahloul, Adham. "Obituary: A Hospital in Aleppo (2013–2016)." *TIME Media*, December 14, 2016.

Sahloul, Zaher. "Aleppo Abandoned: A Case Study on Health Care in Syria." *Relief Web (PHR)*, November 18, 2015.

Syria Civil Defence. "Official Statement: A Joint Statement by the Syria Civil Defence and the Health Directorate." April 4, 2017.

Syria Civil Defence. "Statement on the Killing of Three Volunteers from the UXO Removal Team in Hama Countryside." WhiteHelmets.org, May 22, 2025.

TRT World Media. "Omran Dagneesh's Father Speaks Out." June 8, 2017.

TRT World Media. "Syria's Assad Says Iconic Photo of Omran Dagneesh is 'Fake'." June 23, 2017.

Turnbull, Anya. "How Putin's Propaganda Works, Explained by a Russian." YouTube, 2024.

United Nations. 2011 Treaty Event Media Documentation.

United Press International. "Opposing Ground Zero Mosque Rallies Calm." September 11, 2010.

Vanessa Beeley. Twitter [X] post, February 25, 2018.

VOA. "Russia Uses Ex-UN Weapons Inspector's Ukraine Misinformation for Domestic Propaganda." Leonid Martynyuk, April 24, 2023.

Westcott, Lucy. "Khaled Omar Harah, Syrian 'Miracle Baby' Rescuer, Killed in Aleppo." *Newsweek.com*, August 12, 2016.

Synopsis

In the spring of 2011 peaceful protests demanding liberty by the Syrian people were met with swift and wicked retaliation by their dictator leader. President al-Assad wasted no time in declaring full scale war on his people, starting a systematic bombing campaign that would last nearly 14 years and raze Syria to the ground. The people, forsaken by their own government and the outside world, were left in survival mode - hungry, homeless and routinely massacred. When the bombs rained down, a group of men, regular people from all walks of life, ran to the mountains of destruction to rescue the victims trapped in the rubble. They made it their new vocation to save the lives Assad wanted dead. Garnering the nickname the White Helmets for their white hard hats, these humanitarian first responders would quickly find themselves in the crosshairs of Assad's war, becoming his dedicated bullseye. They had a choice. They could flee for their own safety or stay and help their fellow civilians. Making the ultimate sacrifice, they stayed. Nearly 400 White Helmets volunteers have lost their lives in their bid to help the innocent. To date, they have saved upwards of 130,000 lives....and counting.

About the Author

Born in Toronto, Ontario, Jennifer Krausewitz was a volunteer writer and editor for the Syria Civil Defense social media platforms from 2016 to 2022. She works full time at her editing company and is the author of an artist-commissioned work, *Conversations with Lilith.* This is her first non-fiction book. She is the mother of two daughters and lives at home with her husband and dog Fritz.

Index

A

al-Dyab, Anas – 4, 131, 210–220, 259, 280, 282, 288, 295–296, 299–300, 303, 367

Al-Nusra Front – 108, 179, 181, 187, 247, 356

al-Saleh, Raed – 4, 173, 231, 303, 360

Alabdullah, Ismail – 341, 345

Aleppo – 8, 12, 38–39, 44–45, 47, 50, 64–69, 71–75, 77, 82–84, 86–90, 106, 120, 139, 146–149, 153–163, 165, 172, 240, 300, 306, 315, 317, 328, 331, 342–343, 351

Assad, Bashar al- – 5–6, 9, 11, 14–15, 19–20, 22–24, 26, 29–30, 32–37, 41–44, 47, 50, 58–59, 61, 69, 75–76, 81–82, 91–94, 98, 101–103, 107–108, 119–121, 126–127, 133, 136–137, 139–140, 143, 146, 148, 150–152, 154, 160–161, 163, 166–174, 178, 181, 183, 190–191, 193–197, 199–201, 203–204, 207–209, 223, 225, 233, 235, 237, 242, 244, 247, 250, 260–261, 263, 277, 282, 284, 289–290, 297, 300–301, 304, 306, 308, 311, 313, 316–318, 320–321, 331, 338, 349–350, 352–354, 357–359, 361, 365–366

B

Barrel bombs – 11, 69, 76, 148–149, 155–156, 161, 169, 206, 301–302, 306

Beeley, Vanessa – 167–169, 173–176, 181–182, 193–196, 205, 248

C

Caesar Act / Caesar's Law – 150

Chemical attacks – 123, 127, 186, 188, 193, 195–196

Cluster bombs / Grads – 68, 107, 148, 283

D

Damascus – 23–24, 34, 66, 74, 106, 118, 121, 125, 149, 151, 169–170, 178, 195, 242, 262, 351, 353–358, 362–363, 370–371

Daraa – 17–20, 22, 24–27, 29, 31–32, 34, 37, 106, 183, 185, 259–262, 266, 300, 314, 356

Douma – 186, 190

Endnotes

[1] "Syria: Crimes Against Humanity in Daraa", Human Rights Watch News Release, June 1, 2011

[2] "Syria: Crimes Against Humanity in Daraa", Human Rights Watch News Release, June 1, 2011

[3] "Dead Syrian Children's Images Fuel Opposition Fury", CBC News, June 1, 2011

[4] Statement by the Syria Civil Defence (White Hemets) on the Killing of Three Volunteers from the UXO Removal Team in Hama Countryside, whitehelmets.org, May 22, 2025.

[5] "Last Men in Aleppo", Larm Film And Aleppo Media Centre, Documentary Film, January 23, 2017

[6] Richard James Havis, European Cinema Post Mag, September 21, 2018

[7] White Helmet Najib, Conversation with Jennifer Krausewitz via Facebook Messenger, February 22, 2023

Lucy Westcott, "Khaled Omar Harah, Syrian 'Miracle Baby' Rescuer, Killed in Aleppo", Newsweek.com, August 12, 2016

"The United Nations Briefing on Syria Featuring Eva Bartlett, Independent Canadian Journalist",(alternately named: "Press Briefing by Syrian Mission"),YouTube, R & U Videos, Uploaded by eShafandy, December 27, 2016

"Sara Flounders", Discover the Networks.org, Undated

"Opposing Ground Zero mosque rallies calm". *United Press International.* September 11, 2010.

"Film, Lecture Examines Potential War with Iran", Daily Freeman.Com, July 21, 2021

[13] In 2020 a former Sednaya prison worker who had for many years been tasked with marking the corpses at the prison and photographing each one, to a total on average of fifty bodies per day. This individual was able to get out of Syria with a tiny hard drive bearing the massive evidence of 30,000 deceased persons, all photographed. Codenamed "Caesar", he would take his evidence and go incognito in a blue raincoat, hood covering his head and his face never shown for fear of retaliation, to the American Senate where he would present his gruesome evidence of the horrors occurring daily inside Sednaya Prison at Assad's bidding. The photographs were eventually released online and become a sort of online cemetery for those whose loved ones had gone missing. Moms, dads, wives were able to identify their loved ones and have knowledge of what their outcomes were at long last. Caesar's Law would come into effect [.....]. Not unlike the Nazi documentation of their dead, the Assad Regime's need for meticulous data of those they had murdered will become a vast and integral body of evidence should his crimes ever seen the inside of the Hague.

[14] "Aleppo's reality – Daily life under barrel bombs" – Medecins Sans Frontieres Report from MSF website dated March 11, 2015

[15] "Aleppo's reality – Daily life under barrel bombs" - Medicins Sans Frontieres Report from MSF website dated March 11, 2015

[16] Between 2011 and 2015, Dr. Sahloul led the transformation of the Syrian American Medical Society (SAMS) into a globally-recognized medical NGO representing the Syrian American diaspora, serving hundreds of thousands of Syrian patients and refugees. He co-founded SAMS Global Response to address the refugee crisis in Europe, as well as the American Relief Coalition for Syria (ARCS), a coalition of 14 humanitarian organizations.

Dr. Sahloul is a leading advocate in the Syrian humanitarian crisis and the role of diaspora communities among medical circles, the media, the U.S. government, and the UN. He has authored many articles on the impact of the war in Syria on public health, healthcare workers, civilians, and children, and has been published in outlets such as the New York Times, CNN, WP, WSJ, Foreign Policy, the Chicago Tribune, and the Guardian.

[17] Geneva Convention Article #35 declared civilian hospitals are off limits.

[18] "Obituary: A Hospital in Aleppo (2013-2016)"; TIME Media; Adham Sahloul (Advocacy Officer of S.A.M.S); December 14, 2016

[19] *Aleppo Abandoned: A Case Study on Health Care in Syria;* Relief Web (PHR); November 18, 2015

[20] Oxfam quotes taken from article, dated November 17, 2016, off their website Oxfam.org.

[21] "Charlie Hebdo Provocation"; Vanessa Beeley; The Wall Will Fall; September 14, 2015

[22] "Barrel Bombs are Back!"; Vanessa Beeley; Substack media; January 15, 2025

[23] The Wall Will Fall, article dated November 30, 2019, The War on Syria; Vanessa Beeley's Lecture Tour in Canada.

[24] 'Conspiracy Theorist' Vanessa Beeley Faces Backlash As Universities Cancel Her 'Journalism' Talks; Chris York; Huff Post; December 6, 2019

[25] "Vanessa Beeley Lecture in Ottawa – The Role of the So Called White Helmets"; Vanessa Beeley; YouTube video; December 17, 2019

[26] Sourced from the United Nations 2011 Treaty Event media documentation.

[27] U.S. and European Sanctions on Syria, cartercentre.org September 2020

[28] Twitter [x] @Vanessa Beeley, February 25, 2018

[29] "First Footage from the Khan Shaykhun Chemical Attack", Dr. Shajul Islam, YouTube, April 4, 2017

[30] "Former UN weapons inspector guilty in sex case", Associated Press, CBC, April 15, 2011

[31] "Former UN weapons inspector guilty in sex case", Associated Press, CBC, April 15, 2011

[32] "Russia Uses Ex-UN Weapons Inspector's Ukraine Misinformation for Domestic Propaganda", VOA, Leonid Martynyuk, April 24, 2023

[33] How Putin's propaganda works, explained by a Russian, You Tube, Anya Turnbull, 2024

[34] Official statement by the Syria Civil Defence organization: A Joint Statement by the Syria Civil Defence and the Health Directorate April 4, 2017

[35] "SYRIA: President Assad Speaks to AFP on Alleged Khan Sheikhoun Chemical Attacks", 21st Century Wire, Vanessa Beeley, April 13, 2017

[36] "Syria forces behind Khan Sheikhoun gas attack: UN probe", Aljazeera, September 6, 2017,

[37] "Marie Colvin Wins 2000 IWMF Courage in Journalism Award", Courage in Journalism Awards New York October 2000, International Women's Media Foundation, YouTube, February 20, 2013

[38] "Marie Colvin: Syrian regime deliberately targeted journalist, US court rules", Independent, Samuel Osborne, February 1, 2019

[39] "Marie Colvin Targeted and Killed by Assad, Judge Rules", CNN, YouTube, February 1, 2019

[40] "Marie Colvin: Syrian Government Found Liable for US Reporter's Death", BBC, January 31, 2019

[41] "Marie Colvin targeted and killed by Assad regime, judge rules", Jennifer Hansler, CNN, February 1, 2019

[42] "Journalists' Death Toll in Syrian Revolution", Doha Centre for Media Freedom Website, UNDATED

[43] "Syria War: White Helmets Group Says Aid Centre Hit by Barrel Bomb", Faith Karimi and Jomana Karadsheh, CNN, October6, 2016.

[44] "Seven White Helmet Members Shot Dead in Northwest Syria", Middle East Eye, August 12, 2017

[45] "Pro-Syrian Regime 'Conspiracy Theorist' On A Canada Speaking Tour", Emilie Clavel, HuffPost, December 5, 2019

[46] "James Le Mesurier Talks About the White Helmets, the Syrian Civil Defence", BBC Radio 4, YouTube The Syria Campaign, November 14, 2014

[47] "James Le Mesurier Talks About the White Helmets, the Syrian Civil Defence", BBC Radio 4 interview, November 13, 2014

[48] BBC Radio 4, "Mayday" Podcast, Episode #6 "The One with Sean Penn", Chloe Hadjimatheou, November 9, 2020.

[49] "Russia Behind Litvinenko Murder, Rules European Right Court", BBC.Com World News, September 21, 2021

[50] "Russia Behind Litvinenko Murder, Rules European Right Court", BBC.Com World News, September 21, 2021

[51] *"Intrique Podcast – Mayday"*, Chloe Hadjimatheou, BBC Radio, November 9, 2020

[52] *"Intrique Podcast – Mayday"*, Chloe Hadjimatheou, BBC Radio, November 9, 2020

[53] *"Intrique Podcast – Mayday"*, Chloe Hadjimatheou, BBC Radio, November 9, 2020

[54] "Key backer of Syrian 'White Helmets' found dead in Istanbul", Ali Kucukgocmen, Reuters, November 11, 2019

[55] Malcolm Brabant, "Mysterious Death of White Helmets Co-Founder Spotlights Toxic Propaganda", PBS New Hour article, December 24, 2019

[56] "The Story of the Destruction of an Aid Organization", Christoph Reuter, Spiegel International, September 12, 2021

[57] "Remembering Photographer Anas Al-Dyab", Kyle Almond, CNN, March 1, 2019

[58] "Remembering Photographer Anas Al-Dyab", Kyle Almond, CNN, March 1, 2019

[59] "Remembering Photographer Anas Al-Dyab", Kyle Almond, CNN, March 1, 2019

[60] "As He Had Done Dozens of Times Before, Anas Al-Dyab Rushed to Film the Aftermath of an Airstrike", CNN, YouTube Video, uploaded by Fared Al Mahlool, September 12, 2018

[61] "As He Had Done Dozens of Times Before, Anas Al-Dyab Rushed to Film the Aftermath of an Airstrike", CNN, YouTube Video, uploaded by Fared Al Mahlool, September 12, 2018

[62]"Citizen journalist among 11 civilians killed by air raids in northwest Syria", MiddleEastEye.Net, July 21, 2019

[63] Firstpost Media, UNICEF Report, "Syria Among 'Most Dangerous Places on Earth' for Children, March 11, 2014

[64] Joe English, Unicef Media, March 15, 2020

[65] *"Omran Dagneesh's Father Speaks Out"*, TRT World Media, June 8, 2017

[66] *"Syria's Assad says Iconic Photo of Omran Dagneesh is 'Fake'"*, TRT World Media, June 23, 2017

[67] In various interviews, the Syria Civil Defence has responded to the interview given by Omran's father, saying they are not surprised, not do they blame him for saying what he did, although it is contrary, to the truth, as a visit from the President himself, to any victim, ensures the regime narrative is the one told on threat of severe penalty. Mr. Dagneesh was afraid.

[68] "This Syrian Father Helps his 3-Year-Old Daughter Face the Fear of Bombings with Laughter", Reuters.com, February 18, 2020

[69] "Children in War: How Trauma Wires Developing Brains", UNICEF Europe and Central Asia, YouTube, February 2025

[70] *"Scars Unseen: The Enduring Effects of War on Children's Mental Health"*, Maria Arini Lopez, Psychiatry haveAdvisor.com, February 16, 2024

[71] *"Scars Unseen: The Enduring Effects of War on Children's Mental Health"*, Maria Arini Lopez, Psychiatry Advisor.com, February 16, 2024

[72] "After 13 years of conflict in Syria, more children than ever in need of humanitarian assistance and a chance", UNICEF.COM, March 14, 2024

[73] '*14th anniversary of Syrian Revolution | Nearly 657,000 persons killed since the onset of the revolution in March 2011*', SOHR, March 20, 2204

[74] Joe Hernandez, Geoff Brumfiel, NPR Science.org, February 7, 2023

[75] Joel Day, "One Tragedy, Four Stories: How the Earthquake in Syria Played Out Around the World", Express.co.uk, February 13, 2023.

[76] Rosie Farthwaite, BBC News Arabic, BBC. Com, March 7, 2023

[77] Rosie Farthwaite, BBC News Arabic, BBC. Com, March 7, 2023

[78] Rosie Farthwaite, BBC News Arabic, BBC. Com, March 7, 2023

[79] Rosie Farthwaite, BBC News Arabic, BBC. Com, March 7, 2023

[80] Rosie Farthwaite, BBC News Arabic, BBC. Com, March 7, 2023

[81] Ismail Abdullah, "A message from Ismail Alabdullah from the White Helmets", thesyriancampaign.org, February 7, 2024

[82] Ismail Abdullah, "A message from Ismail Alabdullah from the White Helmets", thesyriancampaign.org, February 7, 2024

[83] Scott Neuman, NPR, The Two-Way Podcast, July 26, 2015

[84] "New President of Syria: Ahmed al-Sharaa", Rory and Alistair, Interview from "The Rest is Politics", February 10, 2025

[85] "New President of Syria: Ahmed al-Sharaa", Rory and Alistair, Interview from "The Rest is Politics", February 10, 2025